VARIETIES OF CIVIL RELIGION

Varieties of Civil Religion

Robert N. Bellah

Phillip E. Hammond

1817

Harper & Row, Publishers, San Francisco

Cambridge, Hagerstown, New York, Philadelphia
London, Mexico City, São Paulo, Sydney

In memory of Talcott Parsons

VARIETIES OF CIVIL RELIGION. Copyright © 1980 by Robert N. Bellah and Phillip E. Hammond. All rights reserved. Printed in the United States of America. No part of this book may be used or reproduced in any manner whatsoever without written permission except in the case of brief quotations embodied in critical articles and reviews. For information address Harper & Row, Publishers, Inc., 10 East 53rd Street, New York, NY 10022. Published simultaneously in Canada by Fitzhenry & Whiteside, Limited, Toronto.

FIRST EDITION

Designed by Jim Mennick

Library of Congress Cataloging in Publication Data

Bellah, Robert Neelly
VARIETIES OF CIVIL RELIGION.

Includes index.
1. Religion. 2. United States—Religion.
I. Hammond, Phillip E., joint author. II. Title.
BL48.B38   1980   306'.6   80–7742
ISBN 0–06–060776–9

80 81 82 83 84 10 9 8 7 6 5 4 3 2 1

Contents

Introduction

ROBERT N. BELLAH

My initial essay on civil religion in America opened a debate that
has continued to this day.[1] Much of that debate has been rather
sterile, focusing more on form than content, definition than substance. From the beginning, however, Phillip E. Hammond has
entered the discussion with significant and original substantive
points of his own.[2] It is therefore a pleasure for me to join with
him in this volume in an effort to extend the consideration of civil
religion to societies and issues that have not been prominent in
the discussion hitherto. This volume seeks to be broadly comparative. It does not, however, attempt to avoid the United States.
Both authors continue to be fascinated by the American case in
its sometimes baffling intricacies. It is our hope that the present
comparative treatment will deepen the understanding of American civil religion at the same time it opens up issues that can be
explored in many other societies.

While the exact application of the term *civil religion* can be
debated, the ubiquity of what can be called "the religio-political
problem" can hardly be doubted. In no society can religion and
politics ignore each other. Faith and power must always, however
uneasily, take a stance toward one another. The polity, more than
most realms of human action, deals obviously with ultimate
things. With respect to both internal deviants and external enemies, political authority has claimed the right to make life-and-
death decisions. Religion, on the other hand, claims to derive
from an authority that transcends all earthly powers. The possi-

bility of conflict between these potentially conflicting claims is always present, yet collisions are not necessarily constant. At various times and places politics may be little more than the pragmatic art of getting things done and religion may confine itself to "spiritual" matters. Or religion and politics may simply be two different pragmatics concerned with distinct spheres of existence.

One area of overlap and potential conflict is what sociologists call the problem of legitimacy, which includes among other things the question whether existing political authority is moral and right or whether it violates higher religious duties. Most societies have institutionalized ways of dealing with this potential tension. Whether we wish to call all such forms of institutionalization civil religions or confine that term to only some of such forms, it is here that we must locate the problem of civil religion.

Fairly distinct types of solution to the religio-political problem (or fairly distinct types of civil religion) seem to correlate with the phases of religious evolution as I have described them.[3] In primitive society neither politics nor religion is very well differentiated, so there is not much point in talking about the relationship between them. Still, persons with high status and influence on collective decision-making are often seen in such societies as possessing more sacred power than others. Hierarchy in such societies is not well developed, but what there is of it is simultaneously religious and political.

In archaic societies, by which I mean typically the great Bronze Age monarchies of the old world in the second millennium B.C., political power has become highly developed and centralized. State structures at least partly independent of kinship have been established and a hierarchy of religious specialists has appeared. Characteristically, the focus of both political and religious attention is on the single figure of the ruler, often identified as a divine king. In such societies political submission to the divine king is often equated with entry into the realm of cosmic order, and political opposition is equated with alliance with the demonic forces of cosmic chaos. The realm of the divine king may be equated with the realm of cosmic harmony, and those beyond the borders may be felt to live in outer darkness.

Though in the first millennium B.C. this fusion of political and religious power was broken through by the emergence of what I have called the historic religions, it remains a permanent possibility in human history. The Egyptian pharaoh and the Shang emperor were not alone in considering their political enemies to be cut off from the source of divine order. Even within the historic religions, archaic forms reassert themselves, as when Christians divide the world into "Christendom" and the pagan realms of devil worshipers, or when Muslims divide the world into "the house of Islam" and "the house of war"—that is, all those domains beyond the reach of Muslim political power. The American tendency to divide the globe between "the free world" and the Communists, and the Communist tendency to reverse the picture, are only recent versions of the same thing. Similarly, elements of divine kingship tend to develop around strong political leaders whenever they appear. In totalitarian societies such tendencies may be very marked, as in the cases of Hitler, Stalin, and Mao Tse-tung. But even in democratic societies some such tendencies may appear: The cases of Abraham Lincoln and John F. Kennedy come to mind in our own history. The Japanese case discussed in Chapter 2 of this book is particularly interesting because it is an example of a full-fledged archaic solution to the religio-political problem (or a full-fledged archaic civil religion) that has survived into the twentieth century.

The emergence of the historic religions, though never fully overcoming archaic tendencies (or primitive ones either, for that matter), does mark a new degree of differentiation between the religious and the political. Whereas in archaic society ordinary people relate to the divine through the mediation of the divine king, once the historic religions arise there can be a direct relation to the divine, unmediated by political authority. The new situation is often expressed through a radical reorientation of divine-kingship symbolism. Confucius, a minor official in a small state, is declared in retrospect to be the uncrowned king of the whole Chinese realm. Plato offers us the ironic picture of the philosopher-king who ought to be but never will be the actual ruler. Irony turns to tragedy in the case of Jesus, whose throne is a cross and whose crown is thorns. What all these symbolisms suggest is that there is a much more problematic relation between political authority and ultimate meaning than had ever been thought before.

Correlative with these new symbolisms of religious meaning is the emergence of structures of religious authority that are in principle independent of the state. The Christian church and the Buddhist sangha are the clearest examples. In situations where clearly differentiated religious structures do not emerge, as in the Confucian case and in quite different ways the Jewish and Muslim as well, there is a strong sense that political authority is illegitimate as long as it does not conform to transcendent ethical norms, as in almost all empirical instances it does not.

Whether or not there is a clearly differentiated religious structure, there tends to be in societies with historic religions a particularly sharp tension between the representatives of religious truth and political authority. This tension can on occasion break out in prolonged power struggles. The conflict between pope and emperor in medieval Europe, the tensions between Confucianism, Buddhism, and Taoism at the T'ang court, and the struggle between the mullahs and the politicians in Iran today are all examples. The most stable solution to these conflicts in historic societies is a division of labor in which the religious authorities recognize the legitimacy of the state in return for political recognition of their own dominant position in the realm of religion. Under such conditions the state expects the church to help maintain social tranquility and the church expects the state to conform to at least minimal ethical norms. Even at their most harmonious, the Buddhist principle that "a monk does not bow down before a king" is maintained.

During periods of intense struggle, however, the division of labor breaks down. Political authority falls back on archaic archetypes. The Israelite king claims to be the Lord's anointed even when denounced by the prophet speaking in the name of Yahweh. The Chinese emperor reminds the critical Confucian literati that it is he who is the Son of Heaven. The Shah of Iran turns to ancient Persian symbols of kingship to suggest in only slightly veiled ways that it is he who is God's agent, not the mullahs. On the other side, religious authorities in the moment of conflict with the state may claim political authority themselves.

The pope in the early Middle Ages comes close to claiming to be the head of an international superstate to which all secular political authorities had to bow. Brigham Young enters the wilderness to become the ruler of his own church-state. The Ayatollah Khomeini is in effect the arbiter of political power in Iran. As the example of present-day Iran suggests, these conflicts have not disappeared from the contemporary world. We will see them still operative in some of the examples discussed at length in this book.

Nonetheless, in terms of my scheme of religious evolution, there is another possibility that emerges in the early modern and modern phases. This is the possibility that a distinct set of religious symbols and practices may arise that address issues of political legitimacy and political ethics but that are not fused with either church or state. It is this rather special case for which Phillip Hammond wishes to reserve the designation "civil religion."[4] Without necessarily agreeing that the term should be so restricted, I nevertheless do agree that this solution to the religio-political question, the solution that characterizes the American case, is quite unique and requires special conditions to bring it about. Hammond's essays in this book suggest what some of those conditions are. They have to do with the dominant form of religion in the formative period (in the American case, Protestantism) and perhaps even more with the pluralism of American religious life. In addition to these factors one would probably also need to mention, following Sidney E. Mead, the importance of enlightenment thought in the formative period.[5] Since most of the chapters in this volume concern themselves with the special conditions and ambiguities of the American solution, this is not the place to examine them further. It does seem, however, from Chapters 3 and 4, that we take the differentiated civil religion as at least a hypothetical norm for modern society and seek to explain the conditions that may block its emergence in the case of such societies as Mexico and Italy. (This is not to say that the American case is in any sense ideal. Some of its specific pathologies are discussed in this volume, and I shall refer to them again in this introduction.)

The case of Italy is an interesting one, for it is a society in which church and state have long existed in uneasy balance, with occasional bitter periods when one attempted to subordinate the other. As will become clear in detail in Chapter 4, liberalism, socialism, and fascism in modern Italy have each shown tendencies toward an archaic regression in which political authority claims its own sacrality. "Nationalism" in its various modern forms frequently shows this tendency in its effort to break the hold of all sacred traditional loyalties. On the other hand, Italian liberalism and socialism, especially since World War II, have tended to give up their totalistic claims and opt for a civility and a tolerance of difference that Hammond sees as essential in a modern civil religion. Italian Catholicism in the same period has gone at least halfway in the same direction. It thus seems possible that if the forces of particularism, what I will call the "ground bass" of Italian society, do not prevent it as they often have before in Italian history, a differentiated pattern of symbols and practices emphasizing individual liberty, social justice, and Christian charity might emerge to underpin a more legitimate and more effective Italian state than has hitherto been known.

The Mexican case as Hammond analyses it has certain parallels to the Italian. Here too both a strong Catholic Church and a secular liberal state have existed side by side for quite a while. In Mexico, however, there seems to be less diversity and less movement toward a differentiated symbol system. Only in its effervescent stage, and then only partially and fitfully, did the revolutionary state make ultimate claims for itself. On the other hand, the Mexican church seems to have remained aloof from the major forces of social transformation in modern Mexico. Although it has not given up its dramatic claims to social authority, it has not articulated them in ways that are socially effective. It is my reading of the Mexican case that this situation creates something of a stalemate. From the religious point of view the state is faintly illegitimate. But it lacks the courage of its own secular liberal convictions and so does not pursue a strong political policy of social and moral reform. This situation of impasse and weakened claims of legitimacy seems to be less severe than in other Latin American societies, but Mexico also suffers from this malaise to some extent.

Both church and state are unitary in Mexico, whatever the difficulty in linking them or mediating the linkage through a differentiated civil religion. North of the United States border there is another case that contrasts sharply with both the American and the Mexican. Canada is unitary neither politically nor religiously. But pluralism in the Canadian case, unlike the American, has not aided in the development of a differentiated civil religion. The lack of a revolutionary experience, the long history of special ties of English Canadians with England and English symbols of civil religion, and the existence of a large province that is linguistically, ethnically, and religiously distinct from the rest of Canada—all these conditions have militated against not only the emergence of a Canadian civil religion but of any very clearly defined sense of national identity. Serious doubts have been expressed about the survival of the Canadian union that would make no sense in the case of Mexico or the United States.[6]

Hammond suggests in Chapters 3, 6, and 8 that American civil religion has resided significantly in the educational and particularly the legal systems in ways that have led to a distinct tradition of civility, openness, and tolerance. Other aspects of the American tradition have not been so benign. The church-state fusion of early New England, together with ideas of a special providential chosenness of the American colonists, has exercised a pull toward archaic regression in the American civil religion.[7] Notions that America is God's country, and that American power in the world is identical with morality and God's will, have not died even today. Fortunately, these ideas never shaped the normative documents of the American civil religion, nor have they characterized its greatest heroes—men like Jefferson, Lincoln, and Martin Luther King—but they have formed an important tradition of interpretation, one carried by nationalistic clergymen more often than by jingoistic politicians. The best antidote to this tendency toward archaic regression is the critical tradition that has characterized American political life from its beginning. This critical tradition has been expressed in what Martin Marty called a public theology and what Walter Lippmann called a public philosophy. A strong public theology has opposed our more unjust wars, especially the Mexican-American, Spanish-American, and Vietnamese wars, demanded racial and social justice, and insisted on the fulfillment of our democratic promise in our economic as well as our political life. The role of public theology has remained vigorous even up to the present, but the intellectual validity of religion among the intelligentsia has been steadily undercut for a century or more.

In the formative period of the American republic a vigorous public philosophy complemented our public theology. It justified a strong normative concern for the common good that was implied in the symbolism of the differentiated civil religion. But public philosophy faded with the founding generation. It was largely replaced by the overwhelmingly private philosophy of liberalism, which justified public action almost exclusively on the grounds of private interest. The common good was expressed in religious terms or not at all. Fitful expressions of public philosophy have occurred in our history, perhaps most notably in the twentieth century in the work of John Dewey, but no continuous tradition has developed. At a moment when civil religious symbols are more and more co-opted by ultraconservatives and the philosophy of liberalism seems less and less adequate as a guide to our public or private lives, a revival of public philosophy seems urgently needed.[8] One of the tasks of such a revival would be to make the religious aspect of our central tradition understandable in a nonreactionary way.

It is not only the American republic that seems bewildered and at sea in the late twentieth century. We live in a troubled world in which the danger of nuclear holocaust constantly grows. Nation-states are still the most important power-centers in our world, but none of them alone seems able to accomplish much. Clearly military, economic, and environmental problems demand a global concord for our very survival. We have at last for many purposes a world *civitas,* but it does not have much civility. American civil religion with its tradition of openness, tolerance, and ethical commitment might make a contribution to a world civil religion that would transcend and include it. Any archaic claims to our own special righteousness or messianic mission, however, can only further the process of global disintegration. In this book we have concentrated on problems of religion and politics at the national level. It is time that we raise our sights to consider the relation of religion and politics in a global order of civility and justice.

NOTES

1. "Civil Religion in America," *Daedalus,* 1967. Reprinted in Robert N. Bellah, *Beyond Belief: Essays on Religion in a Post-Traditional World* (New York: Harper & Row, 1970).
2. "Commentary on *Civil Religion in America,* " in *The Religious Situation: 1968,* ed. Donald R. Cutler (Boston: Beacon Press, 1968), pp. 381–388.
3. "Religious Evolution," *American Sociological Review,* 29 (1964), pp. 353–374. Reprinted in Bellah, *Beyond Belief.*
4. See Chapter 3 of this volume. John A. Coleman has developed a useful typology on which Hammond in part relies. See Coleman's "Civil Religion," *Sociology Analysis,* 31 (1970), pp. 67–77.
5. Sidney E. Mead, *The Nation with the Soul of a Church* (New York: Harper & Row, 1975).
6. A much fuller discussion of Canadian civil religion or the lack thereof is contained in a doctoral dissertation on the subject currently in progress at the Graduate Theological Union in Berkeley, California, by William A. Stahl.
7. Among the many discussions of this aspect of the tradition, perhaps the most interesting is Sacvan Bercovitch's *The American Jeremiad* (Madison: The University of Wisconsin Press, 1978).
8. William M. Sullivan has made an important contribution in this direction in his *Reconstructing Public Philosophy* (Berkeley: University of California Press, forthcoming).

I. Civil Religion:
The American Case

1. Religion and the Legitimation of the American Republic

ROBERT N. BELLAH

Civil Religion, Term and Concept

In 1967 I published an essay I have never been allowed to forget.[1] In it I suggested there is such a thing as civil religion in America. My suggestion has roused passionate opposition as well as widespread acceptance. The opposition to the idea has shown little unity. Some of my opponents say there is no such thing; I have invented something that does not exist. Some say there is such a thing but there ought not to be. Some say there is such a thing but it should be called by another name, "public piety," for example, rather than civil religion. Unfortunately for me, my supporters are in even greater disarray. The term "civil religion" has spread far beyond any coherent concept thereof, or at least beyond anything I ever meant by the term. Perhaps the commonest reaction is a puzzled, "Yes, there seems to be something there, but what exactly is it?" Among the professional specialists in American studies there is another reaction: "We knew it all the time. What Bellah says is nothing new." And then there is perhaps a vague reference to Tocqueville. But, with one or two exceptions, little in the way of conceptual clarity has been forth-

This chapter originally appeared with the same title in *Society*, 15, no. 4, pp. 16–23. Copyright © 1978 by Transaction, Inc. It is published here by permission of Transaction, Inc.

coming from the specialists. I would like to try once again to
clarify this most troublesome problem. The burden of what I
want to say is that the confusion about civil religion is rooted in
a confusion about the nature of the American republic and that
genuinely to clarify the nature of American civil religion would
involve a reform of the American republic.

I must admit I am partly to blame for the confusion by my
choice of the term "civil religion," which turned out to be far
more tendentious and provocative than I at first realized. I think
now the choice of the term was fortunate and the controversies
it generated are fruitful. More neutral terms such as "political
religion" or "religion of the republic" or "public piety" would
not have churned up the profound empirical ambiguities "civil
religion," with its two thousand years of historical resonance,
inevitably did.

On the face of it, what would be more natural than to speak
about civil religion, a subject that has preoccupied theorists of
republican government from Plato to Rousseau? The founders of
this republic had read most of those theorists and were concerned with the problem, even though they did not use the term.[2]
The difficulty arises because for most of those two thousand years
there has been a profound antipathy, indeed an utter incompati-
bility, between civil religion and Christianity. There is even a
question, which I cannot explore here, whether there has not
been a historic antipathy between republican government and
Christianity. Most Christian political theorists down through the
ages have considered monarchy the best form of government
(Christian religious symbolism would seem to be much more
monarchical than republican) and the great republican theorists
—Machiavelli, Rousseau, even Tocqueville—have wondered
whether Christianity can ever create good citizens.[3] Augustine in
the opening books of the *City of God* denounced Roman "civil
theology" as the worship of false gods and the Roman Republic
as based on false ideals and therefore as finally no commonwealth
at all. Rousseau, in arguing for the necessity in a republic of a civil
religion other than Christianity, wrote, "Christianity as a religion
is entirely spiritual, occupied solely with heavenly things; the
country of the Christian is not of this world. . . . imagine your
Christian republic face to face with Sparta or Rome: the pious

Christians will be beaten, crushed, and destroyed. . . . But I am mistaken in speaking of a Christian republic; the terms are mutually exclusive. Christianity preaches only servitude and dependence. Its spirit is so favourable to tyranny that it always profits by such a regime. True Christians are made to be slaves, and they know it and do not much mind: this short life counts for too little in their eyes."[4] And yet at the beginning of our history we were that mutually exclusive thing, a Christian Republic. (Samuel Adams even called us a Christian Sparta.) Or were we? Christianity was never our state religion, nor did we have in Rousseau's strict sense a civil religion, a simple set of religious dogmas to which every citizen must subscribe on pain of exile. What did we have? What do we have now? That indeed is the question.

Religion and Politics

Tension between church and state lies deep in Christian history. The idea of a nonreligious state is very modern and very doubtful. Through most of Western history some form of Christianity has been the established religion and has provided "religious legitimation" to the state. But under that simple formula lie faction, intrigue, anguish, tension, and, on occasion, massacre, rebellion, and religious war. Through much of history the state has dominated a restless church, exploited it, but never destroyed its refusal of final allegiance. On occasion the church has mastered the state, used it for its own ends, and temporalized its spiritual loyalties into a kind of religious nationalism. In all this Christianity is no different from other religions I have characterized as being at the historic stage.[5] Even religions that seem to be much more intrinsically political, such as Islam or Confucianism, have for most of their histories been involved in uneasy and unhappy alliances with state power. Relative to the first four caliphs all Muslim rulers have been viewed as at least faintly illegitimate by the religious community. Relative to the ancient sage kings all the Chinese emperors have lacked fundamental legitimacy in the eyes of the Confucian scholars.

The very spirituality and otherworldliness of Christianity has provided a certain avenue for reducing the tension not always open to other historic religions: the differentiation of functions, the division of spheres. Yet no solution has ever dissolved the underlying tensions described by Augustine and Rousseau. The tendency has been for every solution to break down into religion as the servant of the state or the state as the servant of religion.

Yet there have been great periodic yearnings in Western history to overcome the split, to create a society that would indeed be a Christian republic, where there would be no split in the soul between Christian and citizen. Savonarola had such a dream in fifteenth-century Florence, as did the Anabaptists in sixteenth-century Germany and some of the sectarians during the civil war in seventeenth-century England. Most of these experiments were highly unstable and illustrated rather than refuted Rousseau's argument for mutual exclusiveness. Yet John Calvin in sixteenth-century Geneva created a city that was Christian and republican in an organic way that had few precedents (and that stood curiously behind Rousseau's own republican theorizing). Church and state were not fused; indeed, formal distinctions were sharply maintained. Yet Christian and citizen were finally two ways of saying the same thing. Even more to the point, the New England colonies in the seventeenth century were Christian republics in a comparable sense. In Massachusetts, for example, only Christians could be citizens, though the church did not control the state and both church and state were governed by their members. Even though the reality of this experiment had evaporated by the early eighteenth century, the memory was still strong in the minds of the founders of the republic.

The civil theology of the youthful Hegel in Germany during the decades after the French Revolution shows the yearning for the union of Christian and citizen was still vigorous at the end of the eighteenth century.[6] These youthful speculations stand behind Hegel's mature political theory as well as, curiously, behind the thought of Marx about man and citizen.

Could there be a sense in which the American republic, which has neither an established church nor a classic civil religion, is, after all, a Christian republic, or should I say a biblical republic, in which biblical religion is indeed the civil religion? Is that what it means to say we are "a nation with the soul of a church"?[7] The answer, as before, is yes and no. The American solution to the problem of church and state is unprecedented, unique, and con-

fused. I shall turn from external speculation and from the introduction of tendentious terms like "civil religion" to the way the
tradition has understood itself.

The Work of the Founders

Today the almost Pavlovian response applied to all problems in
this area is "the separation of church and state." That phrase,
especially when it is intensified with the unfortunate Jeffersonian
image of the "wall of separation," is pernicious precisely to the
degree it seems to offer a clear solution when in fact it creates
more difficulties than it eliminates. The first thing to remember
is that the phrase "separation of church and state" has no constitutional standing. The first clause of the first amendment states,
"Congress shall make no law respecting an establishment of religion." That clause has a long history of interpretation that I shall
not review here, but it certainly does not mean and has never
meant the American state has no interest in or concern for religion, or churches either, for that matter, and it certainly does not
mean religion and politics have nothing to do with each other.[8]
To the extent the "wall of separation" image leads to those
conclusions it distorts the entire history of the American understanding of religion and leads to such absurd conclusions as that
religious congregations should have no tax exemption and legis-
lative bodies should not be opened with prayer. To attribute such
intentions to the founders of the republic is not only a historical
error but a political error about the nature of the republic. In-
spection of the second clause of the first amendment, "or prohibiting the free exercise thereof," should begin to dispel the distor-
tions of the extreme separationist position.

The Constitution, while prohibiting a religious establishment,
protects the free exercise of religion. It is this second clause to
which that other common phrase, "religious freedom," refers, a
phrase that has often been used to sum up the American teaching
about religion. This phrase too has a significant Jeffersonian
source, for Jefferson pointed to his authorship of a bill for "establishing religious freedom" in Virginia as one of the three things
he most wanted to be remembered for. The phrase "establishing
religious freedom," which is not constitutional but which expli-

cates the free exercise clause, suggests the positive institutionalization in this area. Indeed, religious freedom or free exercise is the controlling idea. The prohibition of the establishment of a particular religion is required because it would be an infringement on religious freedom. Even so, today it is not uncommon for the religious freedom concept to be swallowed up in the separation concept because freedom here as elsewhere is interpreted in purely negative terms, as the liberal philosophical tradition tends to treat it. Religious freedom becomes then merely the right to worship any God you please or none at all, with the implication that religion is a purely private matter of no interest or concern to political society. I will argue that "establishing religious freedom" means something much more than that, indeed, that it has a powerful positive political significance. But the difficulty of interpretation is not entirely in the mind of the analyst. It is not just a question of reading late twentieth-century ideas about religion into the minds of the founders, though there is much of that. The difficulty is rooted in certain fundamental unclarities about the American political experience and the nature of the American regime, unclarities that go back to the formative period of the republic.

The basic unclarity rests on whether we are a republic in recognizable relation to the republics of classical and modern times and dependent on that inner spirit of republican character and mores that makes for republican citizenship or whether we are a liberal constitutional regime governed through artificial contrivance and the balancing of conflicting interests. What we wanted was to have our cake and eat it too, to retain the rhetoric and spirit of a republic in the political structure of a liberal constitutional state. In so doing we blurred every essential political consideration, including the place of religion in our public life. Indeed, we artfully used religion as a way of evading the incompatibilities in our political life. For as long as the religious bodies remained vital and central in our public life, the evasion was (at least partially) successful. Today, when religion, more even than our other institutions, is uncertain about itself, the evasion is no longer tenable. But I am getting ahead of myself.

The great political philosophers from Aristotle to Machiavelli to Montesquieu (who had such an influence on the founders of the republic) all believed a political regime is an expression of the total way of life of a people, its economics, its customs, its religion. The way of life correlates with the type of person the society produces and the political capacities that inhere in that person. As Montesquieu said, a despotic society will have despotic customs—the arbitrary use of power, dependence of inferiors on superiors, slavery—that will produce a person primarily motivated by fear, just the right kind of subject for a despotic polity. But a republic will have republican customs—public participation in the exercise of power, the political equality of the citizens, a wide distribution of small and medium property with few very rich or very poor—customs that will lead to a public spiritedness, a willingness of the citizen to sacrifice his own interests for the common good, that is, to a citizen motivated by republican virtue. It would be as absurd to expect a people long inured to despotism to create a successful republic as for a republican people to tolerate a despotic regime. And yet these patterns are not fixed. There is indeed constant flux and a tendency toward degeneration—good customs become corrupted and republican regimes become despotic. Since republics go against gravity, so to speak, it is essential if a republic is to survive that it concern itself actively with the nurturing of its citizens, that it root out corruption and encourage virtue. The republican state therefore has an ethical, educational, even spiritual role, and it will survive only as long as it reproduces republican customs and republican citizens.[9]

But the much newer form of political organization, which I am calling liberal constitutionalism though it grew in the very seedbeds of modern republicanism, developed a markedly different idea of political life, partly in response to a newly emerging economic order. Though formulated by some of the toughest minds in the history of modern philosophy—Hobbes, Locke, Hume, and Adam Smith—this tradition gave rise to what would appear to be the most wildly utopian idea in the history of political thought, namely, that a good society can result from the actions of citizens motivated by self-interest alone when those actions are organized through the proper mechanisms. A caretaker state, with proper legal restraints so that it does not interfere with the freedom of the citizens, needs to do little more than

maintain public order and allow the economic market mechanisms and the free market in ideas to produce wealth and wisdom.

Not only are these political ideas, republicanism and liberalism, different; they are profoundly antithetical. Exclusive concern
for self-interest is the very definition of the corruption of republican virtue. The tendency to emphasize the private, particularly
the economic side of life in the liberal state, undermines the
public participation essential to a republic. The wealth the liberal
society generates is fatal to the basic political equality of a republic. And yet the American regime from the beginning has been
a mixture of the republican and the liberal regimes and has never
been a pure type of either. The republican moment emerged
first, however, out of the revolutionary struggle and crystalized
in a document, the Declaration of Independence. The liberal
moment emerged second, during the complex working out of
interests in the new nation, and crystalized in the Constitution.
Even that division is too simple, for there are liberal elements in
the Declaration of Independence and republican elements in the
Constitution, but it does suggest from the very beginning the
balance has never been very easy or very even. The Declaration
of Independence has several central references to God and the
Constitution has none at all. It is time, then, to turn to religion
as a means of mediating the tensions within the American regime.

Religion in the Early Republic

In the early republic religion had two vital locations: in the superstructure and in the infrastructure of the new political regime. It
is to the superstructural location of religion that the Declaration
of Independence points. By superstructural I mean a locus of
sovereignty taken to be above the sovereignty of the state. Perhaps the most striking recognition of this superordinate sovereignty comes from the hand of Madison in 1785 during the
debate on the bill establishing religious freedom in Virginia: "It
is the duty of every man to render to the Creator such homage,
and such only, as he believes to be acceptable to him. This duty
is precedent both in order of time and degree of obligation, to
the claims of Civil Society. Before any man can be considered as

a member of Civil Society, he must be considered as a subject of the Governor of the Universe: And if a member of Civil Society, who enters into any subordinate Association, must always do it with a reservation of his duty to the general authority; much more must every man who becomes a member of any particular Civil Society, do it with a saving of his allegiance to the Universal Sovereign." Here Madison confines himself to the superordinate sovereignty of God over the individual citizen, which precedes the sovereignty of political society over him.

The Declaration of Independence points to the sovereignty of God over the collective political society itself when it refers in its opening lines to "the laws of nature and of nature's God" that stand above and judge the laws of men. It is often asserted that the God of nature is specifically not the God of the Bible. That raises problems of the relation of natural religion to biblical religion in eighteenth-century thought that I do not want to get into here, but Jefferson goes on to say, "We hold these truths to be self evident, that all Men are created equal, that they are endowed by their Creator with certain unalienable Rights, that among these are Life, Liberty and the pursuit of Happiness.—That to secure these rights, Governments are instituted among Men, deriving their just Powers from the consent of the governed,—That whenever any Form of Government becomes destructive of these ends, it is the Right of the People to alter or abolish it." We have here a distinctly biblical God who is much more than a first principle of nature, who creates individual human beings and endows them with equality and fundamental rights.

It is significant that the reference to a suprapolitical sovereignty, to a God who stands above the nation and whose ends are standards by which to judge the nation and indeed only in terms of which the nation's existence is justified, becomes a permanent feature of American political life ever after. Washington and Jefferson reiterate, though they do not move much beyond, the language of the Declaration of Independence in their most solemn public addresses, such as their inaugural addresses or Washington's Farewell Address. The existence of this highest level religious symbolism in the political life of the republic justifies the assertion that there is a civil religion in America. Having said that, I must also say American civil religion is formal and in a sense marginal, though very securely institutionalized. It is formal in the sparsity and abstraction of its tenets, though in this it is very close to Rousseau's civil religion. It is marginal in that it has no official support in the legal and constitutional order. It is in this connection that I must again point out the absence of any reference to God, and thus of any civil religion, in the Constitution of the United States. Belief in the tenets of the civil religion are legally incumbent on no one and there are no official interpreters of civil theology. Indeed, because of the formality I have just pointed out, there was very little civil theology to interpret, although we did produce at a critical juncture in our history at least one great civil theologian, Abraham Lincoln.

The marginality of the American civil religion is closely connected with the liberal side of our heritage and its most important expression, the Constitution. This side has led many to deny there is a civil religion or there ought to be in America. And indeed, from the point of view of the liberal political idea there need not and perhaps ought not to be. The state is a purely neutral legal mechanism without purposes or values. Its sole function is to protect the rights of individuals, that is, to protect freedom. And yet freedom, which would seem to be an irreducible implication of liberalism on etymological grounds alone, no matter how negatively and individualistically defined, does imply a purpose and a value. Since I believe a pure liberalism is a *reductio ad absurdum* and a sociological impossibility, I would locate here at least one of the reasons a pure liberal state has never existed and why in America the rhetoric and to some extent the substance of republicanism has always existed in uneasy tandem with liberalism.

Precisely from the point of view of republicanism civil religion is indispensable. A republic as an active political community of participating citizens must have a purpose and a set of values. Freedom in the republican tradition is a positive value that asserts the worth and dignity of political equality and popular government. A republic must attempt to be ethical in a positive sense and to elicit the ethical commitment of its citizens. For this reason it inevitably pushes toward the symbolization of an ultimate order of existence in which republican values and virtues make sense.

Such symbolization may be nothing more than the worship of the republic itself as the highest good, or it may be, as in the American case, the worship of a higher reality that upholds the standards the republic attempts to embody.

Yet the religious needs of a genuine republic would hardly be met by the formal and marginal civil religion that has been institutionalized in the American republic. The religious superstructure of the American republic has been provided only partially by the civil religion. It has been provided mainly by the religious community entirely outside any formal political structures. Here the genius and uniqueness of the American solution is to be found. At the 1976 Democratic convention Barbara Jordan called for the creation of a national community that would be ethical and even spiritual in content. This is what Talcott Parsons calls the "societal community." It is what might be called in Europe the nation as opposed to the state. It is in a sense prepolitical, but without it the state would be little more than a mechanism of coercion.

The first creation of a national community in America, it is now widely recognized, preceded the revolution by a generation or two. It was the result of the Great Awakening of the 1740s, a wave of religious revivalism that swept across the colonies and first gave them a sense of general solidarity. As the work of Professor Nathan Hatch has shown, this religious solidarity was gradually given a more political interpretation from within the religious community in the 1750s and 1760s with the emergence of what he has called "civil millennialism," namely, the providential religious meaning of the American colonies in world history.[10] It is the national community with its religious inspiration that made the American Revolution and created the new nation. It is the national community that was, in my sense of the term, the real republic, not the liberal constitutional regime that emerged in 1789.

The liberal regime never repudiated the civil religion that was already inherent in the Declaration of Independence and indeed kept it alive in our political life even though the Constitution was silent about it. From the point of view of the legal regime, however, any further elaboration of religious symbolism beyond that of the formal and marginal civil religion was purely private. From the point of view of the national community, still largely religious in its self-consciousness, such elaboration was public even though lacking in any legal status. Here we can speak of public theology, as Martin Marty has called it, in distinction to civil religion. The civil millennialism of the revolutionary period was such a public theology and we have never lacked one since.

As a number of scholars have begun to recognize, the problems of creating a national community in America did not decrease with the establishment of the constitutional regime but in a sense became more severe. With the formation of the new nation the centrifugal forces that were restrained during the revolutionary struggle came to the fore and a sense of national community actually declined. To some extent a national community in the new nation was not fully actualized until after the trauma of the Civil War, though that event set in motion new problems that would later create even greater difficulties in maintaining a genuine national community. But, as Perry Miller has pointed out, to the extent we began to create a national community in the early national period it was again religious revivalism that played an important role.[11] I would not want to minimize the role of enlightenment thought in complicated relation with the churches that Sydney Mead has so brilliantly emphasized. From my point of view enlightenment religion and ethics were also a form of public theology and played a significant role. Yet Jefferson's hope for a national turn to Unitarianism as the dominant religion, a turn that would have integrated public theology and the formal civil religion much more intimately than was actually the case, was disappointed and public theology was carried out predominantly in terms of biblical symbolism.

Even though I have argued that the public theology that came out of the national community represented the real republic, I do not want to idealize it. As with all vigorous young republics it had an element of self-intoxication that has had ominous consequences for us ever after. The "chosen people" or "God's new Israel" symbolism that was pretty well eliminated from the formal civil religion was common in the public theology, though it also had its critics. The public theology provided a sense of value and purpose without which the national community and ultimately even the liberal state could not have survived, but it was never entirely clear what that value and purpose was. On the one hand it seemed to imply the full realization of the values laid down in the Declaration of Independence but certainly not fully implemented in a nation that among other things still legalized slavery. On the other hand it could imply a messianic mission of manifest destiny with respect to the rest of the continent. It may be a sobering thought, but most of what is good and most of what is bad in our history is rooted in our public theology. Every movement to make America more fully realize its professed values has grown out of some form of public theology, from the abolitionists to the social gospel and the early socialist party to the civil rights movement under Martin Luther King and the farm workers' movement under Caesar Chavez. But so has every expansionist war and every form of oppression of racial minorities and immigrant groups.

The clearest and probably the purest expression of the ethical dynamism I have located in the realm of the public theology broke through at one crucial moment in our history into the civil religion itself in the person of our greatest, perhaps our only, civil theologian, Abraham Lincoln. Basing himself above all on the opening lines of the Declaration of Independence, in the Gettysburg Address he called us to complete "the great task remaining before us," the task of seeing that there is a "new birth of freedom" and that we make real for all our citizens the beliefs upon which the republic is based. In the Second Inaugural Address Lincoln incorporated biblical symbolism more centrally into the civil religion than had ever been done before or would ever be done again in his great somber tragic vision of an unfaithful nation in need above all of charity and justice.

It has not been my purpose here to evaluate the whole checkered story of civil religion and public theology in our national history but only to point out they have been absolutely integral to one aspect of our national existence, namely, our existence as a republican people. But so far I have spoken only of what I have called the superstructural role of religion in the republic. Now I would like to turn to the infrastructural role.

Religion and the Creation of Citizens

As I have already pointed out in describing the classical notion
of a republic, there is a necessity in such a regime not only for
asserting high ethical and spiritual commitments but also for
molding, socializing, and educating the citizens into those ethical
and spiritual beliefs so they are internalized as republican virtue.
Once again, however, when we look at the liberal constitutional
regime we will see a complete lacuna in this area. The state as a
school of virtue is the last thing a liberal regime conceives itself
to be. And yet here too what the liberal regime could not do the
national community as the real republic could.

The problem was partly handled through federalism. What
would not be appropriate on the part of the federal government
could appropriately be done at lower jurisdictional levels. Just as
religion was much more open and pervasive at local and even
state levels through most of our history than it ever was at the
federal level, so the state as educator, and educator in the sphere
of values, was widely accepted at lower jurisdictional levels. Robert Lynn has brilliantly shown how the McGuffy readers purveyed
a religious and republican ideology, including a powerful stress
on the common good and the joys of participation in the public
life, during much of the nineteenth century.[12]

And yet, as important as the public schools have been, the real
school of republican virtue in America, as Alexis de Tocqueville
saw with such masterful clarity, was the church. Tocqueville said
religion is the *first* of our political institutions. It was a republican
and a democratic religion that not only inculcated republican
values but gave the first lessons in participation in the public life.
More than the laws or the physical circumstances of the country,
said Tocqueville, it was the mores that contributed to the success
of the American democracy, and the mores were rooted in religion. As a classic theorist of republican government would,
Tocqueville saw that naked self-interest is the surest solvent of
a republican regime, and he saw the commercial tendencies of
the American people as unleashing the possibility of the unre-
strained pursuit of self-interest. But he saw religion as the great
restraining element that could turn naked self-interest into what
he called "self-interest rightly understood," that is, a self-interest

that was public spirited and capable of self-sacrifice. In this way Tocqueville showed how religion mitigated the full implications of American liberalism and allowed republican institutions to survive. Late in his life he began to doubt that such a compromise would really work in the long run, and his doubts have been all too fully confirmed by our recent history. Yet for its time and place Tocqueville's analysis was undoubtedly right. It gives us an essential clue to understand this strange, unique, and perhaps finally incoherent society in which we live.

What Tocqueville saw about the role of religion in such a society as ours was well understood by the founders of the republic. It is significant, for example, that John Adams, during his first year as our first vice-president under the new liberal constitutional regime, said, "We have no government armed with power capable of contending with human passions unbridled by morality and religion. Our constitution was made only for a moral and a religious people. It is wholly inadequate to the government of any other."[13] And Washington in his Farewell Address wrote, "Of all the suppositions and habits which lead to political prosperity Religion and morality are indispensable supports. In vain would that man claim the tribute of Patriotism, who should labour to subvert these great Pillars of human happiness, these firmest props of the duties of Men and citizens. The mere Politician, equally with the pious man ought to respect and cherish them." Perhaps the recognition by our first and second presidents of the necessity of religion and morality, of the basis in the mores and religious beliefs of a people, for a successful republic, in the rather negative, circuitous, and almost apologetic terms of the quotations, expresses the uneasy compromise between republicanism and a liberal regime I am arguing was characteristic of the new nation. But it also suggests the founders of the republic fully understood the relation between the way of life of a people and their form of political organization.

The Corruption of the Republic

It is inevitable, having celebrated only several years ago the two hundredth anniversary of our republic, that we should look around us to see how well our heritage is understood and how

much of it is still operative in our public life. We might have
hoped that a political campaign for the presidency in that bicentennial year or the recent 1980 campaign would have been educa-
tive in the high republican sense of the term. We have had such
campaigns in the past. In the Lincoln-Douglas debates the deepest philosophical meaning of our republic and of our history was
plumbed by two men of enormous intelligence and sensitivity to
the crucial issues. Alas, we did not get that in 1976 or in 1980.
Perhaps the Illinois farmers who drove into the towns from miles
around to hear the Lincoln-Douglas debates were a different kind
of people from the millions in their living rooms in front of the
television screen. Perhaps there were other reasons. But in recent
campaigns what we got was vague and listless allusions to a
largely misunderstood and forgotten past and an attitude toward
the present that seemed to be determined, above everything else,
not to probe beneath the thinnest of surfaces. And yet the great
themes I have been probing here were present, not in any articulate form but present in the uncertainty, the groping, the yearning for something that has so slipped out of memory as to be
almost without a name. It is the ethical purpose of our republic
and the republican virtue of our citizens, or rather the loss of
them, that has haunted our recent political life.

Our rhetoric speaks in the terms of another day, another age.
It does not seem to express our present reality. And yet our
politicians and those to whom they speak are surprised and troubled by the lack of fit, concerned less to find a new rhetoric than
to find an easy formula to make the old rhetoric apt again. Such
an easy formula is the assertion that we must restrain, control,
and diminish government, as though the enormous growth of
our government were some fortuitous thing and not a sign and
symptom of the kind of society in which we live.

To ask the questions the 1976 and 1980 campaigns did not ask
is to ask whether under the social conditions of late twentieth-
century America it is possible for us to survive as a republic in any
sense continuous with the historic meaning of that term. If we
discover the republican element in our national polity has been
corroded beyond repair, we must consider whether a liberal constitutional regime can survive without it, a question it seems to
me not too difficult to answer, but I am prepared to listen to

contrary arguments. Finally we must ask, if we have the courage, if both our republic and our liberal constitutional regime lack the social conditions for survival, what kind of authoritarian regime is likely to replace them, remembering that republican and liberal regimes have been in the history of the planet few and brief. Perhaps we can even discern, beneath the battered surface of our republican polity, the form of despotism that awaits us. Of course, I would hope to discover how to do what Machiavelli says is that most difficult of all political things, reform and refound a corrupt republic. But we must not flinch from whatever reality is to be discovered.

I have mentioned corruption. Corruption is a great word, a political word with a precise meaning in eighteenth-century discourse even though its use has become narrowed and debased with us. Corruption is, in the language of the founders of the republic, the opposite of republican virtue. It is what destroys republics. It might be well for us today to remember what Franklin said on the last day of the Constitutional Convention, 17 September 1787. Old, sick, tired, he had sat through that long hot Philadelphia summer because his presence was crucial to the acceptance of the new document. He was the very symbol of America. He rose on that last day to call for unanimous consent in hopes that that too might help the document be accepted, and he said, "In these sentiments, Sir, I agree to this Constitution with all its faults, if they are such; because I think a general government necessary for us, and there is no form of Government but what may be a blessing to the people if well administered, and believe further that this is likely to be well administered for a course of years, and can only end in Despotism, as other forms have done before it, when the people shall have become so corrupted as to need despotic Government, being incapable of any other."[14] Can we not see in those words the sentiments of an old republican, aware of the compromises contained in the new Constitution but hoping almost against hope that the republican virtue of the people would offset them, at least for a time?

Corruption, again using the eighteenth-century vocabulary, is to be found in luxury, dependence, and ignorance. Luxury is that pursuit of material things that diverts us from concern for the public good, that leads us to exclusive concern for our own good, or what we would today call consumerism. Dependence naturally follows from luxury, for it consists in accepting the dominance of whatever person or group, or, we might say today, governmental or private corporate structure, that promises it will take care of our material desires. The welfare state—and here I refer to the welfare that goes to the great corporations, to most above the median income level through special tax breaks, and to the workers whose livelihood depends on an enormous military budget as much as to the welfare that goes to the desperately poor to keep them from starving—in all its prolixity is the very type of what the eighteenth century meant by dependence. And finally ignorance, that is, political ignorance, is the result of luxury and dependence. It is a lack of interest in public things, a concern only for the private, a willingness to be governed by those who promise to take care of us even without our knowledgeable consent. I would need to explore throughout our society the degree and extent to which corruption in these forms has gone in order to assess whether there is strength enough in our republic for its survival.

Sources of Revival

I would also need to look at religion, following today the brilliant sociological analysis Tocqueville made of the role of religion in our public life, a role all the founders of the republic discerned. To what extent do our religious bodies today provide us with a national sense of ethical purpose? Certainly here there are some notable recent examples. The religious opposition to the Vietnam War was certainly more effective than the opposition of those who spelled America with a "k." And if we have made some significant progress with respect to the place of racial minorities in our society in the last twenty years, it is due mostly to religious leadership. Yet is the balance of American religious life slipping away from those denominations that have a historic concern for the common good toward religious groups so privatistic and self-centered that they begin to approach the consumer cafeteria model of Thomas Luckmann's invisible religion? And to what extent is the local congregation any longer able to serve as a school for the creation of a self-disciplined, independent, public-spirited, in a word, virtuous citizen? Have not the churches along with the schools and the family, what I have called the soft structures that deal primarily with human motivation, suffered more in the great upheavals through which our society has recently gone than any other of our institutions, suffered so much that their capacity to transmit patterns of conscience and ethical values has been seriously impaired? I am not prepared to say the religious communities, among whom I would include the humanist communities, are not capable even today of providing the religious superstructure and infrastructure that would renew our republic. Indeed, I would look to them, as always before in our history, for the renewing impulse, the "new birth" any ethical institution so frequently needs. But the empirical question as to whether the moral capacity is still there on a sufficient scale seems to me open.

If we look to my own community, the scholarly community, there is not a great deal to be proud of. We have left the understanding of our basic institutions, as we have left everything else, to the specialists, and with notable exceptions they have not done a very good job of it. Somehow we have never established a strong academic tradition of self-reflection about the meaning of our institutions, and as our institutions changed and our republican mores corroded, even what knowledge we had began to slip away. On the whole it has been the politicians more than the scholars who have carried the burden of self-interpretation. The founders were all political thinkers of distinction. Lincoln's political thought has moments of imaginative genius—his collected works are still the best initiation into a genuine understanding of the regime under which we live. Even as late as Woodrow Wilson and Calvin Coolidge we had presidents who knew our history in intricate detail and understood the theoretical basis of our institutions. In contrast we have never produced a political philosopher of the first rank. The only profound work of political philosophy on the nature of the American polity was written by a Frenchman. Still we have produced works of the second rank that are not without distinction, though they are usually somewhat isolated and eccentric and do not add up to a cumulative tradition. Such works are Orestes Brownson's *The American Republic*

and Raymond Croly's *The Promise of American Life.* But in a barren
time we must be grateful for such works as we have. If we turn
to these works, we will be referred once again to the great tradition with which I began this chapter. Croly quotes the European/
American philosopher George Santayana: "If a noble and civilized democracy is to subsist, the common citizen must be something of a saint and something of a hero. We see, therefore, how
justly flattering and profound, and at the same time how ominous, was Montesquieu's saying that the principle of democracy
is virtue."[15] How ominous indeed! In that context we can understand the bicentennial epigram written by Harry Jaffa, one of the
few political scientists who continues the great tradition today:
"In 1776 the United States was so to speak nothing; but it promised to become everything. In 1976, the United States, having
in a sense become everything, promises to become nothing."[16]

One would almost think the Lord has intended to chastise us
before each of our centennial celebrations so we would not rise
up too high in our pride. Before the centennial he sent us Grant,
before the bicentennial, Nixon (in whom we can perhaps discern
the dim face of the despotism that awaits us—not a despotism of
swastikas and Brownshirts but a despotism of game plans and
administrative efficiency). It is not a time for self-congratulation.
It is a time for sober reflection about where we have come from
and where we may be going.

NOTES

1. Robert N. Bellah, "Civil Religion in America," *Daedalus,* 96 (Winter 1967).
    Reprinted in Robert N. Bellah, *Beyond Belief: Essays on Religion in a Post-
    Traditional World* (New York: Harper & Row, 1970).
2. Benjamin Franklin came close when he spoke of "Publick Religion" in his
    pamphlet of 1750 entitled *Proposals Relating to the Education of Youth in Pensil-
    vania.* See Ralph L. Ketcham, ed., *The Political Thought of Benjamin Franklin*
    (Indianapolis, Ind.: Bobbs-Merrill, 1965), p. 55.
3. Tocqueville wrote in a letter to Gobineau of 5 September 1843: "The duties
    of men among themselves as well as in their capacity of *citizens,* the duties
    of citizens to their fatherland, in brief, the public virtues seem to me to have
    been inadequately defined and considerably neglected within the moral
    system of Christianity." Alexis de Tocqueville, *The European Revolution and*

Correspondence with Gobineau, John Lukacs, ed. and trans. (Garden City, N.Y.: Doubleday Anchor, 1959), p. 192.
4. Jean Jacques Rousseau, *The Social Contract,* trans. Willmoore Kendall (Chicago, Ill.: Gateway, 1954), book 4, chap. 8, pp. 204–223.
5. See Robert N. Bellah, "Religious Evolution," *American Sociological Review,* 29 (1964), pp. 353–374. Reprinted in Bellah, *Beyond Belief.*
6. See Raymond Plant, *Hegel* (Bloomington: Indiana University Press, 1973), chap. 1.
7. See Sidney E. Mead, *The Nation with the Soul of a Church* (New York: Harper & Row, 1975).
8. It is worth noting that while the Constitution specifically forbade a non-republican form of government in any state, the First Amendment did not forbid the states to establish religion.
9. Jean Jacques Rousseau, *The Government of Poland,* trans. Willmoore Kendall (Indianapolis, Ind.: Bobbs-Merrill, 1972), pp. 29–30, is contemptuous of a people who are not ethically prepared for it espousing liberty:

"I laugh at those debased peoples that let themselves be stirred up by agitators, and dare to speak of liberty without so much as having the idea of it; with their hearts still heavy with the vices of slaves, they imagine that they have only to be mutinous in order to be free. Proud, sacred liberty! If they but knew her, those wretched men; if they but understood the price at which she is won and held; if they but realized that her laws are stern as the tyrant's yoke is never hard, their sickly souls, the slaves of passions that would have to be hauled out by the roots, would fear liberty a hundred times as much as they fear servitude. They would flee her in terror, as they would a burden about to crush them."

10. Nathan O. Hatch, *The Sacred Cause of Liberty* (New Haven, Conn.: Yale University Press, 1977). See especially chap. 1.
11. Perry Miller, *The Life of the Mind in America* (New York: Harcourt, Brace and World, 1965), chap. 1.
12. Robert Wood Lynn, "Civil Catechetics in Mid-Victorian America: Some Notes about American Civil Religion, Past and Present," *Religious Education,* 68, no. 1 (1973), pp. 5–27.
13. Quoted in John R. Howe, Jr., *The Changing Political Thought of John Adams* (Princeton, N.J.: Princeton University Press, 1966), p. 185.
14. Ralph L. Ketcham, ed., *The Political Thought of Benjamin Franklin* (Indianapolis, Ind.: Bobbs-Merrill, 1965), p. 401.
15. Raymond Croly, *The Promise of American Life* (New York: Macmillan, 1909), p. 454.
16. Harry V. Jaffa, *How to Think About the American Revolution* (Durham, N.C.: Carolina Academic Press, 1978), p. 1.

II. Civil Religion in Comparative Perspective

2. The Japanese and American Cases

ROBERT N. BELLAH

Sidney Mead has emphasized the uniqueness of the American solution to the religiopolitical question. In so doing he has contrasted America to the long preceding history of "Christendom." The American republic has not had a state church in part because it has not had a state or church of traditional type. The "religion of the republic" is to be identified with neither state nor church in their conventional form.[1] Phillip Hammond in Chapter 3 and John Coleman elsewhere argue American civil religion is distinct from other forms of civil religion in that it is differentiated from both church and state.[2] Indeed, Hammond wonders whether the term "civil religion" ought not to be restricted to situations typologically similar to the American case, which would make the term rather restrictive and perhaps therefore stronger in comparative perspective. Both Coleman and Hammond offer suggestions for a typology of possible civil religions. James Wolfe has developed a typology of civil religions linked to my typology of the stages of religious evolution.[3] This chapter builds on these previous efforts to develop a comparative perspective. Not only are comparisons interesting in themselves; they often reveal new dimensions to the cases being compared. I hope some refractory features of the American case may be illuminated by a comparative context.

It has seemed useful, following Wolfe, to consider civil religions as varying with the stage of religious evolution. In this regard the contrast between Japan and the United States may be especially instructive since in Japan in the recent past and to a certain extent even today there seems to have survived a civil religion of archaic type (involving a fusion of divinity, society, and the individual), whereas the United States has a civil religion of distinctly modern type (with a high degree of differentiation between divinity, society, and the individual).[4]

In setting up my problem this way I am tentatively rejecting Hammond's restrictive use of "civil religion." There is warrant for this broader usage in the origin of the term itself, in that "civil religion" is pretty clearly an outgrowth of the term "civil theology" that Augustine used to characterize the religion of pre-Christian Rome.[5] That religion was, in terms of my typology, distinctly archaic. Whether the term may be usefully generalized beyond these two types of cases remains to be seen. Now I assert every society must link religion and politics somehow, though that assertion itself, I have learned, is somewhat tendentious.

One way to contrast archaic and modern society, or rather the modern West and all traditional societies, archaic or historic, is to point out, as Louis Dumont following Alexis de Tocqueville has been doing in recent years, that traditional societies are characterized by hierarchy whereas modern societies are characterized by equality—at least in ideal.[6] This contrast is rooted not just in political ideology but in fundamental conceptions of the nature of reality. It will therefore affect the nature of civil religion in the contrasting cases. Indeed, hierarchy or equality may be at the core of the respective civil religions. I can illustrate the difference by quoting from two fundamental documents from Japanese and American civil religion.

The first is article three of Shōtoku Taishi's seventeen-article "constitution" of A.D. 604 (though it may be later). This is one of the earliest conscious documents of what we might call Japanese civil religion. It is more a declaration of principles than what we would normally consider a constitution and in this regard is comparable to the American document I will turn to shortly.

> Article Three. When you receive the imperial commands, fail not scrupulously to obey them. The lord is Heaven, the vassal is Earth. Heaven overspreads, and Earth upbears. When this is so, the four seasons follow their due course, and the powers of Nature obtain their

efficacy. If the Earth attempted to overspread, Heaven would simply fall in ruin. Therefore is it that when the lord speaks, the vassal listens; when the superior acts, the inferior yields compliance. Consequently when you receive the imperial commands, fail not to carry them out scrupulously. Let there be a want of care in this matter, and ruin is the natural consequence.[7]

In contrast consider a long sentence from the charter document of American civil religion:

> We hold these truths to be self-evident; that all men are created equal; that they are endowed by their creator with certain inalienable rights; that among these are life, liberty, and the pursuit of happiness; that to secure these rights, governments are instituted among men, deriving their just powers from the consent of the governed; that whenever any form of government becomes destructive of these ends, it is the right of the people to alter or abolish it, and to institute new government, laying its foundations on such principles, and organizing its powers in such form, as to them seem most likely to effect their safety and happiness.

It is clear in the Japanese case that all men are *not* created equal. Society is embedded in the natural cosmos. Just as heaven is naturally above the earth so are superiors naturally above inferiors. Any attempt to tamper with this natural hierarchy can only produce chaos and ruin. The ideas expressed in article three are clearly Confucian, but this ideology blended easily with Shintō mythology in terms of which the Japanese emperor is descended from the sun goddess and takes his preeminence on earth just as she takes hers among the gods. Hierarchy is rooted in genealogy, which goes back to the so-called age of the gods.

Article two of the "constitution" of 604 brings in still another element of legitimation. It begins "Sincerely reverence the three treasures" and goes on to speak of the Buddha, the dharma, and the sangha. Here the emperor as protector of the sangha is the recipient of the divine protection of the Buddha and the dharma. But Buddhism, with its doctrine of individual enlightenment and its recurrent teaching that a monk should not bow down before a king, is only ambiguously supportive of political hierarchy. Even Confucianism, with its doctrine that the lowliest peasant could become, through virtue, a sage, has a nonhierarchical side, one that would be realized much later in the Tokugawa period when someone like Ishida Baigan could proclaim, "Every man is a small heaven and earth" and thus a focus of individuality and dignity.[8]

It is true that in Japan monks usually did bow down before political authority and sages from the common people were rare indeed. But one could give examples to show that nonhierarchical tendencies were never entirely absent. There are clearly egalitarian elements even in the overwhelmingly hierarchical context of Japanese culture and civil religion.

Conversely, there are hierarchical elements in the American symbolism. Human equality is asserted not only as self-evident but as the result of the action of a divine creator. Further, the declaration has spoken in its opening lines of "the laws of nature and of nature's God." There is thus a cosmic, divine hierarchy in which human values, including equality, make sense and there is a clear notion that God is above and superior to men just as the laws of nature transcend and take priority over the laws of political society.

If the Japanese case has egalitarian components, even if relatively minor ones, and the American case has hierarchical components, even if largely confined to the background, we might wish to consider that the contrast hierarchy/equality is a polarity or a continuum rather than an absolute antinomy.

It is easy for us as Americans and for modern Japanese influenced by Western ideologies to view the hierarchical aspect of Japanese ideology and civil religion as sheer defensive rationalization for political rule. There is much to support such a view. For one thing Japanese civil religion seems to be subject to conscious manipulation at least as early as the sixth or seventh centuries. The degree of self-consciousness in the process does not fit well with the picture of traditional *Gemeinschaft* society, changing by slow unconscious accretion. Neither does it fit well with the claims of modern spokesmen for state Shintō that it has existed "for ages eternal" and has been "true at all times and in all places." Conscious rational manipulation seems more "modern" than "traditional." And yet conscious rational manipulation characterizes Japanese civil religion at crucial turning points throughout its history.

Not only do we find in the seventh century the conscious importation of the continental religious ideologies of Confucianism and Buddhism—mainly to bolster the position of the imperial lineage—we find considerable evidence of conscious manipulation of Shintō mythology. Indeed, the significance of the sun goddess, Amaterasu, and her shrine at Ise may have been sharply upgraded at this period to strengthen the position of the imperial lineage relative to other aristocratic lineages claiming divine descent. This flurry of conscious manipulation continues in the eighth century with the codification of the Shintō myths in the *Kojiki* and the *Nihongi* and with the further spelling out of the implications of Confucianism and Buddhism for the Japanese context.

Another period of conscious concern for matters of civil religion extends from the later Sengoku period in the sixteenth century to the early Tokugawa period in the seventeenth century. Here particularly the development of an ideology of public Confucianism helped to bureaucratize the samurai—turn them from private military henchmen into public servants—and to bring the common people actively into the Tokugawa consensus through the idea of benevolent rule *(jinsei)*. The rulers, who, as in Shōtoku's constitution, represent heaven, are to provide a nurturant and paternal regime under which the people can flourish. In addition, thinkers associated with the Tokugawa House refurbished the somewhat tarnished image of the imperial line and derived the legitimacy of the Tokugawa regime from an emperor who was himself an embodiment of heaven and even, in Shintō terms, a divine king. Thus much that we attribute to the Meiji period at the end of the nineteenth century was prefigured two and a half centuries earlier.

But clearly the prime example of conscious manipulation is modern Japanese civil religion, composed of the modern emperor system and its pervasive ideological influence, of which state Shintō was only a part. Winston Davis, one of the chief American students of this development, has recently given a condensed account:

> During the decades of hyperventilated nationalism which preceded the Pacific War, being Japanese was itself a kind of religious affiliation.

One of the major problems for the new Meiji government was how to generate a truly national spirit that would be strong enough to rechannel the particularistic loyalties symbolized by the local *ujigami* [village deities]. The government was also concerned to prevent the growth of class consciousness in villages which were being exploited by landlords, industry and government alike. The aim of the government's ideological program during these turbulent years was the creation of a patriotic but depoliticized village symbolized by the so-called "imperial farmer." After the effects of the world depression of 1929 began to be felt in Japan, many of the urban unemployed sought to return to their families in the countryside. Often they found the way barred by the elders of the village who claimed that the village was too poor or its land too scarce to support the urban refugees. They feared that city ways might corrupt village morals. For this reason, many of the uprooted were unable to return to the village *Gemeinschaft* which had been the traditional solace of the Japanese folk. Instead, at every turn —in factories, schools, and on the street—they were treated to the Siren's song of the family-state. Officially at least, the nation came to regard itself as one extended family or village. Since both family and village had been in some sense religious corporations, the sacred nature of the emerging family-state was obvious.

The "immanental theocracy" which the government concocted in order to achieve these ends was as artificial and contrived as the mythology of the *Kojiki* itself. While the imperial family had existed for well over a millennium, the imperial *system* which now emerged as an ideological technique for controlling the entire populace was something rather new. Mass media were employed to spread among commoners the archaic imperial mythology which in the past had been the serious make-believe of aristocratic and military alone.

After 1887 when Japan failed to win a revision of her "unequal treaties" with Western powers, a host of religio-political societies began to spring up throughout the land until, by 1936, they numbered nearly 750. By seeking to reassert the spiritual unity of the nation in the face of the double threat of Western imperialism and internal disintegration, these groups mediated between traditional religious and political outlooks and the emerging state cult. Since nearly all religious and political bodies contributed to the generation of the symbols and slogans of the new ideology, clearly more was involved in prewar Japanese patriotism than "State Shintō" or "Shintō Nationalism." Too complicated to be identified with Shintō alone, the halo of symbols and slogans and emotions which congealed around Japan in those years would better be denoted by some more general term

such as "civil religion." The pivotal symbols in this religion were the
sacred ancestors of the imperial family. By homologizing these deities
(i.e., the lineage ideology of ancient Japan) with the ancestor worship
of the common people, the government thought to create a feeling of
national unity and dedication. The machinations of Japan's new industrial and military leaders which caused such suffering and depriva-
tions among the rural masses, were now beautified as the "wish" of
the imperial ancestors.[9]

This description is suggestive in the vehemence of its hostility.
In the face of such a powerful attack from the point of view of
modern egalitarian ideology it is a thankless task to defend the
hierarchical aspect of Japanese civil religion, and I will not attempt to do so. Nonetheless, since modern ideology obscures
many of the meanings of the system it criticizes, I shall reiterate
some of those meanings. Hierarchy in Japan as elsewhere is
linked to an ethical system and a set of values. Clearly, from the
Confucian point of view, which has been most explicit about
these matters, the legitimacy of rule is contingent upon the embodiment of values. Rulers who are not benevolent and righteous
do not deserve to rule. Only virtuous rulers deserve respect.
Though in Japan the enormous importance of lineage muted this
ethical conception of politics, it did not entirely destroy it. Not
only did ethical conceptions moderate the behavior of rulers, but,
very explicitly in the Tokugawa period, complaints from commoners and even revolts were justified in the name of ethical
failure of those above—their lack of "benevolent rule." Finally,
as I have already noted, the assertion of values left open the
possibility that those of any class or status might claim to embody
them. The rise of new popular religions in the nineteenth century
and again after 1945 gave practical expression to that possibility.

I have shown that the strong assertion of individual equality in
America took place against the background of religious hierarchical ideas—the Christian conception of divine/human relations—
and classical philosophy, as in the idea of natural law, also ultimately hierarchical. Both Christianity and classical philosophy
had clear sets of values around which society could agree as well
as a principle of equality in that anyone, however humble, who
embodied those values was worthy of dignity and respect.

But the Declaration of Independence does not spell out those

ethical values very clearly. What is essential is the inherent right
to life, liberty, and the pursuit of happiness and the necessity of
government by the consent of the governed. "Liberty" is as close
as we get to an ethical norm, and that term is deeply ambiguous,
depending on whether it is, in John Winthrop's words, freedom
to do the just and the good (Christian freedom) or freedom to
do what you list (the freedom of natural man).[10] While American
civil religion remained extremely vague with respect to particular
values and virtues, the public theology that fleshed it out and
made it convincing to ordinary people fused it with more explicitly Christian, particularly Protestant, values. But even here the
great stress of the Protestant clergy on the providential, indeed
millennial, meaning of the American republic was on the triumph
of "civil and religious liberty," with all the usual ambiguity about
that central term.

Sydney V. James has indicated one important way traditional
conceptions of virtue could be reconciled with the new civil religion.[11] He speaks of a shift from organicist to individualist conceptions of religious unity. In the organicist view (almost inevitably traditional and hierarchical) all must agree on common
conceptions of ultimate truth and good. But in the individualist
conception religion is seen as contributing to social order not
through the assertion of truths all must believe but, with acceptable theological variations among all the religious groups,
through the inculcation of virtues in individuals that would make
them good citizens. Certain common beliefs remain—such as
belief in God. Sidney Mead even speaks of "some conceptions of
the nature of man and his relation to the cosmos" as characteriz-
ing the "cosmopolitan, universal theology of the republic."[12] But
if so, they remain sufficiently abstract and general that plenty of
room is left for the churches as schools of virtue for the creation
of democratic citizens—as Tocqueville saw so clearly.

The egalitarian potentialities we saw as implicit and incipient
in Japanese religion became explicit and fulfilled in modern
Christianity—without, however, breaking the hierarchical religious mold and its assumption that values have an objective
existence in the world. Modern egalitarianism owes at least as
much to modern secular philosophy as it does to Christianity. But
when we look at the conceptual basis of modern secular individu-

alism and egalitarianism, we find the hierarchical mold and with it any objective set of beliefs and values just about gone.

The degree to which modern philosophy represents a radical break with all traditional ideas is only gradually becoming clear, in part because the early modern philosophers were concerned to disguise the full implications of their teachings. John Locke in particular was extremely devious, and the theoretical incoherence of his *Second Treatise on Government*, so often noted, is produced in part by his attempt to obscure the Hobbesian radicalism of his thought with a cloak of references to the Bible and the Anglican theorist Hooker. For us as Americans, Locke's ambiguity may have been fortunate, for it allowed biblical Christianity and classical republicanism to coexist with what we might call radical liberalism, that is, secular atomistic individualism.

But for a variety of reasons the cloak has been more and more torn away in recent American history, leaving in its stead a radical secular individualism whose implications for social coherence are ominous indeed. Beneath the benign visage of John Locke the harsher face of Thomas Hobbes has grown ever clearer. And it is Hobbes's choice between the war of all against all and the absolute rule of the Leviathan state that begins to haunt us in the closing years of the twentieth century.

It has recently been argued that Locke's *Second Treatise* was itself an effort to provide a myth of modern society, indeed, a civil theology. If so, in its stark uncloaked form it is a strange civil theology indeed. Its first tenet is that individuals are equal not by dint of divine creation but because of their sheer biological similarity. Locke does not reiterate but perhaps implies Hobbes's argument for equality because each of us is capable, as a biological entity, of killing any other under the right circumstances. The primary relation is not that between individuals but between the individual and nature. Economics is prior to society. Our appropriation of property is logically prior to our entry into political society, and indeed, the purpose of our entering into political society is "the protection of our property." Thus society is not an organic unity embedded in a divine or divinely created cosmos but rather a conscious creation of adult individuals designed for the rational end of the mutual protection of their interests. It is significant that the words "moral" and "morality" do not appear

in the entire *Second Treatise*. Hobbes had already taught us there
is no such thing as *the good*. "Good" is only a word individuals use
to designate what they desire. Desires are as various as individuals. Thus it is possible to create a society based on the interests
of individuals but not on common values or ethical norms, for
there are none.

The Lockean doctrine of toleration that made such sense in
eighteenth-century America, with its plethora of churches and
sects, could actually operate to undermine any sense of common
values or public morality, hardly a consequence anticipated by
the Christians who embraced it. If matters of ultimate religious
and moral truth are declared to be essentially private—of concern only to individuals and not to society at large—then their
claim of public truth is sharply undermined. There is little doubt
the modern philosophers considered the teachings of the religious bodies untrue.

Of course civil religion and, even more, public theology—the
noncoercive religious truths addressed by particular confessions
to the nation at large or on occasion articulated by a great political leader such as Abraham Lincoln—for a long time postponed
the implication of modern philosophy that religious teachings are
publicly untrue. But the rise of what Peter Berger calls the "cognitive elite" in the twentieth century, particularly in the universi-
ties and the mass media, has created a powerful group asserting
the radical beliefs of modern philosophical liberalism. Indeed,
through the pressure of such groups as the American Civil Liber-
ties Union, philosphical liberalism is rapidly becoming our orthodox civil religion, if I may indulge in a contradiction in terms, and
traditional American views of the relation of religion and society
are declared unconstitutional. The implication of philosophical
liberalism is that all matters of religious and moral belief are
purely private. Any attempt to articulate common beliefs and
practices is an infringement on individual freedom.

The result is we have individuals in society linked not by common beliefs and morals but only, if at all, through common interests. But whereas Locke could speak of the natural harmony of
interests, that harmony has become dubious indeed today.
Where common values and common religious beliefs have been
banished and the natural harmony of interests has proven illu-

sory, only naked interest is left and a society where there are great disparities of wealth and power. The great philosophy of liberation, classical liberalism, turns out to be a justification of the rule of the stronger. The ultimate individual right is the right to commit suicide. And the alternatives seem to be, as I have said already, anarchic social war or authoritarian rule.

But in spite of the cognitive elite, philosophical liberalism has not completely destroyed biblical religion as public theology or republicanism as the ideology of the common good and the public interest. It has thus not wholly vitiated the traditional civil religion. Indeed, in the face of recent crises rearticulation of our traditional views has taken place. In response to the grave challenge of Watergate to the survival of our constitutional regime we reasserted the rule of law. But if law is, as the liberal utilitarians and positivists have told us, only the expression of the interests of individuals and groups, how could it prove superior to the machinations of Watergate? If law is only the rule of the stronger, how can it check the executive power? If the "rule of law" in the context of Watergate is to have any meaning, it is law as grounded in morality and morality as grounded in ultimate reality. It is the "higher law" of the eighteenth century, the laws of nature and of nature's God, to which we have to return.

Whatever we may think of the political consequences, it was probably not accidental that the first man to be elected president after Watergate was also the first in a long time to use the language of evangelical Christianity. Outside the cognitive elite beliefs in the objectivity of religion and morality are widespread. Tocqueville said religion is the first of our political institutions and our freedom depends on it, and perhaps that is still true. It is doubtful that any society, certainly any free society, could long persist on the basis of secular liberalism alone.

I have suggested that hierarchy and equality are interrelated poles rather than absolute opposites and their relation to freedom is dialectical and not linear. Too exclusive an emphasis on hierarchy results in the authoritarianism Japanese society in most of its history displays. But we would not understand the dynamism and vitality of Japanese society if we did not see that within the ideology justifying hierarchy there has been an ethic that encouraged a kind of moral heroism among the common people.

Japanese society has seldom been a system of amoral exploitation, and individual Japanese have not been reduced to the fearful and spiritless automatons despotism classically creates. Indeed, the presence of public spirit and concern for the common good in Japan rivals the public consciousness of the great republics. Without facing this paradox Japan remains an enigma. And only in this context can we see the seriousness of the vacuum of moral values in Japan today.

But America, the very homeland of political freedom, has pushed egalitarian individualism almost to the point of no return. As Tocqueville pointed out so clearly, emphasis on individual interest with no ethical or moral restraint so each is "shut up in the solitude of his own heart"[13] is the road to a new despotism, perhaps far harsher than traditional authoritarianism.[13]

If this analysis is correct, the subject of civil religion and its environing climate of religious and moral belief is not something of mere antiquarian interest, a concern for a past now irrevocably lost. On the contrary, the health of our civil religion may be a subject intimately linked to the survival of our republic.

NOTES

1. Sidney E. Mead, *The Nation with the Soul of a Church*, (New York: Harper & Row, 1975), esp. chap. 4.

2. John A. Coleman, "Civil Religion," *Sociological Analysis*, 31 (Summer 1970), pp. 67–77.

3. James Wolfe, "The Kennedy Myth: American Civil Religion in the Sixties," Ph. D. dissertation, Graduate Theological Union, Berkeley, Calif., 1975.

4. For a fuller development of this terminology see Robert N. Bellah, "Religious Evolution," in Robert N. Bellah, *Beyond Belief: Essays on Religion in a Post-Traditional World* (New York: Harper & Row, 1970), pp. 20–50.

5. Augustine, *City of God* (Harmondsworth, England: Penguin Books, 1972), book VI, chap. 5, pp. 234–236.

6. Louis Dumont, *Homo Hierarchicus* (Chicago: University of Chicago Press, 1967), and *From Mandeville to Marx* (Chicago: University of Chicago Press, 1977).

7. Ryusaku Tsunoda, William Theodore de Bary, and Donald Keene, *Sources of the Japanese Tradition* (New York: Columbia University Press, 1958), p. 50.

8. Robert N. Bellah, *Tokugawa Religion* (New York: Free Press, 1957), chap. 6.

9. Winston Bradley Davis, *Toward Modernity: A Developmental Typology of Popular*

Religious Affiliations in Japan, East Asia Papers Series (Ithaca, N.Y.: Cornell University Press, 1977), pp. 68–70.

10. Winthrop in Edmund S. Morgan, ed., *Puritan Political Ideas* (Indianapolis, Ind.: Bobbs-Merrill, 1965), pp. 138–139.
11. Sidney V. James, personal communication.
12. Sidney E. Mead, *The Nation with the Soul of a Church* (New York: Harper & Row, 1975), p. 69.
13. Alexis de Tocqueville, *Democracy in America,* trans. George Lawrence (Garden City, N.Y.: Doubleday Anchor, 1967), vol. 2, pt. 2, chap. 2, p. 508.

3. The Conditions for Civil Religion: A Comparison of the United States and Mexico

PHILLIP E. HAMMOND

The discussion of civil religion often permits a mischievous conclusion that the existence of a civil religion is fortuitous, a mere cultural "choice." Thus Ferdinand Mount, in an otherwise astute essay on America's bicentennial, comments on the shock effect of Watergate: "What Europeans are bewildered by is the American's *affectation* of pained surprise on receiving a specific proof of the corruption he knows to be endemic to his political system. This amiable *hypocrisy* surely derives from a more intense commitment to that system (italics added)."[1] Such word choice suggests a dash of reality or a sprinkling of cynicism is all that is required to keep Americans from having a civil religion or at least believing in it. The "intense commitment" Mount refers to is apparently seen as voluntary only, an individual matter of taste. However, such a view is hardly tenable if one regards a civil religion—like any religion—as more than a public relations matter. More is at stake than that, a point nicely exemplified in the following description of Shintō: "traditionally speaking, a Japanese person could not divorce himself from Shintō. Until recent times Shintō has tended to define the weight of his cultural and religious heritage. On both the local and national plane Shintō hallows his homeland and his people, as well as the nexus of the religious, political, and natural order. Given this situation, we can understand why Shintō scholars proudly emphasize that Shintō is a natural expression of Japanese life, rather than the product of a definite set of doctrines or a conscious conversion."[2] In other words, civil religion is a social phenomenon; sacred citizenship for Robinson Crusoe is not possible. In fact, a civil religion in a strict sense may be quite unusual.

The American Civil Religion

That there is a civil religion in America seems generally accepted. However, such assertion does not mean a single, overarching ideology serves to legitimate—in a functional sense—whatever the United States and/or its leaders do, since the ideology also provides the language in terms of which they are judged. Nor does the assertion mean all Americans believe equally in the ideology or mean by it the same thing in all respects. (There were probably some agnostics among the Arunta, too.) What the assertion does mean is a widespread acceptance by Americans of a few religiopolitical tenets regarding their nation's history and destiny. And it also means an attention by the leader-elites—perhaps especially the cultural elite but including the religious and political elite—to the more elaborate implications of these tenets. Thus Wimberley and his associates have found in the 1970s, among a large if not absolutely representative sample of North Carolinians, 74 percent agreement with the statement: "Human rights come from God and not merely from laws." Fully 78 percent claim the U.S. flag is "sacred." And remarkably, inasmuch as this particular tenet has undergone considerable challenge since 1964, a third of the people assent to "America is God's chosen nation today."[3] As for the greater civil religious commitment of the elites, evidence is less clear perhaps but generally supportive.[4]

Irrespective of percentage agreements however, which have to be vulnerable to headline influences, politics and religion in America "from the beginning . . . contracted an alliance which has never been dissolved."[5] The ideology underlying this alliance might be summarized as follows: (1) There is a God (2) whose will can be known through democratic procedures; therefore (3) democratic America has been God's primary agent in history, and (4) for Americans the nation has been their chief source of identity.[6]

America's civil religion is not all benevolent and approving, of course. God's "New Israel" is not without fault in this doctrine, but it does have a special mission, even if that mission brings paradox and agony. There is the likelihood, moreover, as Ahlstrom concludes in his massive religious history of the American people, that by the 1970s "Americans, whether conservative, liberal, or radical, found it increasingly difficult to believe that the United States was still a beacon and blessing to the world. Even less were they prepared to understand themselves as chosen to suffering and servanthood."[7]

The folly of Vietnam accompanied by a failure of nerve in civil rights and followed by Watergate no doubt put American civil religion to severe test. The challenge at the cultural level may be too great, and Americans may be undergoing a profound change in the way they relate their society to the realm of ultimate meaning. Certainly one is more inclined to think so to the degree civil religion is viewed as mere individual choice, since one can observe cynicism replacing faith, pessimism replacing hope. But I am arguing civil religion depends upon conditions independent of particular individuals and events. As with all institutions, civil religion is the accretion of many individuals and events and may be eroded by them as well, but if the American civil religion is on the wane, an institutional analysis is required if one is fully to understand what is occurring.

The Concept Revisited

It is instructive to reflect on why Rousseau was concerned about civil religion, advocated it, and coined the term for it. No doubt part of the reason was to provide a substitute belief system for those whose faiths had been shattered by the forces of Enlightenment. But there is a more important reason. Civil religion was not to be just another religion; its purpose was precisely to *harmonize* religion and politics. Pagan religions had been so co-extensive with their political orders that "there was no way of converting a people but by enslaving them." Christianity, by projecting a "kingdom of the other world," changed all that. "Jesus came to establish on earth a spiritual kingdom, which, separating the religious from the political system, destroyed the unity of the State. . . . [A] perpetual conflict of jurisdiction has resulted from this double power, which has rendered any good polity impossible in Christian States; and no one has ever succeeded in understanding whether he was bound to obey the ruler or the priest."[8]

Authority, then, is the crux of the matter—more precisely, authority to set jurisdictional boundaries and invoke transcendental sanctions. For these twin problems Rousseau offers a single solution: civil religion. Civil religion is *religious* because it is necessary that citizens be disposed to "love their duties," and it is *civil* because its sentiments are those of "sociability, without which it is impossible to be either a good citizen or a faithful subject." Therefore, "the dogmas of civil religion ought to be simple, few in number, precisely fixed, and without explanation or comment. The existence of a powerful, wise, and benevolent Divinity, who foresees and provides the life to come, the happiness of the just, the punishment of the wicked, the sanctity of the social contract and the laws: these are its positive dogmas. Its negative dogmas I would confine to one—intolerance. . . ."[9]

Rousseau's overall concern in *Social Contract* is to identify an effective but nondespotic government, a vehicle for expressing the general will. In the book's final part, he discusses several means for "strengthening the constitution of the State," and it is in this context he introduces the notion of civil religion, an aid in governing. Clearly, by calling it "civil," he intended it in some sense to be independent of the church, and, by calling it "religion" he likewise intended it to be independent of the ruling regime. These two features, when cross-classified, not only identify Rousseau's notion of civil religion but also suggest two other ideological situations that have sometimes been regarded as civil religions.[10]

The two dimensions are continuous variables, not dichotomous; so one may speak of "degrees" of Rousseau's civil religion. There are shadings—between civil religion and ecclesiastical legitimizing or between civil religion and secular nationalism. For example, the "political religions" observed in some developing nations would appear to be more than secular nationalistic

Table 1. **Two Dimensions of Civil Religion**

		Is the civil religion independent of the church? (Is it *civil* and not just ecclesiastical?)	
		YES	NO
Is the civil religion independent of the state? (Is it *religious* and not not just secular?)	YES	Rousseau's civil religion	Ecclesiastical legitimacy of the state
	NO	Secular nationalism	

ideologies. Yet having little in the way of any "theology" independent of the state, they are not fully civil religions in Rousseau's meaning of that term.

The point is not to be arbitrary about definitions, however, but rather to reveal the following theoretical issue: All three kinds of ideologies in Table 1 have been called civil religions, but there are obvious differences among them. All represent "links," as Coleman calls them, by which persons may connect their "society's place in space, time, and history to the conditions of ultimate existence and meaning."[11] But these various links emerge from different social conditions. The conditions are what I explore here.

The point is furthered when it is recognized that, like all belief systems, civil religions must be "carried" by organizational "vehicles." The question is which organizations do the carrying. Rousseau seems to suggest the most fully developed civil religion relies exclusively on neither the church nor the state but to a significant degree at least counts on independent vehicles for its support. Whether this occurs depends not only upon the existence of such independent vehicles but also upon the capacity of church personnel and state personnel to cooperate. In the case of the former, can they *relinquish* a monopoly on "God talk" about the nation? In the case of the latter, can they *adopt* a theological rhetoric? If civil religious ideologies are thought of as balloons, I am asking who is able and willing to hold the balloon strings.

Conceived in this fashion the study of civil religion shifts some distance out of the Durkheim camp, where it has generally been. All communities of people may project their "collective representations," as Durkheim had it, but how they do so—and whether in the manner of Rousseau's civil religion—depends upon particular conditions. These conditions are made clearer by a comparative analysis of the United States and Mexico.

Factors Conducive to a Mexican Civil Religion

The day following the inauguration of President Carter, *Excelsior,* a leading newspaper of Mexico City, reported the event in a story filed by its Washington correspondent. "More than political," the headline read, "it was an act almost religious." The story then detailed not only certain obvious religious features of the event, such as the use of a Bible and the invoking of God's name, but it went to extraordinary length in describing the "mysterious silence," the "intense expressions" as if in a "trance" on the faces of some participants, and the "patriotic tears" among many in the audience.[12]

By itself the story is not strange, perhaps. But less than two months before, Mexico had inaugurated President José Lopez Portillo in a ceremony no less resplendent and public. And the following day *Excelsior* devoted many pages to stories and pictures of the event. But nowhere is there mention of "mystery," "intense emotion," or "tears." The president's address is fully reported and the clothing worn by all the participants is carefully described, but no hint is given that Mexico was experiencing an event "almost religious."[13]

In some respects this absence of a religious flavor in the Mexican inauguration is puzzling because so much in Mexican history would augur a robust civil religion. As a result of immigration and intermarriage it early became an ethnically plural society. Its urge for independence became a reality, and without entangling alliances. For nearly as long as the United States, in other words, Mexico has been—with the exception of a few years under Maximilian—a politically autonomous nation-state.

Like the United States, Mexico fought a long and bitter civil war, a war in which ever inclusive rights to full citizenship were claimed and in principle at least were won. This war, begun in 1910, is called The Revolution, and Mexico even today exalts in its revolutionary past, so much so that the historian Brandenburg was able to identify what he calls the "creed" or set of values that emerged from the revolution and to which verbal commitment is nearly universal.[14] This creed is embodied in the only political party to rule since the revolution, the Institutional Revolutionary Party or PRI. It has had no serious challenge at the polls, although opposition parties exist and are encouraged by the ruling regime.

Numerous heroes are remembered from this history, beginning with Hidalgo and Morelos, two Catholic priests who led the war for independence. Those who helped forge constitutionalism in the nineteenth century, especially Benito Juárez, who engineered the 1857 constitution and served as president, are regarded as "fathers" of the country and frequently compared with Washington or Jefferson. The revolution contributes many names to the patriotic platform: Madero, whose challenge to the Díaz dictatorship triggered the civil war; those generals, Zapata and Villa, whose exploits are now so romanticized; and those who led the transition to peace and established a stable government —Carranza and Obregón. Even as recent a president as Cárdinas (1934–1940) is remembered heroically, in part because he accomplished some of the land reform the revolution promised but also because he brought about the nationalization of the oil industry, thereby flexing Mexico's muscle in front of United States and English power. These are only the biggest of the heroes, however. Dozens of others are honored by statues, parks, fountains, and in the naming of streets, cities, and states. These combine with ubiquitous wall slogans, holidays, and the flag to give Mexico an overwhelmingly nationalistic flavor. Whether in city or remote countryside, the nation's history is constantly remembered.

More pertinent to civil religion is the great influence Comte and Spencer exercised with Mexican public educators. Public education was practically nonexistent until the final decades of the nineteenth century, schools being largely church operated and attended by the well-to-do. But then education became a national endeavor, designed by men who have shared something of an outlook ever since.[15] The first of these educational philosophers shared the positivism that marked the Díaz regime, the extreme "human engineering" view. Included was the idea that schools were to mold citizens for society, independent of church and home. Christianity could no longer be taught as such, but, said Ignacio Altamirano, "democracy as religion" should be. In the 1890s Justo Sierra became the center of an intellectual movement that has been called the "Athaeneum of Youth." While trying to temper the positivism of their predecessors with a non-churchly "spiritualism," Sierra and his adherents continued to regard education in terms of the "positivist sociology of Comte, Littré, and Spencer."[16] Sierra oversaw the opening (in 1910) of the National University out of what had been the Pontifical University. This he did "to nationalize learning, to Mexicanize knowledge." But as minister of public education he also "wanted to 'realize the religion of the motherland in the soul of the child,' to create what he called 'the civic religion, the religion which unites and unifies.' "[17] Toward this end Sierra even drew up a list of American "saints," which included Washington and Lincoln from the north, Bolivar and Martí from the south, and Hidalgo and Juárez from Mexico.[18] This group who controlled public education during the decades prior to the revolution clearly *wanted* to create a civil religion.

The interruption for internal war disrupted public educational development for about ten years, but when President Obregón took office in 1920, he appointed as Minister of Education José Vasconcelos, who had been a young member of Sierra's Athaeneum. Indeed, Vasconcelos had created the motto for Sierra's national university—"By virtue of my race the spirit shall speak" —and he attacked the problem of public education with the same religio-national zeal as had his predecessors. He was the "apostle of the new secular religion" as he sought teachers of comparable fervor who would join what he called "a holy crusade for civilization."[19] Vasconcelos never accepted his predecessors' positivism —wherein are studied only "phenomena," he said, and not "noumena"—but he advanced their goal of an education with strong national flavor.[20] Under his leadership the federal constitution was revised to permit greater federal participation and centralization. (Today a uniform curriculum and free textbooks for the primary grades are supplied by the government.) Federal appropriation rose from 1 percent of the budget just prior to 1920 to 15 percent in 1923.[21] Vasconcelos wrote *La Raza Cósmica*

[The cosmic race], in which he imagined "the white, the Indian, the Negro, and the yellow, united in a synthetic ideal . . . the final inclusive race."[22]

With the new pride in things Mexican, the sixteenth-century Cuauhtémoc, the last Aztec commander, joined the parade of heroes, even as Cortés was forever condemned.[23] And in the effort to exalt in the indigenous, the grandeur of local artists was recognized and utilized. Vasconcelos, for example, commissioned the first of the famed Mexican murals. "Nowhere was the religious fervor of the Revolution more apparent than in the secular propagandistic painting of José Clemente Orozco, Diego Rivera, and David Siqueiros. In the colonial era, with the Catholic Church in its ascendence, the native artistic genius found its outlet in the building and decorating of churches. Under the Revolution this genius burst forth again, but now to glorify and explain the new gospel of the secular rival of the Church—the nationalistic government."[24]

It is clear that Mexico has had not only a dramatic past to exalt and an optimistic future to portray but also a means—public education—for doing so. Moreover, for decades it has operated with an educational theory that encourages and justifies a worshipful attitude toward the state. As recently as 1941 the Organic Law of Public Education was revised to direct the Ministry of Education to "weld Mexicans into a single spiritual nucleus."[25]

Catholicism as a Means to Civil Religion

Mexico is a Roman Catholic society. Franciscans, beginning in 1528, followed by Jesuits and Dominicans, swarmed over New Spain and "in an amazingly brief period, completely replaced the native priests as the natural leaders of Indian society."[26] This spiritual conquest was made easier by the number of similarities between the Indian religion and Christianity, similarities in theology, organization, and especially ritual. If the friars had to bend a little in their European orthodoxy, they nevertheless found parallel practices regarding the cross, baptism, confession, communion, feast days, and fasting. Assimilation of Catholicism was relatively easy and nearly complete.

It was assimilation, however, and not wholesale substitution of

Catholicism for its native predecessor. The result was (is) a "strange hybrid of superstition and idolatrous religious concepts."[27] (Good discussions of this hybrid are in Quirk and especially Brenner.[28]) Since any imported religion is likely to take on characteristics of its host society, the hybridization of Catholicism in Mexico would not ordinarily be worth remarking. However, in this case the superstitions and idol worship have remained uncommonly *independent of church and priest,* a point whose importance will become clear presently.[29]

With independence Mexico remained Catholic. During the war both the loyalists and the rebels invoked the name of the church, and clergy were active on both sides. While it is true that the two prominent priest-leaders, Hidalgo and Morelos, were denounced, excommunicated, and shot as traitors, they had no intention of giving up the Church. Indeed, Hidalgo was filled with remorse for all the blood he and his soldiers had spilled and, after his capture in 1811, returned to the bosom of the "Holy Mother Church."[30] And when Morelos drew up a constitution in 1814—the year before his execution—he "specifically guaranteed the sanctity of Roman Catholicism as the only religion to be tolerated in Mexico."[31]

While Morelos's Constitution of Apatzingán was never put into practice, the plan of Iguala (1821), drawn up by Iturbide after independence, also confirmed the official status of Catholicism as the state religion and denied toleration to all other religions.[32] The war for independence, in other words, was reasonably conservative in purpose, especially with respect to the church. The rebel priests would have abolished clerical *fueros* (special legal jurisdictions whereby canon law courts superseded civil courts), but chiefly they wanted, as native-born priests, the same rights as Spanish-born priests. By extrapolation they wanted to abolish as well the marked distinction between the wealthy, land-owning (Spanish-born) class and the Mexican-born and *mestizo* peasant classes.

A few years later (1824) Mexico's first Constitution reaffirmed both the relative conservatism of the independence movement and its commitment to a state church, which "will be perpetually the Roman Catholic Apostolic."[33] Such ecclesiastical concern was not surprising in view of the near-universal identification of

Mexicans as "Catholic," along with church control of 20 percent
to 70 percent of Mexico's wealth. (The larger estimate is older
and entrenched, but the smaller is probably more accurate.)[34]

Even with the rise of "liberalism" in the 1820s and the formation of a so-called "anticlerical" party, clergymen were to be
found among the leaders' ranks. That is to say, while all liberals
favored curtailment of the Church's worldly power and proclaimed the supremacy of civil power, they were not necessarily
"antireligious."[35] The role of Freemasonry in Mexican liberalism
has been asserted, for example, but, while its presence is undeni-
able, its "anti-Catholicism" is by no means obvious. Instead, what
the liberal reformers wanted was a classic separation of church
and state, allowing each institution freedom within its own
sphere—"as long as the government could define the spheres."[36]

For a forty-year period this issue of church-state separation was
fought over. Benito Juárez, supreme court justice and then president, was the liberals' foremost leader and engineer of the 1857
constitution (for which he is now honored by schoolchildren as
the first among national heroes).[37] Earlier outlawed had been any
but "secular" education and the use of civil machinery to enforce
religious vows and payment of church tithes. In 1857 the Church
was stripped of all real estate except worship centers, and the
registration of births, marriages, and deaths was made a civil
affair. Two years later a number of other curtailments on the
Church—known as the Reform Laws—were passed. They officially separated church and state, forbade public officeholders
from attending religious services "in any official capacity," made
marriage a civil act, and legalized divorce.[38] (Rousseau saw the
importance, in the struggle between church and state, of the
authority to marry. Should the church succeed in claiming this
sole right, he commented on the last page of the *Social Contract,*
"it will render ineffectual . . . the Prince, which will no longer have
any subjects except those which the clergy are pleased to give it.
. . . [I]s it not clear that by behaving prudently and keeping firm,
the church alone will dispose of heritances, offices, citizens, and
the state itself, which cannot subsist when only composed of
bastards?")

Admittedly, these laws (and others yet to come) were anticlerical. But while there was some "atheistic" support for them, such

sentiment was not controlling. The chief desire was to create a representative, republican, and democratic government. Most of the liberals remained Catholic. The 1857 constitution preamble, after all, began, "In the name of God and by the authority of the Mexican people." And when Gomez Fariás approached the document as first signer, he knelt and "swore by the Holy Gospel to recognize and obey the Constitution." As Simpson says of the reformers' leader: "To postulate an irreligious or atheistic Juárez is to make him a consummate hypocrite, which he most assuredly was not. He believed in God and Order. With the early Jesuits, he believed that government had its sanction in God's will expressed through the will of the people. In thus elevating the popular will he naturally ran afoul of the clerical prejudices of the time, but he did so from religious conviction."[39]

The Díaz regime followed (1876–1910). Freemason Porfirio Díaz was married to a devout Catholic, and his handling of the church-state matter reflected the ambivalence of this common situation. He confiscated Church property one day and permitted the Church to buy new property the next; "anti-clerical legislation was enforced by his left hand, retracted by his right."[40]

Even in the extreme the constitution of 1917 following the revolution, while undeniably influenced by some delegates bent on destroying the Church, is best described also as "anticlerical" only. That is, like its precursors of 1824 and 1857, it recognized implicitly that the Mexican people are "Catholic" and will have churches; it simply asserted unquestioned governmental authority to set the limits on the churches' domain.

Because of the nature of church-state relations in the history of Mexico, therefore, a current of anticlericalism has been a major force for over a century. Yet Mexico remains profoundly Catholic in its hybrid way. By 1960 Protestants still amounted to only 1.6 percent of the population and Jews 0.3 percent.[41]

Has Mexico a Civil Religion?

Given such an overwhelmingly monolithic and continuing religious heritage and given such an intense national experience, has Mexico blended them into a civil religion? Do politics and religion harmonize in Mexico? They do not in the sense of Rousseau's meaning of that term. There is no transcendental ideology at once independent of both church and state. Mexico has a rather vibrant nationalism, but it is secular; it is not transcendent but remains the domain of the state. And Mexico continues to have a widespread appreciation for the transcendental, but this appreciation is largely apolitical; it remains, in a peculiar way, the domain of the church.

Consider, first, nationalism as a potential civil *religion.* That it is intense is hardly questioned.[42] And it grows year by year, largely as a result of government effort to use education as a unifying, pride-producing agency.

[T]he goals of leadership groups have been successfully wedded with the values and attitude of the people. There is a good deal of pride in the political and economic institutions in Mexico, despite Mexico's still "developing nation" status. Though the average Mexican's cognitions of the political world and his ability to affect political decisions are low, he nevertheless has an unusual faith in his country. The revolutionary turmoil of 1910–1930 has been well integrated into the national memorabilia and, perhaps, is second only to the Bolshevik Revolution in representing a striking example of the impact of an historical occurrence.[43]

Scott estimates that the proportion of Mexican citizens without even a concept of the nation has declined from 90 percent in 1910 to 25 percent in 1963.[44] Inasmuch as the population nearly tripled during that period, the expansion of nationalistic sentiment has been enormous.

But this pride, this nationalism, is decidedly secular. It is not believed God authored the laws of Mexico or "chose" Mexico as a divine instrument. At least that is my estimate. These kinds of questions have not been asked in opinion surveys in Mexico, as nearly as I could determine. Personnel at the Mexican affiliate of International Research Associates doubted that such questions would even have meaning to the Mexican public, a judgment shared by several prominent Mexican social scientists with whom I talked. The ruling party covers almost every available wall on main streets with political slogans (for example, "Fatherland is first," "To serve is the highest duty," "We work for the causes of Mexico," or "We follow the road of the Revolution"), but not one refers to God or any other sacred idea.

Another potential source of civil religious sentiment is the *corrido,* the ballad or poem detailing some event in the nation's history. Existing both as an oral tradition and in print on cheap paper for wide distribution, these *corridos* are often sagas of heroic daring or noble suffering and thus candidates for expression of links between religion and politics. A careful review of a random sample of *corridos* from the revolutionary period (drawn from Vincente T. Mendoza, *El Corrido de la Revolucion Mexicana* [The corrido of the Mexican Revolution], and Armando Maria y Campos, *La Revolucion Mexicana a Travez de los Corridos Populares* [The mexican revolution through popular ballads]) reveals little or nothing to suggest that the troubadours saw Mexican destiny in any transcendental manner. As sponsor of the nationalism, in other words, the state makes no use of transcendental language nor, apparently, do citizens in thinking about their nation. The distance between this nationalism and a civil *religion* thus appears great.

Consider next the context of sacred ideas and language as a potential *civil* religion. There remains the church, which is still attended by some on a regular basis and by many on an occasional basis. More broadly, there is the vast "cultic" activity surrounding saints, giving rise to assessments of Mexico as the leading Catholic country in Latin America. The display of religious symbols is very common. It is not unusual to read on the dashboard of a taxi "God goes with us" or "Holy virgin, protect me." Shrines are not rare—in homes, of course, but also in bus depots, in flower markets, alongside the melon stand, on the highway, and so forth. The most popular of these shrine figures is the Virgin of Guadalupe, a dark-skinned (Indian) Mary whose veneration goes back to 1531.[45] A basilica in her honor stands now at the place where she first appeared to a humble Indian, Juan Diego; and hundreds of thousands of Mexicans from all over the nation make pilgrimages there on the edge of Mexico City. They implore her and thank her, for in such manner a certain "predictable" order enters their lives. As Brenner says, "Countlessly, every day, Guadalupe is on the lips and in the thoughts of all Mexico."[46] Her cult is the strongest and most widespread.

There is no doubt the cult is *national,* moreover. Not only is the dark virgin "the single most powerful element in Mexican Catholicism," but her very darkness has enabled her to symbolize the postcolonial, miscegenized *mestizo* nation.[47] It is not uncommon today for recent immigrants (for example, from the Spanish Civil War) and their children to be targets of discrimination. One epithet for them is "whitey" and indicates not so much skin color as "incompleteness" as a Mexican. The educated and the wealthy may not publicly honor the Virgin of Guadalupe. Certainly they do not walk for miles to make her a pilgrimage, let alone cover the last hundred yards walking on bare knees, as do many poor people. But hers is a national symbol nevertheless. Her banner led in the war of independence and appeared again in the revolution. Not everyone believes the myth about Juan Diego and the miraculous image on his cape, but everyone recognizes the national character of the cult. Guadalupe's basilica is, as Brenner puts it, "the Mexican navel."

But while the cult of Guadalupe is national, it is not particularly "civil" or political. Zapata's armies may have carried her image into battle, but they did so knowing they had no monopoly on her. The other side carried her, too, and for the same reasons: to ensure one's own safety, a loved one's fidelity, improved health, and so forth. In other words, the cult of Guadalupe involves more personal than civic or political acts. The dark virgin's office is implored so that God is on *my* side, not on *our* side. And so it is, to a large extent, with the other saints' cults as well, a point vividly illustrated in the testimony of several of the children of Sanchez, for whom the Lord of Chalma (another cult, centered about sixty miles southwest of Mexico City) was the focus of their spiritual life.[48] Even when the cult is community oriented—as in the case of agricultural saints—it remains largely apolitical. Under these circumstances the distance between this theology and a *civil* religion also appears great.

So Mexico has no civil religion of the sort Rousseau discussed. It had in its history an ecclesiastical legitimizing of the state, a religious heritage that lingers now as cultish attention to saints and shrines; and it has now a vibrant secular nationalism. But these two ideological forces have not merged as they must if a single ideology—which is both *civil* and *religious*—is to occur. Mexico would seem to have been ripe for such a development; so why it did *not* appear requires an explanation. In the search for this explanation we shall discover something more of the conditions for civil religion.

El Cid Versus Cuauhtemoc: Church versus State in Mexico

Cuauhtémoc, the last Aztec leader to defend against the Spanish invaders, has already been introduced here as a national hero, a symbol of the secular state. El Cid, for whom an occasional restaurant in Mexico is named and about whom Robin Hood–type movies sometimes appear, is somewhat more obscure. He was an eleventh-century Spanish figure who helped drive the Moors from Valencia. In a burst of religiopatriotic zeal in 1924, Father Cantú Corro tried to put these two characters together and extol them as joint symbols of the Mexican spirit: the true church *and* the true nation. He failed because while for centuries church and state did make common cause in New Spain, for the past century and a half the situation has clearly been one of church *versus* state. Therein lies the failure to develop a Mexican civil religion, but the explanation is not as clear-cut as it might first appear.

Mexican church-state mutuality—an instance of what I have called "ecclesiastical legitimation of the state"—began to deteriorate in the eighteenth century. That deterioration helped bring about the pressure for autonomy from Spain and helps to explain why priests figured prominently in the movement. The struggle between church and state can thus be dated from 1810, when the priest Hidalgo emitted his "Grito de Dolores" and touched off the war for independence. By the 1830s classically "liberal" sentiment was entrenched in Mexican politics. It was often manifested as anticlerical, and indeed some politicians probably were more anticlerical than proanything. But most of its supporters were converts to the Anglo-French-American political theories of liberty and equality. They desired freedom, and the church was one of the barriers. By 1857 these reformers had built significant constraints around the political and economic power of the Church, and by 1876 these constraints were firmly and legally established. Pope Pius IX responded to the 1857 constitution by declaring "null and void the said decrees and everything else that the civil authority has done in scorn of ecclesiastical authority and of this Holy See."[49] But the cause was lost. Maximilian's defeat

in 1867, followed by the presidency of Juárez and the constitu-
tionalization of the Lerdo Law, meant the liberal reformers had
won the *political* battle. For example, two priests in Saltillo in
1882 argued that the law requiring priests to get proof of civil
registry of birth or marriage before performing Christian baptism or marriage violated the constitutional separation of church
and state. They had to argue in *civil* courts, however, using the
amparo (writ of judicial review provided for in the constitution);
and they lost.[50] The Church was not then or ever again to share
hegemony in Mexico.

Losing the political battle and losing the battle over symbols
are two different things, however. It took the Church another fifty
years to acknowledge losing the first battle, but the second battle
has not been entirely decided even today. Former President
Emilio Portes-Gil, who then became attorney general, wrote in
1935: "The Church is the formidable enemy which the Constitution of 1857 had to face. But in 1914 it found itself again facing
that same enemy, and to show this we have had to review anew
its attitude throughout the past. In our review we have shown that
the stand taken by it against the Law and against the civil authority is exactly the same as in colonial time, just as in 1810, 1822,
1833, 1836, and 1865; and that after the lengthy period enjoyed
by it for recovery it has again adopted the same attitude in 1913,
1914, 1917, 1926, and 1934."[51] Portes-Gil exaggerates, however.
The church never "recovered" after the 1857–1876 period; it
had few political weapons, only symbols to fight with. According
to Leopoldo Ruiz y Flores, exiled apostolic delegate to Mexico,
"The Catholic Church recognizes no human power which can
prevent Her from doing anything She Herself deems necessary
for the salvation of souls; therefore in spiritual matters She is
subordinate to no one."[52] The rhetoric dates from the middle
ages, but by 1934 such a statement was *only* rhetoric, an utterance
of symbols.

"Mexican history might have been a different story," writes
Brandenburg, "if Church had broken with State, hailed Hidalgo
and Morelos as Catholic heroes, and encouraged them to lead the
masses."[53] Indeed, it might have been a different story, but a
different story of symbols, not of power. By 1876 the Church *was*
broken from the state politically, whether or not it concurred.

The Church's only options were to join symbols in a combined venture with the state or to withhold them. It took the latter course.[54]

During the years of the revolution, the Church had reason to side with the liberals, but because the latter were joined by anti-clerical radicals (most notably Villa), it chose instead to back the conservative (losing) side. When the constitution of 1917 was drafted, therefore, "Catholic" representation was nonexistent, and the resulting document not only repeated earlier material restrictions on the Church (such as government ownership of all church property, civil registry of priests, and making marriage a civil matter) but also got in a symbolic lick or two (for example, religious garb was not to be worn in public; worship was to be only an indoor affair; alien priests were forbidden; and no religious labels were allowed for political parties). The symbolic nature of the struggle is stated succinctly in Roman's discussion of the 1917 constitutional congress: "Although other arguments were also used against the clergy, the issue returned time and again to the saving and the building of the nation and to destroying the *ideological* domination of the church" (italics added).[55] Article 3, containing the above restrictions, also declared that primary education is to be free and secular. Since parochial schools constituted so large a part of education in Mexico, this goal was slow in developing. By 1974, 7.8 percent of primary students were still enrolled in private schools, of which half are estimated to be Roman Catholic. Private (and thus Catholic) schools figure more prominently in postprimary education. For example, an estimated 75 percent of the students in Normal Primeria (that is, training to be primary teachers) are in Catholic schools.[56] An obvious ambivalence surrounds Catholic education in an overwhelmingly Catholic country whose constitution calls for secular education. Many parents send children to parochial schools because they are believed superior. I was told the attorney general under a recent president did so. When asked how, as chief legal officer of the nation, he justified it, he replied his childrens' education was his wife's concern.

It was a symbolic defiance *par excellence* by the Church that led to the most recent (and probably final) church-state struggle, the so-called Cristero Rebellion of the 1920s. In 1923 the cornerstone was laid for a monument to Cristo Rey (Christ the King) on a peak in the state of Guanajuato, at the approximate geographic center of the nation. A crowd of forty thousand came and heard, among others, the Vatican representative to Mexico proclaim Christ the king of Mexico. The government, to counteract this blatant "outdoor worship," began registering (and limiting the number of) priests, something the constitution allowed but that had not been enforced. The Church responded by shutting down all churches, and military skirmishes broke out, a festering problem that lasted five years.[57]

The Cristero Rebellion was serious, of course, but the outcome was never in doubt. Catholic leaders misjudged the nature of the people's loyalty, for most found it easy enough to honor their saints at shrines whether or not priests were on hand. As Bailey puts it: "[Catholic] loyalty was still very great; few Mexicans had formally abandoned their faith—but they had, like most people in other Western nations, compartmentalized their lives. The Mexican social cosmos by the 1920s was essentially secular. Religion was Sunday Mass, baptisms . . . the last rites . . . but it was not wages, working conditions, food, housing, and land."[58]

Periodic stories circulate even today of Catholic conspiracies. The openly conservative Sinarquista party ("without anarchy") flourished briefly in the 1940s, and the second largest political party during the past several decades (PAN) is generally recognized as a "Christian Democratic" party. But even so, PAN ("National Action Party") gets at most 14 percent of regional votes, and its token seats in the legislature serve more to prove the ruling party operates a "democracy."[59] In the battle of church versus state in Mexico, in other words, the state won. El Cid lost this time to Cuauhtémoc.

Catholic Ambivalence and the Failure of Civil Religion in Mexico

In the opening pages of this chapter, I suggested that development of a Rousseau-type civil religion depends upon the existence of independent organizational vehicles to "carry" it. The independence of those vehicles in turn depends upon whether church personnel are willing and able to relinquish their monopoly on God talk about the nation and whether other persons (in nonreligious roles) are willing and able to adopt such theological rhetoric. I used the metaphor of civil religious balloons and asked who held the strings. Can state (civil) people and church (religious) people grasp the same string, use the same language? For two hundred years in Mexico the general answer has been "no."

To a significant degree persons from the "church" side in Mexico have in recent decades made peace with a government that steadfastly refuses to sponsor them, that insists on religious tolerance instead. These persons have, so to speak, adjusted to a secular, constitutional system; they speak *its* language. But a comparable shift by civil officials has not occurred. Perhaps the last public official to conduct his office in ecclesiastical language was Octavio Véjar Vásquez, minister of education in the early 1940s. An avowed Catholic conservative, he "confessed his devotion to revealed truth" and wanted schools to train people for their "hierarchic position in creation. . . . There can be no education," he said, "without the sign of the Cross behind it."[60]

But Vásquez was an exceptional case. Without question the larger problem today is for persons in secular roles—especially politicians—to engage in God talk. In the 1890s the dictator, Porfirio Díaz, had commemorative dinner plates drawn up showing his face and that of Juárez along with the Virgin of Guadalupe, a clear instance of how politics makes strange bedfellows. When President Avila Comacho announced in 1940 that he, too, was a "believer," a ripple was observed. And the government today provides money to build churches (for example, the new basilica honoring the Virgin of Guadalupe), since it owns them anyway. But these examples suggest how awkward it is for politicians to appear sympathetic to religion, how difficult it is for political rhetoric to include transcendent references. Other instances show how pervasive is this difficulty, this ambivalence.

1. Ignacio Comonfort was the first president elected under the constitution of 1857, in which the Church was legally restrained. He exemplifies the cross-pressured position of the Mexican politician. He knew it was necessary to limit the powers of the clergy, but he also believed the Mexican people were devoted to the Church and wanted its minis-

trations. His own mother was a devout Catholic who
pleaded with him not to antagonize the priests.[61]

2. I have mentioned the Athaeneum of intellectuals and
educators who gathered around Justo Sierra in the late
nineteenth century and, inspired partly by Spencer and
others, tried to create a civil religion for Mexico. *Their*
ambivalence was obvious. Sierra himself remained a
doubter, making a pilgrimage to Lourdes, France, late in
his life to see if his faith might increase. It did not. The
literary critic, Samuel Ramos, applies the rule more generally. Citing the Nicaraguan poet Rubén Darió, who "once
cried that his soul was the object of contention 'between
the cathedral and pagan ruins,' " Ramos claims, "When
the two heritages met they could not be combined in
. . . a new synthesis. . . . Whenever an [Hispanic] American
of great consciousness raises his voice in sincere protesta-
tion, religious anxiety arises."[62]

3. A youthful member of the Athaeneum later had an opportunity to do something directly about Mexico's civil religion. José Vasconcelos was appointed minister of education in 1920 and became the "apostle of the new secular
religion."[63] But the ambivalence showed through. On the
one hand education was to be concerned with "practical
adjustment and empirical accomplishment . . . [no longer]
a foreign institution artificially grafted onto the body poli-
tic." On the other hand Vasconcelos contended "Dewey's
accent on 'all learning by doing' . . . is only an application
of Anglo Saxon 'Protestantism carried to pedagogy.' "[64]
Thus Vasconcelos distributed free books to schools
throughout the land—but they were translations of Roman
and Greek classics, and schoolchildren could not yet read!
Thus he wrote his visionary *La Raza Cósmica* [The cosmic
race], anticipating a synthetic racial ideal—yet he also
wrote of the synthetic race he was charged with educating:
"the *mestizo* population of our land is far from possessing
the vigor necessary to create ballet." Thus he was the anticlerical designer of Mexico's postrevolutionary educational system—but following a political defeat in 1925 the
"temptation . . . really to give up for good and enter a

monastery, to pray, making up for the years in which I had not prayed, returned in intense and urgent form." The goal, Vasconcelos said, was *"to get back on the track* of simple civilized normality" (italics added), that is to say, an eminently traditional and conservative goal.[65] It is not surprising that a later educator would judge Vasconcelos's work as minister of education "chaotically inconsistent, its accomplishments much more apparent than real."[66]

These vignettes say nothing of a material power struggle between church and state, the sacred and the secular. They reflect instead the symbolic level of social activity. They are therefore trivial by most standards, indicating only the ease or difficulty persons have in grasping one or another ideological balloon by which to articulate their behavior. The argument here is that the civil (political) and religious balloons have not been easy to hold together because of the ambivalence toward the church so widely felt by Mexicans in the civic arena. Two more examples—again symbolic and trivial—can be given to help show the pervasiveness of this dilemma.

4. Probably no Mexican painter is better known than Diego Rivera, whose murals adorn so many public buildings in Mexico. An avid revolutionary, Rivera was a firm nationalist and Communist as well. As president of the Communist party in Mexico, for example, it was he who arranged for Trotsky's exile in that country. The Church suffers terribly in Rivera's depictions of its clergy as avaricious and cruel. In 1923 Rivera had completed the mural at the National Preparatory School, and he and his co-painters were to be honored by a fiesta. The broadside announcing this celebration made a point, however, of saying that, "all this to give thanks to the Lord who kept them from terrible and horrible fall from the scaffold in nearly a year of most painful labor at the height of almost ten meters."[67] What Rivera thought of invoking the Lord's name on this occasion is not known, but his ambivalence can be assumed. When he painted the famed mural in Mexico City's Del Prado Hotel (1947–1948), he had one of his characters holding a sign saying "God does not exist." But a year

before his death in 1957, Rivera replaced that pronounce-
ment with the innocuous message now there. Rivera died
in the "bosom of the church."[68]

5. Finally, it is instructive to read the "official" account of
President Echeverría's European state visits in 1974. As
the first Mexican president ever to have an audience with
the Pope, and indeed the first Mexican politician in a century to deal in any way directly with the Vatican, Echeverría
had to juggle his symbols carefully. His chronicler therefore goes to lengths to acknowledge first the furor created
in Mexico by the papal interview but then lists dozens of
heads of governments received by the Vatican since World
War II, including not only Catholics but "Protestants, An-
glicans, Orthodox, Buddhists, Mohammedans and followers of no religion."[69] One does not yet take lightly the
mixing of the civil and the religious in Mexico.

To summarize, Mexico has no civil religion of the sort Rousseau urged. It has a nationalism, and it retains a religiousness, but
these two cultural themes have not merged. The symbols of the
first have not mixed with the symbols of the second. The explanation for this failure to mix lies in the ambivalence toward the
Church that followed bitter church-state struggles of the nineteenth century.

It is possible to imagine other paths the symbols might have
taken. In Haiti, for example, when the Church excommunicated
President Duvalier, he simply distributed a picture showing himself with God's hand on his shoulder, with the caption "I have
chosen him."[70] Despite hostilities, in other words, it is conceivable that the symbols of ecclesiastical legitimacy might have been
taken over by the Mexican state. Or it is possible Mexican nationalism might have ceased to be secular only and developed its own
sacred symbols, the situation approached in the Soviet Union.[71]

But neither of these happened either. Pablo Gonzalez Casanova, one of Mexico's leading sociologists, suggests the legisla-
tive branch, in sanctioning the executive's actions, fulfills a function similar to that of the divine powers that sanctioned the laws
by which the "rulers of old" governed.[72] Johnson is more accurate in describing the theory of the present Mexican Constitu-

tion, however, when he says, "Human rights were recognized not as inherent but as creation of the nation."[73]

This muted moral rhetorical role for governmental institutions is illustrated by Mexican judicial behavior. The law can speak in profoundly religious ways, especially in matters undergoing judicial review. Mexican courts possess this review capability through the doctrine of *amparo,* a device allowing citizens to bring grievances against authorities directly to judges. Via Articles 14 and 16 of the Mexican Constitution, courts have expanded their oversight capability much as United States judicial power has expanded under the due process and equal protection clauses of the Fifth and Fourteenth Amendments.

Moreover, the Mexican Supreme Court has not been merely a tool of the ruling regime but exhibits considerable independence. It "has pressed officialdom vigorously in several key policy areas. *Amparo* courts appear willing to tackle almost every kind of procedural abuse in the administration and interpretation of laws. . . . The high percentages of cases won by *amparo* plaintiffs and the great volume of cases initiated each year demonstrate that the Mexican judiciary is an important allocator of values, scarce resources, and sanctions in the National political system."[74]

And yet the Mexican Supreme Court, for all its activity, remains passive with respect to great moral questions. For example, Schwartz's examination of the 1917–1971 period

> reveals no instance where the Court ruled on the merits of a civil, criminal, or administrative action involving government favoritism or discrimination against a particular religion. This conspicuous absence is all the more remarkable considering the great religious violence sparked by the so-called *Cristero* Rebellion in 1926. Its turbulent aftermath extended into the early 1940s. The solution to the crisis was indeed political, involving police power and negotiation among contending political leaders but not judicial rule-making, adjudication, or the writ of *amparo.*[75]

Thus the court, though not constitutionally prohibited, has nevertheless been reluctant to adopt any role wherein it expresses the more profound values of the Mexican nation. In other words it articulates no Mexican civil religion.

Although the two quasi-civil religions (ecclesiastical legitimacy and nationalism phrased in sacred terms) were historical options Mexico might have elected, the Rousseau-type civil religion must now be regarded as remote indeed. But in retrospect, it is not puzzling that a civil religion never appeared in Mexico. The history of church and state seems "naturally" to have precluded a transcendent understanding of Mexico's national destiny, an understanding independent of both church and state.[76]

Stated this way, however, the puzzle is why there are situations where such an independent understanding *does* develop. Under what conditions will a civil religion appear? To answer this question I return to the case of the United States.

Having reviewed some of the features of Mexico that explain why no Rousseau-type civil religion is found there, one might be inclined to dismiss the finding with a "What did you expect?" Two things suggest the folly of such a dismissal, however. I mentioned one of these when I cited several characteristics of Mexico that would seem to have facilitated a civil religion: the strong nationalism, the powerful role of religion in its history, the recognition of a "Mexican" people that has emerged out of a diverse ethnic situation, and the deliberate campaign to erect a civil religion.

The other thing making casual dismissal of the Mexican case unwise is the implied assumption that the absence (and therefore the presence as well) of a civil religion can easily be explained, that the conditions for civil religion are not at all problematic. Against this second line of reasoning is the argument that civil religion (at least of the Rousseau variety) is rare, and the conditions for its development are not obvious, just as the explanation for civil religion's absence is not obvious. The case of Mexico therefore redirects attention to the United States and how it is a civil religion developed there, a civil religion independent of both church and regime. An answer comes in several stages.

A Conducive Ideology

Without question the most common method of accounting for an American civil religion consists of tracing the history of the ideas that comprise it. In this view two currents of thought, staffed for the most part by two groups of people, dominated the formative years of the American civil religion. Despite their differences, they converged on the idea that Americans were the new chosen people. One current—generated by the Puritans—believed America was renewing a covenant with God. The other current —originating in the deists or "philosophes"—were fashioning a social contract based on divine law. Both thus imagined God to be intimately involved in national affairs, even as both upheld the separation of church and state and a voluntary religion. This point is very ably advanced by Dohen and many others. Howe, for example, suggests the "wall of separation" between church and state, which the First Amendment is to ensure, was not simply a Jeffersonian deist figure of speech but even more reflected the "evangelical" desire to keep the "wilderness of the world" out of the "garden of the church." Both positions, however, led to an insistence on "voluntarism" or nonestablishment of religion.[77]

Nowhere was the resulting "republican religion" more apparent than in the "Yale theology" of the early nineteenth century, the goal of which was "the moral renovation of the American people through revivalism, reform societies, the religious press, and sumptuary legislation."[78]

> Republican religion did much to lay the historical groundwork for the tradition of religious liberty and limited separation of church and state, as it did to nurture creative minorities like the abolitionists, social gospelers, and civil-rights protesters. While it worked to demean and harass Negroes, Mormons, Catholics, Jews, and agnostics, . . . it also provided Afro-Americans with institutions of their own and bred nearly all black public leaders. Through Lincoln it articulated the ideological meaning of the Civil War. In Wilson it mingled missionary nationalism with a vision of internationalism, and in the eloquence of Martin Luther King, Jr., it found a voice for the revitalization of a civic religion in the context of demands for the renewal of the premises and promises of the ancient covenants.[79]

The beliefs of the founding generations then, whether Puritan or rationalist, whether inspired by Moses and Isaiah or by Locke and Montaigne, were conducive to a perspective that saw the American *nation* as the chief agent in the unfolding of history. Of such, it is said, civil religion is made; America had those beliefs, and Mexico did not.

At best, however, the ideas alone are a necessary but not sufficient explanation. Did they generate the evangelical fervor that made the expanding frontier a mission scene? Yes, but that fervor did not surpass the enthusiasm (and success) of the Franciscans and Jesuits in New Spain. Did those ideas generate a renewed interest in the Old Testament-inspired notion of a "chosen people?" Yes, but so were Catholic missionaries in Mexico imbued with beliefs that the New World was the new occasion to fulfill God's promise.[80] Was the promised land of America found to be bountiful, thus confirming God's compact? Yes, but the silver mines of Mexico were more than adequate substitutes for American milk and honey as signs of God's grace.

One ideological difference does stand out between Protestant America and Catholic Mexico; it is the difference in those belief systems that Max Weber made explicit. In America, for Deist as well as for Puritan, God's involvement was direct; in Mexico God's influence was mediated by church, priest, sacrament, and saint. But even this difference, while obvious and of enormous theological importance, does not by itself explain the appearance of an independent civil religion in the United States but not in Mexico. Recall the balloon metaphor. This ideological difference alone does not reveal what enabled the church in America to relinquish its monopoly on holding the string of the religion balloon and what enabled government officials to grab it.

Other conditions were obviously necessary, conditions not unrelated to Protestant ideology. In this sense the common explanation for America's civil religion—that it arose out of Puritan and other ideas—is not incorrect but only incomplete. It would be more accurate to say certain ideas found institutional roots in the Protestant soil of America that they did not find in Catholic Mexico, and these institutions—not just the ideas—were also necessary for a civil religion. The first of these, institutionalized religious liberty, explains how the church lost its monopoly on religious symbols.

Religious Liberty, Voluntarism, and the Separation of Church and State

One idea that took root early in American soil was that of religious liberty. There is no need to romanticize this chapter of history and make all the Puritans libertarians, "but the remarkable thing about the English settlements in America is that there, in the brief period between 1607 and 1787 these traditionally antagonistic groups of people learned to dwell together side by side in relative peace. First, they learned to tolerate one another, and eventually they began to think of freedom for all as an inherent or natural right."[81]

However, from the beginning that natural right, when institutionalized, became the *government's* responsibility. Thus even during the first century of the Massachusetts colony, while Puritan Congregationalism was "established" and levied taxes, many Anglican, Baptist, and Quaker colonists sought and found relief by appeal to the provincial authorities. Here is but an early instance of what was to become a common American irony: In its efforts to protect religious liberty, civil government enlarges its own role as religious arbiter. Michael Novak puts it this way: "No one church was allowed to become the official guardian of the central symbols of the United States. Instead, the nation itself began to fill the vacuum where in many cultures a church would be. The nation became its own unifying symbol system, the chief bestower of identity and purpose."[82]

The church was left to compete as a voluntary association, a situation foreign observers sometimes interpreted as theological weakness and sometimes as community vitality but always as a blend of the civil and the religious. Clergy did not cease to preach on destiny, worth, and judgment; but they had to share the pulpit. And every time someone's "free exercise" right was upheld, the government "established" further its own religious role. America became, as G. K. Chesterton said, a nation with the soul of a church.

Religious liberty and voluntarism thus led to an unusual "separation" of church and state, a situation in which the organizations are perhaps separated but the symbols are not. In exchange for the right to believe as they wanted, Americans relinquished any church's monopoly on religious symbols and shared them with government. The result is a civil government with a religious flavor, a flavor nowhere more apparent than in the rhetoric of presidential inaugural addresses.[83]

This unusual separation of church and state remains today a

difference between "Protestant" America and "Catholic" Latin America, even where in the latter separation of church and state is secure. Ivan Vallier allows us to understand this difference with his distinction between "religious competition" and "political competition."[84] The Catholic Church in Latin America competed politically with government for a long time (and in some places still does), but only recently has it competed religiously. Churches in America, however, because of the doctrine of religious liberty, have always competed religiously but never politically, that is, over the rules governing competition. This situation is one factor that allowed, indeed encouraged, the emergence of an American civil religion.

To summarize the argument to this point: America's ideological heritage, especially the Protestant idea of covenant and the rationalist idea of social contract, made civil religion possible in the United States. But inasmuch as these and similar ideas are also found in Mexico's ideological heritage, the simple availability of the ideas is not enough to explain the presence of civil religion in the one country and its absence in the other. More is required.

I have suggested an additional factor: The doctrine of religious liberty accompanying Protestantism was institutionalized as an unusual separation of church and state. In this separation the church lost its monopoly on religious symbols, sharing them with civil agencies, and government therefore also dealt in religious symbols. The point is ironically illustrated in a 1935 report of the Congregational Churches of Mexico that attempted to explain the continuing tumult between church and state in that country. Catholicism, the report says, "put the Pope above the State, and finds it impossible to support a Government which no longer consents to be the tool of Romish machinations." By contrast, Protestants can support the state "as long as it does not seek to compel disobedience to God's commands."[85] What the report fails to acknowledge, of course, is that Protestantism (as well as Catholicism) in the United States achieves this harmony by relinquishing to civil agencies the authority to define God's commands. In protecting the "free exercise" of religion, government further "establishes" its own religious role. In return for the guarantee of flying any religious balloon, all churches' balloon strings must be available for handling by government.

Political Activity by Churches

American churches never "competed" politically in that they never set the rules of competition or determined jurisdiction, but this did not keep them out of the political arena. Indeed, it might be argued the peculiar nature of U.S. church-state "separation" meant churches entered the political fray with greater abandon than was the case when they did compete. Even today, as countless studies show, greater political activity characterizes those Protestant groups with the more "republican" religion; groups asserting "the church should stay out of politics" are those whose Christianity rests less easy with religious liberty or the democratic regime generally. At the extreme, religious groups claiming the sole way to truth make common cause with fascist politics. Partly, too, this explains why more liberal political involvement is found in those denominations with more members of high economic standing. Churches serving the rich often take positions some of their individual rich members oppose. Historically, the charge against mainline Protestant churches has not been for political inactivity but for political naivete.[86]

In America, therefore, one observes the role of religion in political life, even as clergy and churches are "nonpolitical" or, as Tocqueville noted, "disestablished."[87] Protestants got there first, of course, and some still level accusations of a *de facto* Protestant establishment. But while top political leadership has come chiefly from members of one of the mainline Protestant groups, that membership has been of little *political* significance. Jews and Catholics have made a similar adjustment and seen their religious affiliation also become politically insignificant.[88] Anthony Trollope, following his visit in 1860, said in America "Everybody is bound to have a religion." But, he added, "it does not matter what it is."[89] Candidate John F. Kennedy, telling the Houston Ministerial Association in 1960 that his first commitment was to the U.S. Constitution, was merely echoing Trollope's sentiment. The ease with which the Catholic hex disappeared following

Kennedy's election provided further confirmation. A politician's membership in one or another denomination may have sizable significance at election time, of course, depending upon the use to which it is put. But so may a politician's photogenic quality, ethnicity, ad lib ability, or money supply. Religious affiliation merely lines up with these other attributes and has no necessary relationship with the politician's substantive record.

Any religion that does influence political life is thus "non" denominational even if its early roots were evangelical Protestantism. It is diffused throughout American institutions, even if it was shaped theologically by New England ecclesiastics. It is a civil religion and inspires clergymen as well as others to political activity, even if it is the unique theology of no denomination. How ingrained this religion became, even early in the nation's history, is illustrated by the religious comments of another foreign observer. Harriet Martineau was a convinced Anglican who, coming to the United States in 1834 for a two-year period, compared the religious situation in America with what she perceived to be the "established" position of the church back home in England: "It appears to me that the one thing in which the clergy of every kind are fatally deficient is faith: that faith which would lead them, first, to appropriate all truth, fearlessly and unconditionally; and then to give it as freely as they have received it. . . . What would Paul's ministry have been if he had preached on everything but idolatry at Ephesus, and licentiousness at Corinth? . . . what kind of an apostle would he have been? Very like the American christian clergy."[90] Further reflection by Martineau would have led her to realize deficient faith was not the source of difficulty but rather the peculiar political role that must be played by disestablished clergy when they are politically active. A more accurate rendering than Martineau's is one made a decade earlier by the Frenchman, August Lavasseur:

> one must be struck at the constant union of religious ideas with patriotic sentiments, which so strongly characterize the [American] citizens . . . ; but what is no less worthy of remark is that their religion, freed from minute ceremonies, resembles a sentiment, as much as their love of liberty resembles a creed. Among them a political orator never closes a preparatory address without invoking or returning thanks to the Almighty; as a minister, when he ascends the pulpit

always begins by reminding his audience of their duties as citizens, and the happiness they enjoy in living under wise institutions. It may be said that this mixture of political morality and theology extends through all the actions of the Americans, a tincture of gravity and profound conviction.[91]

The closeness of religion and politics, more than their separateness, marks the church-state situation in America. Some have seen in this closeness the source of atheism's unpopularity. Others have commented on the absence of a church-based political party in the United States, owing to the "religiousness" of all political parties. Still others point to the essentially "private" role to which church theology is reduced inasmuch as the church cannot compete politically.

All such observations may be true and probably are. From the standpoint of the development of a civil religion, however, the closeness of religion and politics in America has another meaning, a meaning in which a large number of foreign observers of the religiopolitical scene concur: Unlike their counterparts elsewhere, American politicians, government officials, and civil servants have been *favorable* to religion. Not having to compete politically with churches, politicians could draw their language, imagery, and symbols easily and unashamedly from religious ideology. People in the political sphere could hold the strings of religious balloons.

Civil Agents of the Civil Religion

Here then is a second and less obvious explanation for America's capacity to generate a civil religion—the opportunity and inclination of its government agencies to use religious symbols. The first explanation—that the Protestant doctrine of religious liberty led to the kind of church-state separation wherein clergymen, even while politically active, did not "compete" politically—is seen here in mirror image. Thus unlike politicians in Mexico, American politicians have felt little ambivalence toward the church because, unlike the Catholic church in Mexico, the various U.S. churches have competed not with the state but only with one another. Politicians are therefore free to deal in religious symbols.

When government agencies use religious symbols, they are typically not sectarian symbols but those common to all believers in the United States, which means political units (chiefly the nation), not ecclesiastical units, are the units of reference. For example, Bellah observes that presidential inaugural language always includes God but never Christ.[92] God looks favorably (or unfavorably) on *this country,* not simply on the Presbyterians of this country. As noted, therefore, American churches have been politically involved in civil, not just ecclesiastic, affairs, and thus served as agents of the civil religion. But I turn now to the religious involvement of government agencies. For, it seems fair to presume, these agencies have also played a critical role in the development of American civil religion. It is not enough that religion attend to the civil; the civil must also attend to the religious.

I have referred to elected politicians' use of civil religious symbols. Less obvious is the way other civil agents have used the civil religion. The several civil positions in Mexico already described have their American counterparts; comparing the two sets shows how easily in the United States the "civil" position became "religious" as well.

Education

As in Mexico, U.S. public education was seen as a vital agency for any civil ideal. Even before the American Revolution, "education became an instrument, deliberately used, by which dominant groups sought to recreate an ideal unity and minorities struggled to retain their group's identity."[93] Moral inculcation, it was recognized, could not be "tied to sectarian or even religious teaching. . . . In the polyglot cities . . . the establishment of schools with any denominational coloring was sure to alienate some of the families. . . . [Horace] Mann did not—nor did he wish to—abolish the use of the Bible in the public schools. . . . But he was happy to report in 1844 that only a small fraction of the towns used the Bible as a devotional work; the rest used it as a reader."[94] The school promulgated national unity and "nonsectarian" morality. Unlike Mexico, however, public education was not inhibited in this promulgation from using religious symbols as long as they were thought common to all, which again meant politically defined, not denominationally defined, units were the units of reference. Even today in some places the religious symbols used are to Jews unjustly Christian and to Catholics unjustly Protestant. They are therefore not in reality "common" to all. But such an assertion does not negate the civil religious *intention* to use common religious symbols.

Educators

The designers of American public education were believers; schools were the nation's way to do God's will. The father of American public education—the prophet of the common school and counterpart to Mexico's José Vasconcelos—is Horace Mann. During the mid nineteenth century he was secretary of the Massachusetts Board of Education and thus creator of the school system that served as a model for many other states. Mann rejected the sternly orthodox Calvinism of his youth, but who can doubt its impact in the following letter he wrote to a friend three decades later? "If I had a few thousand dollars I know I could, very perceptively, hasten the millennium. God having time enough on his own hands lets these things drag along strangely; but I confess I am so constituted that I feel in a hurry." A few years later he wrote to another friend, "schools will be found to be the way that God has chosen for the reformation of the world."[95]

Mexico's Vasconcelos, we have reason to believe, was incapable of thoughts like these. The goal, he said while minister of education, was "to get back on the track of simple civilized normality." It is true he imagined himself engaged in what he called a "holy crusade" and sought "teachers animated with apostolic fervor," but he "was resigned in advance to seeing the results disappear as soon as the political wheel turned."[96] Mann, it is safe to say, was incapable of thoughts like *that*.

Mann's erstwhile Calvinism and his belief that education was to reform the world became civil religion as it emerged in the schools, most of all in Mann's insistence upon public schools for *all* people. They were to teach and indoctrinate "those articles in the creed of republicanism, which are accepted by all, believed

in by all, and which form the common basis of our political faith."
Mann resisted the pressures to make public schools sectarian,
even as he embraced their need to educate in the "fundamental
principles of Christianity." Just four years before he assumed the
secretaryship, Massachusetts had disestablished the Congregational Church. Now, writes his biographer, "Mann was about to
preach a new religion and convince his constituency of the need
for a new establishment, a nondenominational institution, the
public school, with schoolmasters as a new priestly class, patriotic
exercises as quasi-religious rituals, and a nonsectarian doctrine
stressing morality, literacy and citizenship as a republican creed
for all to confess."[97]

To a remarkable degree he succeeded. Public education flourished in the nineteenth century and schools came to dominate
small town America's landscape in the way cathedrals dominated
the landscape of European villages.

Along with Mann, Henry Barnard has been regarded as a
"founder" of American public education. Barnard served many
years as secretary of the Connecticut Board of Education, but his
impact on the public school movement was perhaps greatest in
the *American Journal of Education,* which he began in 1855 and
edited for twenty-six years. This publication was the only national
journal for pedagogy in the nineteenth century.

Like Mann, Barnard was reared on a New England Puritan
ethic and trained in law, but then the public school movement
"pulsed in his blood as he pictured himself as a missionary 'captured and enlisted for life.'" Friends and frequent correspond-
ents, Barnard and Mann referred to public education as the "Ark
of God" and the "Ark of the Lord." Education for Barnard was
a "holy cause" and a "Christian crusade"; teachers were "the
chosen priesthood."[98]

Persons more committed than Mann and Barnard to the civil
religion cannot be found, but plenty of persons in the public
school movement shared their commitment. What they were involved in was not only a crusade on behalf of the republic; it was
also a religious crusade. Combining intellectual instruction with
moral admonition—the mark of the popular McGuffey readers,
for example—was necessary in their view. "These peculiarities of
our government," wrote Barnard in 1865, "require that the spirit

of the people shall be educated in conformity to them."[99]

This whiggish outlook—that government has responsibility for the morality of its youth because morality is necessarily reflected in behavior—was not (and is not) just a partisan difference, although then (as now) the viewpoint was stronger in one political party. The outlook is rather more American than partisan. One's religious beliefs, everyone agreed, ought to be reflected in one's citizenship. The civil religion is both parent and child to the public school.

The Judiciary

The court system in Mexico, though it possesses the constitutional authority for doing so, has not used judicial review as a moral-religious platform. Although the *amparo* is invoked frequently and judges therefore are put in a "final arbiter" position, they have not become involved in great moral issues. They have unsnarled administrative or procedural disputes, but Mexican courts have neither articulated nor sought to articulate "principles" of human governance.

The contrast with the American judicial system is striking. Puritanism, of course, had the capacity for making every issue a moral issue, as Roscoe Pound said, but Puritanism in religiously plural America transmuted moral issues into legal issues as well.[100] Courts were asked to "interpret" law; they were charged with identifying not only "duties" but "aspirations"; and the result is a judiciary with a (civil) religious character.[101] Here, along with education, is another way Puritanism's innerworldly asceticism indirectly led to the development of American civil religion.

This judicial religiousness is often noted. U.S. Supreme Court justices, for example, have been called "the nine high priests," and the sacredness imputed to the Constitution and other artifacts of the legal order are often commented upon.[102] No single church evokes the breadth of respect enjoyed by the Supreme Court. The reason, no doubt, is that the Court is a "vital national seminar" in ways and on issues that churches never have been in the United States.[103]

It is perhaps more than coincidence that this expanding judicial role and the religious character accompanying it occurred during the same decades that the "republican religion" established theological hegemony in America. If the argument here is correct, the two developments result from some of the same causes: The American kind of church-state separation meant no church monopolized religious symbols; courts were called upon to articulate ultimate purpose and justice; and judges felt little ambivalence in doing so. Religious balloon strings, being no longer the property of the church only, could be grasped by anybody, including (perhaps especially) judges. However, a debate continues on whether judges "ought" to grab the religious balloon strings. This is part of the issue of "judicial activism," on which Alexander Bickel, in *The Least Dangerous Branch,* was so eloquent a spokesman on behalf of the Court's "passive virtues." While the alacrity with which courts are prepared to step into political/moral issues can be questioned, the religious character their actions assume when they do step in cannot be.

As in the case with public education, then, the U.S. judicial system (especially at the federal level) has played a religious role. The nation is the chief agent in the drama, and so both education and the courts promulgate a *civil,* not sectarian, religion. That is to say, it is a religion independent of churches, just as, being little tied to the ruling regime, it is a religion independent of the state. Biased in favor of one or another ecclesiastic outlook at times, this civil religion can also at times be biased on behalf of the political status quo. But it is not just a political or secular ideology; its transcendent references are frequent and clear. Used to justify all manner of errant nonsense, it is nevertheless "essentially prophetic, which is to say that its ideals and aspirations stand in constant judgment over the passing shenanigans of the people, reminding them of the standards by which their current practices and those of their nation are ever being judged and found wanting."[104] It is, in the full Rousseau sense, a "civil religion."

No doubt public education, in its civil religious role, primarily transmits the civil religion—however imperfectly. And courts, in their civil religious role, primarily apply and modify it—however imperfectly. But *in their civil religious roles* both of these institutions derived from a single set of circumstances. First are the ideas that allowed the nation to be understood in a transcendent manner.

Second is the way one of those ideas—the doctrine of religious liberty—gave rise to religious pluralism at the organizational level. Third was the need nevertheless for common symbols of national purpose, which, because of ecclesiastical pluralism, no church could supply. And fourth was the freedom felt by persons outside of church to use religious symbols. The result was that so-called secular institutions were called upon—and their personnel were able—to symbolize the civil religion. The American civil religion is thus a product of certain ideas, but those ideas have been filtered through particular social institutions. Mexico, though it entertained some of the same ideas, failed to create comparable institutions; so it did not develop a civil religion.

Conclusion

History records a number of ways religion and politics have been related, but with the coming of modern nation-states all the traditional ways required modification. Means of accommodating to "secularization" developed, the variety of which is illustrated by Smith in his sample of nations from around the world. It is the "church" that accommodates to the "state," however, at least in power terms; religion declines as power coalesces in the institutions of the state.[105]

Rousseau, contemplating this religious decline and concerned about the consequences, coined the term "civil religion" for what he regarded as a viable solution—an ideology at once transcendent but focused on the nation-state. The handmaiden of neither the church nor the state, this ideology was to have an independent existence. It would provide persons with ultimate meaning by locating them in their society, which in turn would be located in space and history. In such manner, at least in "Christian states," "perpetual conflict of jursidiction" would be avoided.[106]

Civil religions, in Rousseau's meaning of the term, have not routinely developed, however. On the contrary, they are probably quite rare. Nationalisms abound, of course, but they typically are tied to the ruling regime, reflecting little of a transcendent or "ultimate" quality. And there are modern instances of nations enjoying the legitimacy provided them in a relationship with a single denomination, but they, being dependent on a church, are vulnerable to an inhibiting particularism.[107] The strategy advocated by Rousseau, in other words, has not been commonly adopted.

Interest thus shifts to the conditions that allow and/or encourage an independent civil religion. Durkheim may still be correct in suggesting all societies possess a "common conscience," but not all states develop civil religions. In some respects the intrusion of Durkheim-like theorizing has inhibited the analysis of civil religion, even as it undeniably has alerted scholars to civil religious possibilities in the first place. The reason has to do with the nonuniversality of "totemism" or transcendental ideology featuring the state as chief agent. The elusive collective conscience may be a universal phenomenon, but its theological expression is not.

On the basis of the foregoing analysis of Mexico and the United States, perhaps this explanation can be offered: Civil religion depends for its existence upon circumstances allowing persons and institutions to be "religious" and "political" at the same time. The heavenly sphere of theology must blend with the worldly sphere of the civil. It was one of Max Weber's great insights that while "every . . . religion must, in similar measure and for similar reasons, experience tension with the sphere of political behavior," religions differ in how they deal with this tension.[108] Innerworldly asceticism has an edge, at least when it comes to the development of a civil religion.

In most of Christian history the religious and political spheres have been thought separate. Augustine's City of God was believed superior to the earthly city, just as on earth a vocation in the church was preferred over ordinary pursuits. Few had a choice in the second of these matters, and nobody had a choice in the first, but the separateness of spheres was unmistakable. Bishop John Ireland of St. Paul, Minnesota, put it neatly: "When I am asked: Do you put Church before Country, or Country before Church? I reply: I neither put Church before Country, nor Country before Church. Church and Country are in altogether different spheres. . . . The Church is supreme in one order of things; the State is supreme in another order."[109]

Such a viewpoint eases the tension between religion and politics, however, only as long as no dispute arises over boundaries.

When Archbishop Mora y del Rio responded to the 1917 Mexican Constitution by claiming church immunity from government regulation, he was hardly sidestepping an issue. The Church, he said, is "a perfect society, founded by God himself," a statement calculated to infuriate, not appease, the worldly sphere.[110]

What Max Weber saw in the sequence of Protestant developments was a remarkably different way to "ease tension" between religion and politics: "inner-worldly asceticism can compromise with the facts of the political power structures by interpreting them as instruments for the rationalized ethical transformation of the world and for the control of sin."[111] Puritanism in America followed such a course, and the American civil religion was a result. Where medieval Catholicism politicized religion, American Puritanism sacralized politics.

As the foregoing analysis shows, however, the American civil religion resulted not just from the contents of Puritan ideas. In addition, the Puritan method of harmonizing politics and religion led to institutional changes, which in turn facilitated development of a civil religion. I noted several of these institutional changes: (1) Churches became voluntary associations in a strict sense, though lines around religious liberty or "free exercise" were (are) difficult to draw in this "separation" of church and state. (2) Churches engaged in much political activity, though generally in the same manner and with the same weapons as other voluntary associations. (3) Persons therefore found it easy to be simultaneously "religious" and "political." (4) Political institutions became embued with sacred meaning, educational and legal institutions (and their personnel) being the manifestations previously discussed.

In due time the medieval Catholic method failed—as the case of Mexico illustrates—but left the vestigial conception of religion and politics as separate spheres. The Puritan solution may have been worse from the viewpoint of a power-seeking church, but at least it left political institutions and their personnel theologically infused. The Catholic method meant that while church contended with state, individuals had to juggle their loyalties to the "separate" organizations. The Puritan solution did away with church-state struggle at the organization level but shifted the struggle to the personality level. Thus "conscience" enters the legal realm in America as it never does in Mexico. The Puritan way of resolving tension between religion and politics left the church, *qua* church, with no power, therefore, but it meant religious symbols entered politics. The conditions thus existed for a civil religion to develop. And develop it did in America, to a degree of independence perhaps not matched by the civil religion of any other society. The importance of those conditions— and not just the civil religious idea—is what this comparison has shown.

NOTES

1. Ferdinand Mount, "The Last Hurrah?" *Encounter,* 48 (March 1977), p. 61.
2. H. Byron Earhart, *Japanese Religion: Unity and Diversity,* 2nd. ed. (Encino, Calif.: Dickenson Publishing Co., 1974), pp. 19–20.
3. Ronald C. Wimberley and James A. Christenson, "Civil Religion and Church Religions." Paper presented at the 1976 annual meeting of the Association for the Sociology of Religion.
4. See, for example, the particular data of Herbert McCloskey, "Consensus and Ideology in American Politics," *American Political Science Review,* 58 (June 1964), pp. 361–382. For a summary statement see Robert E. Stauffer, "Civil Religion, Technocracy, and the Private Sphere: Further Comments of Cultural Integration in Advanced Societies," *Journal for the Scientific Study of Religion,* 12 (December 1973), pp. 415–425.
5. Alexis de Tocqueville, *Democracy in America,* trans. Henry Reeve (New York: Schocken Books, 1961), vol. 1, p. 300.
6. Three excellent discussions of this creed are John E. Smylie, "National Ethos and the Church," *Theology Today,* 20 (October 1963), pp. 313–321; Sidney E. Mead, *The Lively Experiment* (New York: Harper, 1963); and Sidney E. Mead, "The Nation with the Soul of a Church," *Church History,* 36 (1967), pp. 262–283. Will Herberg, *Protestant, Catholic, Jew* (Garden City, N.Y.: Anchor Books, 1960), focuses on the fourth creedal tenet. Ernest Lee Tuveson, *Redeemer Nation: The Idea of America's Millennial Role* (Chicago: University of Chicago Press, 1968), focuses on the third.
7. Sydney E. Ahlstrom, *A Religious History of the American People* (New Haven, Conn.: Yale University Press, 1972), p. 1094.
8. Jean Jacques Rousseau, *Social Contract,* ed. C. M. Andrews (New York: William H. Wise, 1901 [originally published 1762]), pp. 116; 117–118.
9. Ibid., pp. 123–124.
10. I have benefited from other efforts to classify civil religions, especially John A. Coleman, "Civil Religion," *Sociological Analysis,* 31 (Summer 1970), pp. 67–77, and Martin E. Marty, "Two Kinds of Two Kinds of Civil Religion,"

in R. E. Richey and D. G. Jones, eds., *American Civil Religion* (New York: Harper & Row, 1974), although some of their distinctions are not incorporated in my typology.

11. Coleman, "Civil Religion," p. 70.

12. *Excelsior,* 21 January 1977.

13. Ibid., 2 December 1976.

14. Frank Brandenburg, *The Making of Modern Mexico* (Englewood Cliffs, N.J.: Prentice-Hall, 1964), chap. 1.

15. See Irma Wilson, *Mexico: A Century of Educational Thought* (New York: Hispanic Institute in the U.S., 1941); George F. Kneller, *The Education of the Mexican Nation* (New York: Columbia University Press, 1951); and Josephina Vasquez DeKnauth, *Nacionalismo y Educacion en Mexico* [Nationalism and education in Mexico], 2nd ed. (Mexico City: El Colegio de Mexico, 1975).

16. Samuel Ramos, *Profile of Man and Culture in Mexico,* trans. Peter G. Earle (Austin: University of Texas Press, 1962), p. 164.

17. Leopoldo Zea in Frederick C. Turner, *The Dynamic of Mexican Nationalism* (Chapel Hill: University of North Carolina Press, 1968), p. 93. See also Ramos, *Profile,* p. 165.

18. Wilson, *Mexico,* p. 37.

19. Robert E. Quirk, *The Mexican Revolution and the Catholic Church, 1910–1929* (Bloomington: Indiana University Press, 1973), pp. 116 and 117.

20. Kneller, *The Education,* p. 170.

21. Ibid., pp. 46–47.

22. José Vasconcelos, *A Mexican Ulysses: An Autobiography,* trans. and abridged W. Rex Crawford (Bloomington: Indiana University Press, 1963), p. 156.

23. With bitterness, the contemporary Mexican poet-critic-ambassador, Octavio Paz, points out this move to revere (create?) an indigenous past has led the otherwise magnificent Anthropological Museum in Mexico City to organize its presentation so as to "culminate" with the Aztecs. As Paz points out, however, compared with the Olmecs, Toltecs, or Mayas who preceded them, the Aztecs are not a good model. Octavio Paz, *The Other Mexico: Critique of the Pyramid,* trans. Lysander Kemp (New York: Grove Press, 1972).

24. Quirk, *The Mexican Revolution,* p. 116.

25. Kneller, *The Education,* p. 100.

26. Lesley B. Simpson, *Many Mexicos,* rev. ed. (Berkeley: University of California Press, 1952), p. 70.

27. Manuel Gamio, *Forjando Patria* [Forging the native land] (Mexico City: Editorial Porrúa, 1960), p. 111.

28. Quirk, *The Mexican Revolution,* chap. 1; Anita Brenner, *Idols Behind Altars: The Story of the Mexican Spirit* (Boston: Beacon Press, 1970 [originally published 1929]).

29. See also William Madsen, "Christo-Paganism: A Study of Mexican Religious Syncretism," Ph.D. dissertation, Department of Anthropology, University of California, Berkeley, 1955.

30. Simpson, *Many Mexicos*, pp. 192–193.
31. William Weber Johnson, *Heroic Mexico* (Garden City, N.Y.: Doubleday, 1968), p. 388.
32. W. H. Callcott, *Church and State in Mexico, 1822–1857* (Durham, N.C.: Duke University Press, 1926), p. 39.
33. Cited in Brandenburg, *The Making*, p. 183.
34. See Johnson, *Heroic Mexico*, p. 13, and Jan Bazant, *Alienation of Church Wealth in Mexico: Social and Economic Aspects of the Liberal Revolution, 1856–1875* (Cambridge, England: Cambridge University Press, 1971), p. 13.
35. David Bailey, *Viva Cristo Rey* (Austin: University of Texas, 1974), p. 10.
36. Quirk, *The Mexican Revolution*, p. 22.
37. Rafael Segovia, *La Politización del Niño Mexicano* [The politicization of the Mexican child] (Mexico City: El Colegio de Mexico, 1975), p. 91.
38. Bailey, *Viva Cristo Rey*, pp. 11–13.
39. Simpson, *Many Mexicos*, pp. 243 and 248.
40. Brandenburg, *The Making*, p. 41. A more church-positive Díaz is portrayed in J. Lloyd Mecham, *Church and State in Latin America*, rev. ed. (Chapel Hill: University of North Carolina Press, 1966), chap. 15.
41. Brandenburg, *The Making*, p. 41.
42. See Gabriel Almond and Sidney Verba, *The Civic Culture*, abridged (Boston: Little, Brown, 1965); Robert E. Scott, "Mexico: The Established Revolution," in Lucien W. Pye and Sidney Verba, eds., *Political Culture and Political Development* (Princeton, N.J.: Princeton University Press, 1965); Turner, *The Dynamic*; and Peter Ranis, *Five Latin American Nations: A Comparative Political Study* (New York: Macmillan, 1971).
43. Ranis, *Five Latin American Nations*, p. 227.
44. Robert E. Scott, "Nation Building in Latin America," in K. W. Deutsch and W. J. Foltz, eds., *Nation-Building* (New York: Atherton, 1963), p. 81.
45. Eric Wolf, "The Virgin of Guadalupe: A Mexican National Symbol," *Journal of American Folklore*, 71 (1958), pp. 34–39.
46. Brenner, *Idols Behind Altars*, p. 151.
47. Turner, *The Dynamic*, p. 142.
48. Oscar Lewis, *The Children of Sanchez* (New York: Random House, 1961).
49. Quoted in Simpson, *Many Mexicos*, p. 245.
50. Karl M. Schmitt, "Catholic Adjustment to the Secular State: The Case of Mexico, 1867–1911," *Catholic Historical Review*, 48, no. 2 (July 1962), pp. 187–188.
51. Quoted in Charles S. MacFarland, *Chaos in Mexico* (New York: Harper & Bros., 1935), p. 125.
52. Quoted in ibid., p. 136.
53. Brandenburg, *The Making*, p. 32.
54. Mecham, *Church and State*, chaps. 15–16, is a succinct history of Mexican church-state relations from 1821 to 1965.
55. Richard Roman, "Church-State Relations and the Mexican Constitutional

Congress, 1916–1917," *Journal of Church and State*, 20 (Winter 1978), p. 79. On restrictions of the church see Henry B. Parkes, *A History of Mexico*, 3rd ed. (Boston: Houghton Mifflin, 1960), p. 362.

56. See Alberto Hernández Medina, "El Financiamiento De La Educacion Privada En America Latina" [Financing Private Education in Latin America] (Mexico, D. F.: Centro de Estudios Educativos, A. A., 1976). The estimates of what percent of private school students are Catholic were given to me in a private communication from Hernández Medina.

57. See Quirk, *The Mexican Revolution*, and Bailey, *Viva Cristo Rey*, for accounts of this event.

58. Bailey, *Viva Cristo Rey*, p. 309.

59. Donald J. Mabry, *Mexico's Accion Nacional* (Syracuse, N.Y.: Syracuse University Press, 1973), pp. 52–69.

60. Kneller, *The Education*, pp. 69 and 55.

61. Parkes, *A History*, p. 234.

62. Ramos, *Profile*, p. 85.

63. Quirk, *The Mexican Revolution*, p. 116.

64. Kneller, *The Education*, pp. 61–62; Patrick Romanell, *Making of the Mexican Mind* (Lincoln: University of Nebraska Press, 1952), p. 98.

65. Vasconcelos, *A Mexican Ulysses*, pp. 180, 200, 173.

66. Daniel Cosío Villegas, *American Extremes*, trans. Américo Paredes (Austin: University of Texas Press, 1964), p. 22.

67. Quoted in Brenner, *Idols Behind Altars*, p. 251.

68. Dan Hofstadter, ed., *Mexico 1946–73* (New York: Facts on File, 1974), p. 65; Bertram D. Wolfe, *La Fabulosa Vida de Diego Rivera* [The fabulous life of Diego Rivera] (Mexico City: Editorial Diana, 1972), p. 310.

69. Mario Ezcurdia, *Operacion Europa* [Operation Europe] (Mexico City, 1974), p. 151.

70. Frederick C. Turner, *Catholicism and Political Development in Latin America* (Chapel Hill: University of North Carolina Press, 1971), p. 35.

71. Jennifer McDowell, "Soviet Civil Ceremonies," *Journal for the Scientific Study of Religion*, 13 (September 1974), pp. 265–279; Mary-Barbara Zeldin, "The Religious Nature of Russian Marxism," *Journal for the Scientific Study of Religion*, 8 (Spring 1969), pp. 100–111.

72. Pablo Gonzalez Casanova, *Democracy in Mexico*, 2nd ed., trans. D. Solti (New York: Oxford University Press, 1970), p. 20.

73. Johnson, *Heroic Mexico*, p. 322.

74. Carl E. Schwartz, "Judges in the Shadow: Judicial Independence in the United States and Mexico," *California Western International Law Journal*, 3 (December 1972), pp. 313 and 332.

75. Ibid., pp. 289–290.

76. Ivan Vallier, *Catholicism, Social Control, and Modernization in Latin America* (Englewood Cliffs, N.J.: Prentice-Hall, 1970), p. 43, states a similar thesis although he refers not to civil religion but to "a durable religio-moral foundation within which political processes can be stabilized."

77. Dorothy Dohen, *Nationalism and American Catholicism* (New York: Sheed and Ward, 1967); Mark DeWolfe Howe, *The Garden and the Wilderness* (Chicago: University of Chicago Press, 1965).

78. Elwyn A. Smith, *The Religion of the Republic* (Philadelphia: Fortress Press, 1971), pp. 170–171.

79. Cushing Strout, *The New Heavens and the New Earth: Political Religion in America* (New York: Harper & Row, 1974), p. 343. See also Ahlstrom, *A Religious History*, pp. 552–564.

80. Simpson, *Many Mexicos;* Jacque Lafaye, *Quetzalcóatl and Guadalupe: The Formation of Mexican National Consciousness 1531–1813,* trans. Benjamin Keen (Chicago: University of Chicago Press, 1976).

81. Mead, *The Lively Experiment*, p. 3.

82. Novak, *Choosing Our King*, p. 107.

83. Robert N. Bellah, "Civil Religion in America," *Daedalus* (Winter 1967), pp. 1–21.

84. Vallier, *Catholicism*, p. 150.

85. Quoted in MacFarland, *Chaos in Mexico*, p. 253.

86. See Donald B. Meyer, *The Protestant Search for Political Realism, 1919–1941* (Berkeley: University of California Press, 1960).

87. Tocqueville, *Democracy in America*, vol. 1, p. 364.

88. See Jacob Agus, "Jerusalem in America," in E. A. Smith, ed., *The Religion of the Republic* (Philadelphia: Fortress Press, 1971); Thomas T. McAvoy, "American Cultural Impacts on Catholicism," in Smith, *The Religion;* Thomas F. O'Dea, "American Catholics and International Life," *Social Order*, 10 (June 1960), pp. 243–265; and especially Dohen, *Nationalism*, for details.

89. Quoted in Dohen, *Nationalism*, p. 11.

90. Quoted in Milton Powell, ed. *The Voluntary Church* (New York: Macmillan, 1967), p. 124.

91. Quoted in ibid., p. 64.

92. Bellah, "Civil Religion."

93. Bernard Bailyn, *Education in the Forming of American Society* (New York: W.W. Norton, 1972), p. 99.

94. Robert L. Church and Michael W. Sedlak, *Education in the United States* (New York: Free Press, 1976), p. 90.

95. Quoted in Jonathan Messerli, *Horace Mann: A Biography* (New York: Knopf, 1972), pp. 403 and 441.

96. Vasconcelos, *A Mexican Ulysses*, p. 173.

97. Messerli, *Horace Mann*, p. 253.

98. Quoted in Vincent P. Lannie, ed., *Henry Barnard: American Educator* (New York: Teachers College Press, 1974), p. 13.

99. Quoted in ibid., p. 156.

100. Roscoe Pound, *The Spirit of the Common Law* (Francestown, N.H.: Marshall Jones, 1921), p. 43.

101. These terms are from Lon Fuller, *The Morality of Law* (New Haven, Conn.: Yale University Press, 1964).

102. Max Lerner, "The Constitution and the Court as Symbols," *Yale Law Journal*, 46 (1937), pp. 1290–1319; Alexander Bickel, *The Least Dangerous Branch* (Indianapolis: Bobbs-Merrill, 1962), pp. 29–33.
103. Eugene V. Rostow, "The Democratic Character of Judicial Review," *Harvard Law Review*, 66 (1952), p. 208.
104. Mead, "The Nation," p. 275.
105. Donald E. Smith, *Religion and Political Development* (Boston: Little, Brown, 1970), p. 117; Salo W. Baron, *Modern Nationalism and Religion* (New York: Meridian, 1960), p. 7.
106. Rousseau, *Social Contract*, p. 118.
107. The Afrikaners in South Africa are a good example. See Dunbar Moodie, *The Rise of Afrikanerdom* (Berkeley: University of California Press, 1974).
108. Max Weber, *The Sociology of Religion*, trans. Ephraim Fischoff (Boston: Beacon Press, 1963), p. 223.
109. Quoted in Dohen, *Nationalism*, p. 110.
110. Quoted in Quirk, *The Mexican Revolution*, p. 100.
111. Weber, *The Sociology*, p. 226.

4. The Five Religions of Modern Italy

ROBERT N. BELLAH

This chapter takes as its point of departure and as recurring touchstones several texts of Benedetto Croce and Antonio Gramsci. The method of the chapter pretends to no more than elucidation, interpretation, and commentary on these and certain other related texts. The justification of such a method can only come from the exceptional grasp and penetration of these two men and the great influence they have had—they are probably modern Italy's two most important thinkers. Both were profoundly concerned with the meaning of modern Italian society in the broadest historical and philosophical perspective. It is not a question of accepting their views; indeed, they differed sharply from each other. But I have found that grappling with their views in the context of Italian history has been a serviceable way to understand the place of religion, in the sense of systems of ultimate meaning, in modern Italy.

Benedetto Croce (1866–1952), the son of an aristocratic Neapolitan family, was a philosopher and historian of culture who became a living embodiment of liberal culture during the first half of this century. Believing "history is the history of liberty," he opposed all totalitarianisms. During the Mussolini period he withdrew from public life and, though never silenced, lived on

This chapter was first published in Italian under the title "Le Cinque Religioni Dell'Italia Moderna," in Fabio Luca and Stephen R. Gaubard, eds., *Il Caso Italiano* (Milan: Garzanti editore, 1974), pp. 439–468.

the margins of political toleration. After World War II he was felt to be the greatest living symbol of the old liberal Italy and was as such both honored and disregarded.

Antonio Gramsci (1891–1937) was the son of a poor Sardinian family, ultimately of Albanian extraction. After coming to Turin he became one of the first outstanding leaders of the Italian Communist party. Arrested by Mussolini in 1926, he spent the rest of his life in prison, except for the few days he survived, diseased and physically broken, after his release in 1937. His greatest work was done in prison and became known only when it was published after World War II. Gramsci's work has been widely popular among Italian intellectuals since the late 1940s, but he has had no outstanding continuator or successor.

Both Croce and Gramsci, viewed in the proper light, can be seen as lawgivers and even as prophets. Both were intensely concerned with the ethical and political orders of Italian society. Both had a vision of a good normative order they hoped to persuade their society to adopt. Both based their norm giving or law giving on a fundamental conception of reality to which they gave ultimate respect and that they invoked as legitimation for their normative demands; so they can rightly be called prophets. To Croce the historical realization of liberty was the highest good; to Gramsci it was the dialectic of socialist liberation. But lawgivers require law takers, and prophets require followers. Each in his own way finally found himself alone. Each, though concerned with power, had to renounce power, to reject his society as it was, and to refuse to collaborate with it. Both of them joined that long line of Italians, saints and heroes, who refused the demands of the powers of their day. They are thus not unworthy guides to the study of the meaning of reality in modern Italy.

Croce and Gramsci

Benedetto Croce began his well-known book *History of Europe in the Nineteenth Century,* with a chapter entitled "The Religion of Liberty." After describing various features of liberalism as it came to be expressed in the early nineteenth century, he writes,

Now he who gathers together and considers all these characteristics of the liberal ideal does not hesitate to call it what it was: a "religion." He calls it so, of course, because he looks for what is essential and intrinsic in every religion, which always lies in the concept of reality and an ethics that conforms to this concept. . . . Nothing more was needed to give them a religious character, since personifications, myths, legends, dogmas, rites, propitiations, expiations, priestly classes, pontifical robes, and the like do not belong to the intrinsic, and are taken out from particular religions and set up as requirements for every religion with ill effect.[1]

It is clear that Croce wishes to broaden the definition of religion beyond the traditionally religious elements he heaps together in the last sentence and that point to Catholicism. Croce's argument is close enough to my own that, following him, I will treat modern Italy as a land not of one religion, as common sense would dictate, but of several. Even the varieties I will consider are all but one to be found in Croce's book. In his second chapter, "Opposing Religious Faiths," he discusses Catholicism and socialism as competitors to liberalism, and in his last chapter he discusses a more recent religion he calls activism, which includes, among other things, fascism, though that word is not mentioned.[2] I will add a fifth religion, or class of religions, which I will argue precedes temporally, and in a sense, logically, all the others, and which I will call pre-Christian or sub-Christian religion. But I will not be satisfied, as Croce largely was, to lay out passively and statically the five religions side by side.

Antonio Gramsci criticized Croce's *History of Europe in the Nineteenth Century* for beginning in 1815 and his *History of Italy* for beginning in 1871, that is, just after but not including the French Revolution in the one book or the Risorgimento in the other.[3] He thus excluded "the moment of struggle; the moment in which the conflicting forces are formed, are assembled and take up their positions; the moment in which one ethical-political system dissolves and another is formed by fire and steel; the moment in which one system of social relations disintegrates and falls and another arises and asserts itself."[4] Gramsci's view of the "religions" is instructive because it emphasizes the element of struggle, of process, of politics. His conception of religion modulates from the Crocean to something more recognizably Marxist:

"Note the problem of religion taken not in the confessional sense but in the secular sense of a unity of faith between a conception of the world and a corresponding norm of conduct. But why call this unity of faith 'religion' and not 'ideology,' or even frankly 'politics'?"[5] Gramsci sees two major functions of such "religions." One is essentially defensive or, one might say, "integrative":

> But at this point we reach the fundamental problem facing any conception of the world, any philosophy which has become a cultural movement, a "religion," a "faith," any that has produced a form of practical activity or will in which the philosophy is contained as an implicit theoretical "premiss." One might say "ideology" here, but on condition that the word is implicitly manifest in art, in law, in economic activity and in all manifestations of individual and collective life. This problem is that of preserving the ideological unity of the entire social bloc which that ideology serves to cement and unify.[6]

The other is to provide new forms of consciousness appropriate for new stages of social development. Of particular importance to Gramsci is a religion or ideology that can provide a "national-popular collective will" such as he saw in Protestantism in the Reformation or Jacobinism in the French Revolution.[7] For him the particular problem of Italy arose from the fact that the Renaissance was not in this respect the equivalent of the Reformation nor was the Risorgimento the equivalent of the French Revolution. It thus remained the task of Marxism ("The Philosophy of praxis corresponds to the nexus Protestant Reformation plus French Revolution") to awaken the national-popular collective will so long dormant in Italy.[8] One need not accept fully the terms of Gramsci's dynamic analysis to see it usefully supplements Croce's more static structure.

In addition to the theoretical resources drawn from Croce and Gramsci I would like to apply two of my concepts developed from the analysis of American and Japanese society. In dealing with the religious dimension of American political life I borrowed the notion of "civil religion" from Rousseau and showed the exent to which a rather articulated set of religious beliefs and practices had grown up in the American polity that was independent from though not necessarily hostile to the various church religions that flourish in America.[9] In applying the notion to Italy it becomes important to realize that all five religions are civil religions. This is above all because Italian Catholicism is and has always been a civil religion. Not only is it the nature of Catholicism generally, or at least until quite recently and in certain countries like the United States, to express itself in particular social and political forms, but above all because the papacy, with its ineradicably political implications, has been for centuries an Italian institution. It has therefore, and again until quite recently, been impossible to challenge the Catholic political system without challenging Catholicism as a religion. It is for that reason, especially in Italy, that liberalism, socialism, and activism have had to be civil religions, religiopolitical organisms, in competition with the Catholic civil religion. The interrelations and interpenetrations are important, as we shall see, but the general point still stands. The sense in which the pre- or sub-Christian religions are civil religions is somewhat different and necessitates the application of still another concept, adapted from the language of music, of the "religious ground bass."

I developed the notion of the religious ground bass to get at that aspect of Japanese religion that cannot be subsumed under the headings of "Buddhism" or "Confucianism."[10] It is close to what is meant by Shintō not in the more formal aspects of that not very formal religion but at the point where Shinto shades off into the religion of the basic social structure itself, the religion embedded in the family, village, work group, and so on. What is evident in Japan just because there is such a thing as Shintō is more obscure in Italy but nonetheless important.

The Religious Ground Bass

As a figure of a much more general phenomenon and as an example of its most extreme form let us consider Carlo Levi's description of the religious life of a village in southern Italy in which he lived for a year, a life so alien that he considers it not only pre-Christian but in a sense prereligious.

> To the peasants everything has a double meaning. The cow-woman, the werewolf, the lion-baron, the goat-devil are only notorious and

striking examples. People, trees, animals, even objects and words have a double life. Only reason, religion, and history have clear-cut meanings. But the feeling for life itself, for art, language, and love is complex, infinitely so. And in the peasants' world there is no room for reason, religion, and history. There is no room for religion, because to them everything participates in divinity, everything is actually, not merely symbolically, divine: Christ and the goat; the heavens above, and the beasts of the field below; everything is bound up in natural magic. Even the ceremonies of the church become pagan rites, celebrating the existence of inanimate things, which the peasants endow with a soul, the innumerable earthy divinities of the village.[11]

This passage and the one that follows are interesting not only as descriptions of what Levi saw but of how a cultivated Italian intellectual thought about what he saw. The following is a description of the procession at the local feast of the Virgin Mary:

Amid this warlike thundering [of firecrackers] there was no happiness or religious ecstasy in the people's eyes; instead they seemed prey to a sort of madness, a pagan throwing off of restraint, and a stunned or hypnotized condition; all of them were highly wrought up. The animals ran about wildly, goats leaped, donkeys brayed, dogs barked, children shouted, and women sang. Peasants with baskets of wheat in their hands threw fistfuls of it at the Madonna, so that she might take thought for the harvest and bring them good luck. The grains curved through the air, fell on the paving stones and bounced up off them with a light noise like that of hail. The black-faced Madonna, in the shower of wheat, among the animals, the gunfire, and the trumpets, was no sorrowful Mother of God, but rather a subterranean deity, black with the shadows of the bowels of the earth, a peasant Persephone or lower world goddess of the harvest.[12]

Not only, for Levi, do the peasants live at a level of "subterranean" intensity beneath the "clear-cut meanings" of reason, religion, and history, they are finally and deeply antagonistic to those meanings:

Governments, Theocracies and Armies are, of course, stronger than the scattered peasants. So the peasants have to resign themselves to being dominated, but they cannot feel as their own the glories and undertakings of a civilization that is radically their enemy. The only wars that touch their hearts are those in which they have fought to defend themselves against that civilization, against History and Gov-

ernment, Theocracy and the Army. These wars they fought under
their own black pennants, without military leadership or training and
without hope, ill-fated wars that they were bound to lose, fierce and
desperate wars, incomprehensible to historians.[13]

I would like to take Levi's description of the pre-Christian or
sub-Christian religion of a desperately poor village in the far
south of Italy as standing for that particularistic religious life,
embedded in the roots of the social structure, that I have referred
to metaphorically as the religious ground bass. Here I would
include all those loyalties to family and clan, to pseudokinship
groups like the mafia, to village and town, and to faction and
clique that so often in Italy, as elsewhere, ultimately define reality
more significantly for their members than all the formal religions
and ideologies combined. The musical metaphor of the ground
bass is meant to suggest a deep and repetitive sonority, a drone
bass that continues in spite of all melodic developments in the
upper registers, the more formal theologies and philosophies,
and not infrequently drowns them out altogether.

While something like a religious ground bass is probably universal, its strength relative to other components of the religiocul-
tural system is certainly variable—probably greater in Japan than
in China, in Italy than in France or England. Its strength within
Italy also clearly varies in time and space; it was stronger a century ago than today, stronger in the south than in the north. But
of the latter contrast I have come to suspect that the south stands
not only for a geographical region but for a region in the Italian
soul and that there is something of the "south" everywhere in
Italy. The characteristics of the particularistic religion generally
can be extrapolated from Levi's description: It is emotional and
intense in contrast to the ascetic rationalism of high Italian culture; it is fiercely closed to the outside world (there is not one
such religion but as many as there are groups), as opposed to the
universalism of high Italian thought; and it is presided over by a
woman, an epiphany of the Great Mother of the Mediterranean
world, only partially and uncertainly articulated with the Virgin
of Nazareth.

To borrow an analogy from the political realm, I might say the
religious ground bass has been traditionally the "real religion"

and Catholicism the "legal religion." Certainly the attitude toward the church has often been legalistic and external—one does what one must in terms of the deep loyalties and obligations of the particularistic structure and then squares it as best one can with the demands of the church. The statesman Minghetti, himself a religious man, described the Italian masses in the late nineteenth century as almost devoid of "religious sentiment." For them, he said, "habit counts for more than faith. The latter has little influence on thought, and even less on action."[14] The degree to which a genuine Catholic piety has penetrated the Italian masses has varied in time and place over the last century, but it must certainly be said that Catholic identity has often been more of a shield for particularistic loyalties than an expression of deep inner faith. But then the same thing must be said for the secular religions of liberalism and socialism as well.

Only in this connection can we understand how a society that seems, if one considers its articulate and self-conscious classes, so intensely ideological can show such low rates of political and ideological knowledge and involvement when compared with other modern societies.[15] The gap between intellectuals and masses, between conscious ideology and popular feeling, is probably greater than in most Western countries. This can be and has been interpreted in terms of fragmentation and alienation, but we need more than merely negative terms to describe what is going on here.[16] The ground bass religion involves deep loyalties and even a kind of faith. It is understandable as a defensive reaction to a long history of bad government, oppression, and brutality, especially in the south, and to the partial failure of mass religious and ideological movements to penetrate the masses. But it is also the expression of a cultural continuity with an ancient past, a form of culture not only premodern but also pre-Christian and even pre-Roman. In particular there seems to be something central about the place of the woman in the ground bass culture, a place never quite adequately expressed in the writings of the self-conscious intellectuals. The position of the Italian woman is markedly less equal than in most modern societies, but as the female opposition to the divorce law suggests, there are rewards other than equality for women in the traditional system.

Finally, we may consider the ground bass religion as a civil religion, not of the nation but of the particular group whose essence it expresses. As such it may be a powerful force in combination, alliance, or opposition to one of the great rival civil religions seeking dominance in the state. An Italian professor pointed out to me in Italy there is always a gap between believing and doing and between belief and action comes the political calculus. But here I think political refers primarily to group interest and group loyalty rather than to civic concerns broadly expressed. The priority of particular group loyalties has protected the Italians from the worst extremes of ideological passion of the twentieth century—even fascism never went very deep—but it has also operated to undermine a genuine commitment to democratic and liberal values when these did not seem to pay off for particular groups.

Catholicism

The presence of the papacy in Italy has always been a mixed blessing for Italian spirituality. It has inhibited the development of a national church in the sense that France and Spain have national churches, religious patterns that are at the same time genuinely Catholic and expressive of the national popular culture. The ablest of the Italian clergy have been drawn into the international bureaucracy of the church, not into the formulation of a peculiarly national expression. At the same time the political priorities of the papacy seem to have inhibited in recent centuries the intellectual and devotional creativity the church has sometimes shown in other countries. Until a little over a century ago the papacy was itself a temporal power, one of the major states of Italy, and it remains to this day a sovereign state recognized diplomatically by many nations. It is impossible to understand the history of modern Italian Catholicism without understanding the politics of the papacy.

Gramsci's analysis of Italian history focused on the recurrent problem of the isolation of a cosmopolitan intellectual elite from a national-popular base that the structure of the Italian church exemplified but did not originate. Indeed, he traces this phenomenon back to the formation of a class of "imperial" intellectuals

in the early Roman Empire.[17] Nor did, in his view, the modern
secular intellectuals wholly escape from an analogous position
relative to the mass of the Italian people. But in many respects
the Catholic clergy remain paradigmatic of the place of the intellectual in Italy, and the two-class structure of the church, the clear
distinction between the religiously elite clergy and the common
people, has had enormous general repercussions. It is in part to
this phenomenon, emphasized especially by the presence of the
central organ of the church, the papacy, that I would link the
tendency of Italian thinkers of all persuasions to think in terms
of elites, of governing classes and political classes, more or less
clearly differentiated from the general population.

One of Gramsci's central theoretical problems is the conditions under which an "organic" intelligentsia is formed, that is,
one closely tied to a social group or class, which expresses its
inner needs and aspirations, rather than, as has usually been the
case in Italy, one that remains isolated from effective social involvement. This perspective explains why for Gramsci the lack of
an Italian Reformation is such a significant fact: "The Lutheran
Reformation and Calvinism created a vast national-popular
movement through which their influence spread. . . . The Italian
reformers were infertile of any major historical success."[18] It is
partly in response to that void of an Italian Reformation that we
may understand Gramsci's fascination, and not Gramsci's alone
but that of almost every major modern Italian intellectual, with
Niccolo Machiavelli, the Italian contemporary of Luther and Calvin.[19] Gramsci treats Machiavelli as a Reformer in secular guise,
a "precocious Jacobin," with a vision of a people armed, a national Italy, and Gramsci used the figure of Machiavelli's Prince
to express the unifying and leading function of the modern Communist party. Gramsci does not mention that in the *Discourses*
Machiavelli expresses an admiration for the religion of the ancient Romans, a truly "civil religion" relative to which he found
Christianity largely impotent politically. Nonetheless Machiavelli's *Discourses* were undoubtedly one of the sources for that
political faith that Gramsci so admired under the name of Jacobinism.

The Counter-Reformation in Italy has often been condemned
for its political and cultural effects, for its final confirmation of

absolutism as against any kind of popular sovereignty, and for the stultifying consequences of its cultural policy. Its religious consequences were also negative, as for instance in the crushing of Sarpi's "national-popular" Catholicism in Venice.[20] The externality and legalism of Trent encouraged not a deeply internalized piety but only the theatrical and mannered religious fervor of the baroque.[21] Yet within the pores, so to speak, of Tridentine Catholicism other possibilities were growing. The sober and sincere piety of Alessandro Manzoni in the nineteenth century was perhaps only a harbinger of things to come: a serious lay piety that would penetrate and transform the popular consciousness, at least in certain areas of the north.

But long before the fruits of such an inner transformation could become evident, the church was, in the middle of the nineteenth century, confronted with a major crisis: the emergence of the national question in Italy and the implications of unification for the papacy and the church. After a brief neo-Guelph flurry in 1847 and 1848, the first years of Pope Pius IX, when Italy was momentarily swept by the wild hope of an Italian confederation under the presidency of the pope, it became clear that the papacy would not only not lead the process of unification but would vigorously oppose it. The church was ideologically still locked in an encounter with the French Revolution, which it saw as the work of a liberal sect spawned ultimately by the Protestant Reformation and inimical to the principles of true religion. Throughout the nineteenth century the papacy resolutely opposed every effort to develop a liberal Catholicism, and it always felt closer to absolutist regimes like that of Austria than to any liberal polity. The Papacy was, after all, one of the firmest of the remaining absolute monarchies of Europe, and within Italy after 1848 it felt closer to almost every regime than to that of Constitutional Piedmont, which was to form the territorial base for the unification effort. It was thus not surprising that Italy had to be unified in the teeth of papal opposition and that devout Catholics mourned instead of celebrating when in March of 1861 Cavour proclaimed the existence of the Kingdom of Italy. Italy could not be unified without that large block of territories in the center of the peninsula known as the Papal States, and given its hostility to the nature of the new regime and the continued assertion of temporal sovereignty it would not relinquish for decades, the papacy would not accept the legitimacy of the new state. The aggrieved papacy in effect declared its loyal followers to be without a country. By its famous *non expedit* decree it forbade Catholics to be electors or elected in the new nation. The Catholic press referred to "King Victor Emmanuel" (presumably of Piedmont) and not to "the king" (of Italy). The liberal leaders of the new state did not engage in a religious persecution but neither did they fail to take advantage of their moment of triumph over the temporal power of the church. Many religious orders were dissolved and their properties confiscated. Anticlerical demonstrations were not unknown and a certain anticlerical rhetoric was common to the more radical liberal politicians.[22] A heritage of ill will was created in the first fifty years of the new nation whose full effects would not be evident until the Fascist period when the church, which on every conceivable ideological ground was antithetical to fascism, nonetheless found in it, at least at first, an ally, on the principle that an enemy of my enemy is my friend.

Finally, the church consistently referred to its lay opponents as "sects." The issue was not religion versus politics but two kinds of religion and two kinds of politics or two kinds of civil religion.

Liberalism

Gramsci would have agreed with the Catholic apologists in seeing the French Revolution and its accompanying ideology as simply another stage of what had already been begun in the Reformation, though for him the valence would have been different:

> France was lacerated by the wars of religion leading to an apparent victory of Catholicism, but it experienced a great popular reformation in the eighteenth century with the Enlightenment, Voltairianism and the Encyclopaedia. This reformation preceded and accompanied the Revolution of 1789. It really was a matter here of a great intellectual and moral reformation of the French people, more complete than the German Lutheran Reformation, because it also embraced the great peasant masses in the countryside and had a distinct secular basis and attempted to replace religion with a completely secular ideology represented by the national patriotic bond.[23]

That aspect of liberalism, as I am using the term in this chapter, which Gramsci describes and tends to call "Jacobinism" with a very positive value, Croce, in whose terms this "secular ideology" was certainly a religion, called "democracy" with a rather negative value compared to the "liberalism" with which he identified. Croce contrasted the "democracy" of the eighteenth century as mechanical, intellectualist, and abstractly egalitarian, whereas the "liberalism" of the early nineteenth century was personal, idealistic, and historically organic: "The democrats in their political ideal postulated a religion of quantity, of mechanics, of calculating reason or of nature, like that of the eighteenth century; the liberals, a religion of quality, of activity, of spirituality, such as that which had risen in the beginning of the nineteenth century: so that even in this case, the conflict was one of religious faiths."[24] Transferring these general conceptions to the Risorgimento reveals a characteristic difference of evaluation between Croce and Gramsci. For Croce, Cavour is the great liberal hero of the Risorgimento, the man with a sense of organic continuity, of history, of the necessity of the monarchy. Croce viewed Mazzini as a mechanical democrat whose views would have ruptured the natural growth of Italian society and who justly failed. Gramsci sees the victory of Cavour and the moderates as a "passive revolution," a victory of the ruling classes that the moderates organically and effectively represented but a defeat for the people. His sympathies would have been with Mazzini and Garibaldi had they been able to link their Action party with the organic needs of the masses, especially the rural masses, but it was just this that they failed to do.

> The Action party was steeped in the traditional rhetoric of Italian literature. It confused the cultural unity which existed in the peninsula —confined, however, to a very thin stratum of the population, and polluted by the Vatican's cosmopolitanism—with the political and territorial unity of the great popular masses, who were foreign to that cultural tradition and who, even supposing that they knew of its existence, couldn't care less about it. A comparison may be made between the Jacobins and the Action party. The Jacobins strove with determination to ensure a bond between town and country, and they succeeded triumphantly.[25]

Both Croce and Gramsci underestimate Mazzini, the greatest liberal and popular prophet of the nineteenth century, perhaps because both of them are too imbued with a Hegelian historicism that tends to applaud the winners. In spite of the fact that for nearly forty years Mazzini was the heart and soul of the movement for Italian unity, it was not his ideas that were actualized in 1871 and he ended his days in sadness and disappointment. But Mazzini's significance, as Luigi Salvatorelli has pointed out, is in his effort to reestablish the spiritual unity of the Italian people that had been draining away ever since the time of the medieval communes. His slogan, *"Dio e popolo,"* was not an empty phrase but the expression of a deep national need:

> Every nationalistic conception presupposes the primacy of politics over any other activity of the spirit. The Mazzinian conception of the Risorgimento, on the other hand, completely overcomes the political through the spiritual. Not only is all *ragion di stato* radically rejected, but politics is integrally subordinated to ethics; and ethics is nothing but the application of religious faith. Mazzini took up the Italian religious problem, with a view toward a radical solution. Here we touch the true depths of the Mazzinian revolution. It does not reside in a political rearrangement (which might allow for gradualness and expediency); nor does it reside in insurrection, which is a simple temporary instrument; rather his revolution resides in this inner religious transformation. He speaks explicitly of a new faith, which goes not only beyond the old Christian confessions he now considers impotent, but also beyond the skeptical and materialist nonbelief of the eighteenth century. . . . What remains necessary is otherworldly faith, which for him is faith in God, who manifests himself to humanity through successive revelations; one day, all humanity will be called up to God, just as individuals ascend to him in their successive lives. Until such time as social unity is established, ecclesiastical and political authority must remain as independent of each other as possible. But once the new society has really been constituted, there will be no more reason for the separation of Church and state, or of political and religious institutions. Ethics will conform to faith, and will be realized in politics; so, too, the state shall be the Church and the Church shall be the state. No divorce between heaven and earth; our work on this earth is a sacred task, the realization of the reign of God.[26]

In the end, of course, the Risorgimento did not lead to such a grand national regeneration. It was a revolution "from above,"

a "passive revolution" leaving the Italian masses largely un-
touched. Cavour's formula of "a free church in a free state" was
not only entirely unacceptable to the Vatican, it woefully underestimated the religious transformation that would have been necessary to create the free people for whom the free church and free
state could have had real meaning. This is not to say that Cavour's vision was not ethical and indeed religious in its own right.
But it remained the special property of a ruling elite and was not
really translated into a national culture.

Even when liberalism became so widespread among the educated classes, as it did by the end of the nineteenth century, that
it was almost taken for granted, it was by no means securely
institutionalized among the masses, as the rise of socialist, Catholic, and fascist parties uncertainly or not at all committed to
democratic institutions would subsequently show. But even the
greatest of the twentieth-century Italian liberals, Benedetto
Croce, suffered from the elitist restriction that had always characterized Italian liberalism. Again it is Gramsci who makes the point
when he criticizes Croce for not understanding that

> the philosophy of praxis, with its vast mass movement, has repre-
> sented and does represent an historical process similar to the Refor-
> mation, in contrast with liberalism, which reproduces a Renaissance
> which is narrowly limited to restricted intellectual groups. . . . Croce
> is essentially anti-confessional (we cannot call him anti-religious
> given his definition of religious reality) and for numerous Italian and
> European intellectuals his philosophy . . . has been a genuine intel-
> lectual and moral reform similar to the Renaissance. . . . But Croce
> did not "go to the people," did not wish to become a "national"
> element (just as the men of the Renaissance—unlike the Lutherans
> and Calvinists—were not "national" elements), did not wish to cre-
> ate a band of disciples who . . . could have popularised his philoso-
> phy and tried to make it into an educative element, starting in the
> primary school (and hence educative for the simple worker or peas-
> ant, i.e., for the simple man of the people). Perhaps this was impos-
> sible, but it was worth trying and the fact that it was not tried is
> certainly significant.[27]

Gramsci goes on to criticize Croce's elitist distinction of religion for the masses but philosophy for the educated elite. The
following passage from Croce's *The Philosophy of Conduct* with its

delicately patronizing tone toward the "younger brother" illustrates precisely the weakness to which Gramsci points:

> This function of an idealistic ethical symbol, this affirmation that the
> moral act is an expression of the love and the will of the universal
> Spirit, is characteristic of the religious and Christian Ethic, the Ethic
> of love and of the anxious search for the divine presence, which, as
> a result of narrow partisanship or lack of insight, is spurned and
> vilified today by vulgar rationalists and intellectualists, by so-called
> free-thinkers and similar riff-raff who frequent masonic lodges. There
> is hardly any truth of Ethics that cannot be expressed in the words of
> traditional religion, which we learned as children and which rise spon-
> taneously to our lips because they are the most sublime, the most
> appropriate, and the most beautiful of all: words that are, to be sure,
> still redolent of mythology, yet at the same time instinct with philoso-
> phy. Between the idealistic philosopher and the religious man there
> is undoubtedly a deep rift; but it is no different from that which
> appears in ourselves on the eve of a crisis, when we are mentally
> divided, and yet very close to inner unity and harmony. If the religious
> man cannot help regarding the philosopher as his adversary, indeed
> as his mortal enemy, the philosopher for his part sees in the religious
> man his younger brother, himself as he was but a moment before.
> Hence, he will always feel more strongly attracted to an austere,
> compassionate, allegorical religious ethic than to one that is superfi-
> cially rationalistic.[28]

Liberalism as an articulate movement remains elitist in Italy to
this day. The parties that remain loyal to it in parliament are small
and do not represent the popular masses. Yet who can say the
Catholic and socialist subcultures who represent the Italian
masses have not, over the last century, steadily and continuously
felt the influence of liberalism and been in part transformed by it?
Perhaps Croce was not wrong after all in his claim for liberalism.

> Because this is the sole ideal that has the solidity once owned by
> Catholicism and the flexibility that this was never able to have, the
> only one that can always face the future and does not claim to deter-
> mine it in any particular and contingent form, the only one that can
> resist criticism and represent for human society the point around
> which, in its frequent upheavals, in its continual oscillations, equilib-
> rium is perpetually restored, so that when the question is heard
> whether liberty will enjoy what is known as the future, the answer must
> be that it has something better still: it has eternity.[29]

Socialism

Many historians have described the first decades after the unification of the country as a period of mild disillusionment. The great battles of the Risorgimento had been fought and a victory of sorts had been won. Liberalism in the saddle proved disappointing compared to the heroic days when liberalism was in the opposition. The intense moral idealism of Mazzini was gradually replaced by the rise of positivism as the dominant philosophy—Herbert Spencer was everywhere read and quoted. The unification of the country provided the basis for a gradually accelerating industrial growth, particularly in the north, but this sign of positivistic "progress" seemed to be creating as many problems as it solved. It is these circumstances that make understandable the emergence of socialism as a major force in Italy. As Croce saw it: "The psychological conditions which we have described, uncertainty with regard to aims, doubt as to means, bankruptcy of ideas, all these symptoms from which Italy was suffering explain how it was that her young men were fired with such lively enthusiasm for the doctrines of socialism. Beginning about 1890, the cult of socialism grew rapidly and continued throughout the decade."[30] According to Croce the work of Karl Marx, "who created the new 'religion of the masses' in the same sense in which Paul of Tarsus created Christianity," was at first known only second or third hand.[31] But when Antonio Labriola discovered Marx's writing and popularized his theories, "Herbert Spencer, whom every one had read and quoted as the highest authority, was no longer quoted or read, and was allowed to fall into complete oblivion."[32]

Besides having a strong appeal for many of Italy's educated youth, among whom Croce himself was numbered for a while, Marxian socialism early met success among the industrial workers, especially in the urban north. The Italian Socialist party gradually began to build up not only a network of institutions—labor unions, mutual aid societies, and cultural organizations—but a distinct subculture, what according to Arturo Carlo Jemolo might almost be called "a new religion." Jemolo vividly describes the quality of that early socialist culture:

> The Italian—and in general the Latin—socialist of the first ten years of the century was totally different from his brother of today. He

would never have admitted, for instance, that any question of wages was of greater moment to him than a great abstract question. He longed for the moral and material redemption of the poorer classes, but he believed that this should be achieved by a transformation of the world. Depending on his school of thought and the particular concepts of the section of the Party with which he identified himself, he might differ from his fellows as to the manner in which he hoped to effect his regeneration, but his true aim was the complete obliteration of the past. He even had his special forms of dress, used the appellation "Comrade," and wore a distinctive flower—a red carnation—in his buttonhole. If he was a fanatical believer in the new ideas he did not even observe the rites of civil marriage, but openly lived in "sin." To his ideal system a fundamental reorganization of the economy was not less essential than a humanitarian outlook, anticlericalism, internationalism, anti-militarism, an aversion to all that had its origin in the military spirit or was infected with that spirit— whether it was a question of decorations, even for valour, or of duels.[33]

Just as the policy of various ministries ranged over time from vigorous repression of the socialists to tacit encouragement of them, especially in their efforts to unionize the workers, so the policy of the Socialist party modulated from one of intransigent opposition to the entire "bourgeois regime" to one of gradual acceptance of the framework of democratic institutions. This tendency was set back at the time of the colonial conquest of Libya in 1911, which the socialists bitterly and in some areas violently opposed, and there ensued the dominance for a time of a militantly revolutionary faction led by Benito Mussolini. But all indications were that in the long run the Socialist party tendency to enter the political system and thereby bring the newly emerging working classes into active participation in political society would prevail. The Great War, however, in Italy as elsewhere, shattered the illusion that this and similar trends were "inevitable," as had been widely believed only a short time before.

Activism

The last of modern Italy's five "religions" is what Croce calls "activism." For Croce, activism, which he defines as "morbid romanticism" and links loosely to incipient trends in the same direction in the early nineteenth century, is a parody or perversion of liberalism, a sickness of liberty.[34]

> For if liberty is deprived of its moral soul, if it is detached from the past and from its venerable tradition, if the continuous creation of new forms that it demands is deprived of the objective value of this creation, if the struggles that it accepts and the wars and the sacrifice and the heroism are deprived of the purity of the end, if the internal discipline to which it spontaneously submits is replaced by external direction and commands—then nothing remains but action for action's sake, innovation for the sake of innovation, and fighting for fighting's sake; war and slaughter and death-dealing and suffering death are things to be sought for and desired for themselves, and obedience too, but the obedience that is customary in war; and the upshot is activism. This is, accordingly, in this translation and reduction and mournful parody that it achieves of an ethical ideal, a substantial perversion of the love of liberty, a devil-worship taking the place of that of God, and yet still a religion, the celebration of a black mass, but still a mass.[35]

Such trends were general in Europe in the first years of the twentieth century, according to Croce, but in Italy they focused around the "morbidly romantic" figure of Gabriele D'Annunzio, whom Croce calls libidinous and sadistic.

It was not an accident that D'Annunzio, who would play the role of John the Baptist to the movement that was to be the fulfillment of activism in Italy, namely Fascism, was a poet. Indeed, Fascism attracted many of the leading innovators in Italian literature of the day, men like Marinetti and Pirandello. In this context a remark by Croce about socialism takes on a particular interest: "Thus not only political opinion but the whole of Italian thought and culture was permeated and invigorated by Marxian socialism. Only on literature and poetry it did not, and could not, have effective influence, owing not to lack of enthusiasm, but to its philosophical and practical character, which moved outside the mental process of poetry."[36] The strictly rational tendency of Marxian socialism was characteristic of Italian thought, since both liberalism and Catholicism were, each in its own way, highly rationalistic and, in the early twentieth century, unpoetic. In all these traditions reason and intellect were highly valued, in part for their ability to control emotion and passion. In this regard

activism was closer to the religious ground bass, with its intense
emotional commitments and its relative lack of theoretical complexity, than to the other three traditions. However, in the years
before World War I activism was a largely elite movement appealing to the educated but bored sons of the bourgeoisie, eager
for excitement and glory and disappointed in the Italietta, the
"Little Italy" of the liberal politicians. It seems likely that without
the drastic disruptions resulting from the First World War activism would have remained little more than a literary mood and
Fascism as a major political movement would never have been
born.

There were, however, even before the war, a few connections
between activism as a literary movement and a broader mass
following, connections that would be broadened and strengthened when the Fascist movement emerged after the war. One
such point of connection was the work of Georges Sorel, translated in about 1909 by Croce and enjoying a vogue in Italy, partly
thanks to Croce's efforts, that it never enjoyed in France. Sorel
was the socialist closest to activism and also, not accidently, a
partial exception to Croce's rule that socialism was not "poetic."
Croce's own ambivalent assessment, published after the triumph
of Fascism, suggests Sorel's importance:

> Revolutionary minds, scornful of accommodating reformism and
> impatient of the flabbiness into which orthodox socialism had fallen,
> devoted themselves in Italy also to seeking new formulas, better fitted
> to them; and one was supplied by Sorel with his syndicalism. Sorel
> assimilated socialism, as he conceived it, to primitive Christianity,
> assigned to it the aim of renewing society from its moral foundations,
> and therefore urged it to cultivate, like the first Christians, the senti-
> ment of "scission" from surrounding society, to avoid all relations
> with politicians, to shut itself up in workmen's syndicates and feed on
> the "myth" of the general strike. It was the construction of a poet
> thirsting for moral austerity, thirsting for sincerity, pessimistic with
> regard to the present reality, stubbornly trying to find a hidden fount
> from which the fresh pure stream would well forth; and tested by
> reality, his poetry quickly vanished, even in his own eyes.[37]

Among many others, Mussolini was infected by the mood of
Sorellian apocalyptic activism well before he left the Socialist
party.

According to Gramsci even Marinetti's rather esoteric movement of futurism held some appeal for the workers. In a series of manifestos and theatrical demonstrations Marinetti declared all traditional culture obsolete—one of his most famous manifestos called for the filling in of the canals of Venice and the leveling of her marble palaces to make way for railroads and factories, the true poetry of the future. Gramsci claimed many workers before the war "had seen in futurism the elements of a struggle against the old academic culture of Italy, mummified and alien to the popular masses."[38] Gramsci also claimed four-fifths of the readers of Marinetti's review, *Lacerba,* with a circulation of twenty thousand, were from the working class.

But one thing that differentiated all the activists, D'Annunzio, Marinetti, and Mussolini, from a left-wing socialist like Gramsci and a conservative liberal like Croce was their glorification of war, and more particularly their violent interventionism in the First World War. That war, traumatic for so many nations, was a major disaster for Italy. It seriously disrupted the economy and set off an inflation that was serious for wage earners and all but fatal for small property owners and produced a class of ultrarich war profiteers. It gravely overloaded the political system with serious problems at a time when it had not fully assimilated the consequences of universal male suffrage, voted in 1912. One of the new political elements was the emergence of a Catholic party, the Popular party, for the first time since the unification of the country. The 1919 elections showed the two great popular parties were the Catholics and the Socialists; the Liberals, who had ruled Italy for half a century, were a declining political force.

In the disturbed period just after the war all the tensions and divisions of Italian society were exacerbated. Class conflict was intense; returning veterans were bitter toward the pacifist workers with their draft exemptions based on their essential occupations; small property owners were afraid of losing the last vestige of gentility in the galloping inflation; the Catholic left, genuinely dedicated to nonrevolutionary social reform, did not unite with the socialists, many of whom were coming under the spell of the Russian Revolution, but formed rival "white" labor and peasant unions in competition with the "red" ones. Above all the great wave of strikes and demonstrations of 1919–1920 led to the fear that a Bolshevik revolution was in the making, though nowhere, not even in the best organized Turin group around Gramsci, was there any real revolutionary plan. Under these very severe tensions and pressures Italian politics reverted to its subideological base in the particular loyalties of families and small groups. Only thus can one understand the triumph of Fascism, which never gained what Gramsci called ideological hegemony—indeed, which never had an ideology at anything like the level of articulation and sophistication of the Catholics, liberals, or socialists.

Fascism in the immediate postwar period was a highly personal movement, an eclectic mixture of whatever Mussolini found that worked. Composed of veterans, former socialists and anarchists, and enraged bourgeois youth eager to fight the socialists as a substitute for the war they were too young for, fascism focused around the leader role Mussolini copied largely from D'Annunzio but with effective organizational forms Mussolini had learned in his years as a socialist. In the beginning its program contained a leftist flavor, but the situation dictated that Mussolini shift to the right, for it was the antisocialist violence of his *squadristi* that swelled his ranks. In free elections Fascism never approached the vote of the Catholics and socialists. It only came to power through the tacit conviction of millions of Italians that Mussolini would protect family and home, property, and tradition. That tacit conviction created the possibility of Mussolini coming to power; it took the cowardice of the king and the weakness of the liberal politicians to ensure it.

Even though Fascism remained ideologically eclectic and chaotic—Gentile's systematizations never had any organic connection with the movement—and in large measure it was simply the acting out on the national stage of some of the less pleasant aspects of the Italian underculture—the band of thugs tied to their leader in bonds of personal loyalty—it did develop an ideological style and became, once in power, a church, as Jemolo describes it:

> Fascism, like Bolshevism was itself a Church, claiming the whole man, in all his waking moments and in all his activities. Even in art and literature it prescribed what he must condemn and what he must admire. It had its uniforms, its epistolary style, its formulas, its ges-

tures of salutation, its rites that accompanied the party-member to the grave: the summons to the burial service, the Roman salute with which the Blackshirt greeted even funerals, even religious processions. (For many years the anti-Fascist was easily recognizable by the way he saluted a hearse and by his behavior when passing a cemetery, by his recourse to the traditional forms of greeting and his refusal to adopt the Fascist salute.) As the parish church and its presbytery are a focal point of the activities of the good Catholic, so was the local party headquarters a place of meeting, recreation, and meditation: a place where the new faithful forgathered in the evenings and on feast-days, where all initiatives, whatever their object, had to originate, and where —after 1935—a bride would often go immediately after her wedding to exchange the gold ring which the priest had just blessed for a ring made of iron. The party was a Church that persuaded its zealots to renounce all other interests: a Church that did not concern itself with the life to come, because in the Fascist *Weltanschauung,* as in the Communist, every aspiration has to be fulfilled in this world and there is no place for a future life in which earthly injustices may be set to rights.[39]

Given the hollowness of his ideology, the meagerness of his successes, and the fact that Mussolini never gained the kind of totalitarian control over Italian society that Hitler did over Germany, one must ask about the social and ideological bases of support of his regime. There is no question that the Italian liberal bourgeoisie, convicted of impotence in handling the postwar crisis, surrendered control of the government, though not of the economy, to Mussolini, some of them willingly, some of them reluctantly, but only a few of them going into principled opposition. Even the latter, as long as it remained theoretical, Mussolini tolerated, particularly in the figure of Benedetto Croce, who continued to write and publish all through the Fascist years. But in tolerating it Mussolini largely neutralized that opposition. It was the socialists who took the brunt of Fascism. Already in 1921 and 1922, even before Mussolini came to power, socialism's painfully built up network of institutions had been destroyed by the *squadristi* and many of its leaders murdered. Gramsci himself, by that time the leader of the Italian Communist party, was arrested in 1926 after his parliamentary immunity was violated and died in 1937 after years of bad food and maltreatment in a Fascist prison. Nevertheless, after the hurricane of terror it is probable that a

sector of the working class grasped what comfort it could from
the ideology of the corporative state and gave it its tacit consent.
But, ironically for both parties, Mussolini's securest basis of popular support came from his religious policy and derived from the
Catholic church.

Fascism in its earliest days was both anticlerical and republican,
in continuity with Mussolini's earlier socialist position, but the
Duce soon learned he had to swallow both monarchy and papacy
to become dictator. The latter was for him the bitterest pill of all.
After he had worked out the Concordat of 1929, which was to
signal the high point of his popularity in Italy, Mussolini stipu-
lated that in his audience with the pope he would not have to go
through the ceremony of kissing the ring, and he forbade photog-
raphers when he participated in the religious service in Saint
Peter's during which he had to pray on his knees. There is no
reason to believe Mussolini ever had anything but contempt for
the church in his own personal life. On the other hand there is
very little in Fascist ideology to escape condemnation at the
hands of religious orthodoxy, had the church desired to apply
rigorous standards. The relations between party and church were
indeed not untroubled, and the church successfully resisted Mussolini's efforts, soon after the Concordat, to destroy its lay organization, Catholic Action. After the racial laws of 1938 and especially after the German occupation, the church became
increasingly alienated from the regime, and the role of many of
the clergy in the resistance was a heroic one. Yet the fact remains,
and needs to be explained, that the relation of the church to the
regime was for many years a close, indeed, an intimate one, as can
be seen in Jemolo's description:

> But the government gained far more from this co-operation than
> did the Church—among other things, a sense of legality, almost of
> divine prescription, such as no Government had ever enjoyed in the
> past: and that not merely as a Government, but as a regime. It might
> have seemed of small account that in their processions the boys of
> Catholic Action walked in threes, in imitation of the Fascist militia,
> and not in fours, as they had done up to 1922; that they carried their
> flags with the staffs resting on their stomachs, again in imitation of the
> Fascists, and not on their shoulders, as had been the custom before
> the March on Rome; that even the most obscure parish magazines and

journals of religious associations showed the year of the regime along-side that of the Christian era; and that Catholics habitually observed all the outward forms of Fascism, beginning with the Roman salute and the conversational use of *voi,* abandoning, because the Duce so willed it, the age-old use of the third person as the polite form of address. These things might have seemed unimportant, but they were not. Thus, only thus, by drawing a veil over the past, by keeping lowered the curtain which divided the Fascist world from all that lay beyond its frontiers, could the Government assert itself as a regime, as *the* regime: not merely as a system of government, but as a philoso-phy of life; one might well say, as a Church.

Nor was it a matter of indifference that the Houses of the Fasci, the shrines of those who had given their lives for the Fascist revolution, were invariably blessed by the local bishop; that no party initiative which sought to create a new way of life, a new outlook, ever lacked the co-operation of the clergy; that a course on the *mystique* of Facism could be inaugurated with a speech (albeit of strict religious or-thodoxy) by a cardinal.

All this went far beyond the idea inherent in the precept "Render unto Caesar," far beyond respect for and co-operation with the lawful Government. All this was a sanctification not of the Fascist Govern-ment but of the Fascist outlook, the Fascist way of life. The non-Fascist, the anti-Fascist, was approaching a point at which he would have to ask himself whether the parish church was still *his* church; he was now having to go to mass early in the morning if he wished to avoid the sermon, which too often comprised a full-scale attack on all the democratic, masonic Governments which were opposing the providential plans of the Duce.

And, after 1929, one would have been hard put to it to find a bishop's pastoral or sermon, an inaugural speech at a diocesan confer-ence, that did not contain the word, the invocation, the blessing, the epithet appropriate to the Duce. And the epithets chosen became progressively more sonorous, and the person invoked tended more and more to assume the likeness not of a Head of Government, but of the pioneer of a civilization.[40]

The only thing that can explain how the church clung to this strange alliance for so long is the history of bitterness of the first seventy years of the Kingdom of Italy and the fact that the church was at last coming into its own, legally recognized as a central institution of society instead of existing in some limbo of mar-ginal toleration and occasional minor persecution, that and the fact that the church was, for many people and in many areas, embedded in and serving the interests of the particularistic groups and their essentially pre-Christian group loyalties that regarded Mussolini as their savior.

The Recent Past

The aftermath of the Second World War was remarkably similar to that of the First World War, though the outcome was radically different. Once again there was the threat of revolution, this time from the armed partisans and workers in the north; once again there was the upsurge of a great fear from all those concerned about family and property, stability and tradition. Only this time all such elements coalesced under the leadership of a reborn Catholic party, the Christian Democrats. The 1948 elections were the high water mark of this upsurge, the greatest electoral party victory in modern Italian history.[41] Italy after 1945 was certainly different from Italy before 1922. The Fascist regime itself, whatever its negative features, probably contributed to that "passive revolution" in another of the senses in which Gramsci used the term, in which important social changes can go on even under reactionary and repressive regimes—the gradual erosion of particularistic and traditional authority structures and the development of more egalitarian social forms—though it may be in the nature of the less effective Italian Fascist regime to have served more as a guardian for such structures and less as a corrosive to them than in the more efficient fascist regimes in Germany and Japan. In any case Italy after 1945 was neither a mass society nor a very mobilized one. Never having had a Reformation or a revolution, the formal religions and ideologies continued to float on the surface of Italian society, appealing to a mobile educated elite but not permeating much of the substructure except in certain areas of the country where Catholic piety or socialist fervor were genuine popular phenomena (for example, the Veneto for the Catholics and Romagna-Emilia for the socialists). A culture of decadence reminiscent of the pre–World War I activism was again in evidence in the postwar period, though lacking in vigor and, fortunately so far, in any effective political expression. All the elements remain and remain with a viscosity that leads many to despair of fundamental change in Italian society. Yet there are a number of new factors in the Italian situation that give rise to at least the possibility of creative change.

An important contextual factor for much of the recent past has been a relatively favorable international situation that provided neither the threat nor the temptation of war nor, with the decline of the cold war, any intense external ideological or political pressure either. Thus the kinds of external threats and disturbances that have frequently diverted modern Italian history from what might be thought of as a "normal" course have been on the whole less in evidence. The serious international economic crisis and the renewal of big power rivalry of the late 1970s threaten once again the fragile balances of Italian development.

The electoral triumph of Christian Democracy within the institutional framework of the liberal state created a new situation with respect to the problem of civil religion. The very logic of the early cold war forced the church into a defense of liberalism and democracy to a degree unprecedented since the French Revolution. The liberal state, instead of being the church's persecutor, was now its defender and so had to be evaluated differently. Particularly now that liberalism was not a major independent political force or contender for rule, its values could be accepted as the legitimate norms of the state and given religious approval. On the other hand, in the immediate defensiveness of the first postwar years, instead of a rather clearly differentiated liberal civil religion toward which the church could maintain a nonantagonistic autonomy, there emerged a fusion of religious and political values, as the very term Christian Democracy suggests, which led almost to a clerical democratic state. Under John XXIII the tight bearhold union of party, church, and state began to be broken on the initiative not of the Christian Democratic party but of the church. With the "opening to the left," itself made possible by that incipient differentiation of the party and the church in the early 1960s, the possibility of an autonomous liberal civil religion became more real. It would be based on the symbols of the Risorgimento, inevitably, but it would include the celebration of democratic values to which at several crucial points Catholics had also contributed.

If such a solution to the civil religion problem does eventually emerge, a solution based on the common acceptance of certain political values rather than a struggle to the death between different religiopolitical ideologies, it will depend on changes in both the church and the socialist left. Relevant changes in the church have been clearly evident, as I have already mentioned, from the time of the *aggiornamento* of Pope John. Developments have not been smooth and recent years have seen something of a "reverse course," but the long-range tendencies do not seem likely to change. The basic implications of the changes are a greater freedom of the church from party and state on the one hand and a wider range of political options for Catholics than support of the Christian Democratic party, options that include support of more vigorously reformist or radical parties of the left. It is true that the church in Italy has probably not responded as quickly to the new freedoms of Vatican II as have some other national churches —the habit of authority at the center of power has been too strong—and opportunities have been missed, as when the church responded too defensively and too unsympathetically to the movement of so-called "spontaneous groups" of idealistic youth in the late 1960s. But if the church will not lead the way to new freedoms, it has already lost its power to maintain strict discipline. A purely negative erosion of authority could prove dangerous for the church and for Italy, and there is no assurance that vigorous leadership will again be asserted. But the Italian church in the last fifty years has come a long way out of the wilderness. It faces no formidable secular enemy—even the Communist party prefers not to face it head on—and it has long been close to the sources of secular power. It can afford, as Pope John so well saw, to open up all kinds of new possibilities, not out of weakness but out of strength. Temporary reversals should probably not obscure the long-term trend toward liberalization.

If the Catholics have, in the last half century, gradually moved back into the centers of power, the same cannot be said of the socialists, who have never held effective power in Italy. Indeed, the history of socialism in Italy is a history of persecution from the very beginning, a persecution that reached catastrophic proportions in 1921 and 1922 and the long night that followed. Since the war, socialists have been harassed rather than persecuted, but only in the last few years has a large socialist group,

the left-wing Italian Socialist party, attained a share of political
power, and that certainly not the lion's share. If there has been
no *aggiornamento* within the Italian Communist party, no equivalent to Vatican II, it is certainly in part because an embattled
defensiveness has been objectively warranted. Nevertheless the
Italian Communist party (CPI) has a tradition of flexibility, hu-
manism, and appeal to intellectuals that is perhaps unique in the
Western world. This does not by any means mean the CPI is
clearly committed to liberal democratic values; it only means in
the right circumstances it might be possible to open the door on
that question. There have emerged in recent years a number of
groups to the left of the CPI, disillusioned by its flaccidity and,
if anything, more authoritarian than the orthodox parent. These
groups express a left-wing activism reminiscent of the Sorellian
variety previously discussed. The terrorism a few of these groups
have spawned impedes rather than advances the evolution of a
national community. It rouses once again the anxiety that
strengthens particularistic commitment. The main problem on
the left, however, remains the Italian Communist party, the largest excluded group in modern Italian history. The eventual entry
of the Communists into some share of governmental power, un-
thinkable only a few years ago, has come to be widely discussed.
Such an eventuality would create the possibility for the transformation of Communist values in a way parallel to what has happened to the Catholics. But if such a transformation is to be
something other than a sellout that will just produce a new mass
alienated party to the left of the Communists, it will have to be
accompanied by at least the beginning of the solution to some of
Italy's basic social problems. In other words the only way to
democratize the socialists is to socialize the democracy. How
difficult that will be is already evident from the fruits of the
several efforts at establishing a center-left government.

But in spite of some grounds for optimism, no observer of
Italian society today could call it a happy one. Corruption and
cynicism, as so often in the past, go hand in hand, and basic
demands for justice and welfare go unanswered. These are ge-
neric problems in all modern societies, but the will to meet them
seems more lacking in Italy than in many other advanced Western countries. The immobilism of particularistic interest, far

more than fervid ideological differences, threatens every effort to create a genuinely democratic society responsive to popular need. Centuries of failure to institutionalize the dreams and ideals that again and again have grown up on Italian soil have led to a certain fatalism. Whatever their differences, the greatest of modern Italian novelists—Manzoni, Verga, Moravia, Silone, Lampedusa—share a fundamental pessimism about the human capacity to alter social institutions. All of them opt instead for a certain dignity and integrity in the individual human soul.

And yet modern Italy has not been poor in individual souls who have had the courage to try to alter institutions. Arturo Carlo Jemolo, with his ceaseless struggle to defend religious liberty, critically, polemically, and legally, is such an example.[42] So is Danilo Dolci, with his effort to find, outside of any religious or ideological orthodoxy, forms of social participation that will be neither impersonally bureaucratic nor boss dominated.[43] Nor should the achievements of many such men, working through parties and independently, be underestimated. Croce, who led at several points an active political life, always reminds me of the modest but real institutional successes of modern Italy. And Gaetano Salvemini, another man of conscience who was not afraid to enter the political arena, warns there are no paradises on earth and if we will not settle for some kind of purgatory, we are likely to end up in hell.[44]

Italian history states with stunning clarity the central issues of the sociology of human existence: the very partial institutionalization of morality, the role of the moral hero and the immoral hero, and the problem of when to take power and when to renounce power. Italian history has produced a continuous series, century after century, of men larger than life, extraordinary as intellectuals but above all as moral virtuosi. But at the same time no other society has illustrated so clearly the problem of continuous inveterate corruption and ineptitude.

I shall close by quoting Ignazio Silone, whose words sum up many of the themes of this chapter in the way that they interweave the strands of socialism, liberty, and, implicitly, Christianity:

> Consideration of the experience I have been through has led me to a deepening of the motives for my separation which go very much

further than the circumstantial ones by which it was produced. But my faith in Socialism (to which I think my entire life bears testimony) has remained more alive than ever in me. In its essence, it has gone back to what it was when I first revolted against the old social order; a refusal to admit the existence of destiny, an extension of the ethical impulse from the restricted individual and family sphere to the whole domain of human activity, a need for effective brotherhood, an affirmation of the superiority of the human person over all the economic and social mechanisms which oppress him. As the years have gone by, there has been added to this an intuition of man's dignity and a feeling of reverence for that which in man is always trying to outdistance itself, and lies at the root of his eternal disquiet. But I do not think that this kind of Socialism is in any way peculiar to me. The "mad truths" recorded above are older than Marxism; towards the second half of the last century they took refuge in the workers' movement born of industrial capitalism, and continue to remain one of its most enduring founts of inspiration. I have repeatedly expressed my opinion on the relations between the Socialist Movement and the theories of Socialism, these relations are by no means rigid or immutable. With the development of new studies, the theories may go out of fashion or be discarded, but the movement goes on. It would be inaccurate, however, with regard to the old quarrel between the doctrinaires and the empiricists of the worker's movement, to include me among the latter. I do not conceive Socialist policy as tied to any particular theory, but to a faith. The more Socialist theories claim to be "scientific" the more transitory they are; but Socialist values are permanent. The distinction between theories and values is not sufficiently recognized, but it is fundamental. On a group of theories one can found a school; but on a group of values one can found a culture, a civilization, a new way of living together among men.[45]

NOTES

1.   Benedetto Croce, *History of Europe in the Nineteenth Century,* trans. Henry Furst (New York: Harbinger, 1963), p. 18.
2.   The book was first published in Italy in 1933 and it was necessary for Croce to be somewhat guarded in his language.
3.   Benedetto Croce, *A History of Italy, 1871–1915,* trans. Cecilia M. Ady (New York: Oxford University Press, 1929).
4.   Antonio Gramsci, *Selections from the Prison Notebooks,* ed. and trans. Quintin

Hoare and Geoffrey Nowell Smith (New York: International and London: Lawrence & Wishart, Ltd., 1971), pp. 118–119.

5. Ibid., p. 326.
6. Ibid., p. 328.
7. Ibid., p. 130.
8. Ibid., p. 45.
9. See Robert N. Bellah, "Civil Religion in America," in Robert N. Bellah, *Beyond Belief: Essays on Religion in a Post-Traditional World* (New York: Harper & Row, 1970).
10. Robert N. Bellah, "Values and Social Change in Modern Japan," in ibid.
11. Carlo Levi, *Christ Stopped at Eboli,* trans. Francis Frenaye (New York: Noonday Press, 1970), p. 117.
12. Ibid., pp. 118–119.
13. Ibid., pp. 137–138.
14. Arturo Carlo Jemolo, *Church and State in Italy, 1850–1950,* trans. David Moore (New York: Oxford University Press and Oxford: Basil Blackwell Publisher, Ltd., 1960), p. 39.
15. Joseph LaPalombara, "Italy: Fragmentation, Isolation, and Alienation," in Lucian W. Pye and Sidney Verba, eds., *Political Culture and Political Development* (Princeton, N.J.: Princeton University Press, 1965), pp. 286–288.
16. Ibid.
17. Gramsci, *Selections,* p. 17.
18. Ibid., p. 394.
19. Ibid., p. 123. Croce, *A History,* p. 152, traces this modern interest in Machiavelli to the 1890s and says, "With the Marxists, Machiavelli returned to Italy." By that he meant the Marxists were the first Italians since the mid seventeenth century to take Machiavelli seriously. Croce's own role in reviving Machiavelli scholarship was not negligible.
20. William Bouwsma, *Venice and the Defense of Republican Liberty* (Berkeley: University of California Press, 1968).
21. "The Counter-Reformation in Italy was essentially an authoritarian superstructure raised over indifferent individual consciences, a baroque decoration covering the religious and moral void." Luigi Salvatorelli, *The Risorgimento: Thought and Action* (New York: Harper & Row, 1970), p. 19.
22. Jemolo, *Church and State,* p. 42.
23. Gramsci, *Selections,* pp. 394–395.
24. Croce, *History of Europe,* p. 31.
25. Gramsci, *Selections,* p. 63.
26. Salvatorelli, *The Risorgimento,* p. 96.
27. Gramsci, *Selections,* p. 132.
28. Cited in Jemolo, *Church and State,* p. 95.
29. Croce, *History of Europe,* p. 358.
30. Croce, *A History,* p. 145.
31. Ibid., pp. 145–146.
32. Ibid., p. 154.
33. Jemolo, *Church and State,* p. 141.

34. Croce, *History of Europe,* p. 343.
35. Ibid., p. 342.
36. Croce, *A History,* p. 156.
37. Croce, *History of Europe,* p. 306.
38. Gramsci, *Selections,* p. 93.
39. Jemolo, *Church and State,* p. 191.
40. Ibid., pp. 268–270.
41. For postwar politics generally but particularly for a helpful treatment of the Catholic and socialist subcultures see Giorgio Galli and Alfonso Prandi, *Patterns of Political Participation in Italy* (New Haven, Conn.: Yale University Press, 1970).
42. See H. Stuart Hughes, *The United States and Italy,* rev. ed. (Cambridge, Mass.: Harvard University Press, 1965), p. 241.
43. My visit to Dolci's headquarters in Sicily and my talks with him in Rome during my research visit to Italy in the spring of 1972 were the most impressive moments of that trip.
44. Gaetano Salvemini, *Italy from the Risorgimento to Fascism,* ed. A. William Salomone (Garden City, N.Y.: Doubleday Anchor, 1970), p. 453.
45. Ignazio Silone, *The God That Failed,* ed. Richard Crossman, (New York: Bantam, 1965), pp. 101–102.

III. The Development of Civil Religion

5. The Rudimentary Forms of Civil Religion

PHILLIP E. HAMMOND

Not every nation-state has a civil religion. Whatever the proclivity of enduring groups to project or represent themselves symbolically, not all succeed in doing so in transcendental terms. Only some make sacred their civil rituals; only some create theology out of their political myths. A several-faceted issue is thus raised: What distinguishes those nation-states with a civil religion from those without? Why might a civil religion develop in the first place? What needs, felt by whom, are met by a civil religion? And why are such needs not met by other (prior, noncivil) religions? To answer such questions is to advance our understanding of civil religion. At the very least the question of whether various ceremonies and ideologies *should* be regarded as rituals and theologies is clarified if a plausible reason can be given as to why they *can* be.

In this chapter I attempt only to illuminate some of the conditions that *could* give rise to civil religions, thus making plausible at least their existence. Briefly put, my argument is (1) the condition of religious pluralism prevents any one religion from being

Chapter 5 is a somewhat revised version of "Religious Pluralism, Legal Development, and Societal Complexity: The Rudimentary Forms of Civil Religion," *Journal for the Scientific Study of Religion*, 13 (June, 1974), pp. 177–189. I want to acknowledge the important research assistance of William A. Cole in developing this chapter.

used by all people as a source of generalized meaning, but (2) people nevertheless need to invest their activity with meaning, especially when that activity brings together persons of diverse religious background. Therefore (3) a substitute meaning system is sought and, if found, the people whose activities have been facilitated by it will tend to exalt it.

I suggest a universalistic legal system can be such a substitute meaning system, though, as other chapters in this volume suggest, more than a universalistic legal system is surely involved.

Admittedly, the theory here is abstract. It suffers from the fault of so much of the social scientific study of religion, which in its efforts to show the sociological importance of religion has been forced to deal with global, far-reaching, and historical variables. In so doing, such study has frequently sacrificed the closely specified and carefully measured variables. This one is no exception. And yet I use quantitative data from a number of societies and may for that reason claim to avoid some of the pitfalls of "mere" theoretical analysis. Nevertheless the analysis makes several broad assumptions: regarding the time order of variables, regarding the meaning of "social complexity" (soon to be specified) found among present-day developing societies, and regarding the equating of contemporary nation-states with what in theory are "societies."

I previously identified a second caveat. The overarching theory states that a generalized legal system will be elevated to civil religious status insofar as it facilitates the interaction of religiously diverse people. In fact, however, the information (and thus the narrower theory examined here) pertains only to the first of the two implied assertions—that a generalized legal system facilitates the interaction of religiously diverse people. The second assertion—that such a legal system will then become sacrosanct—remains unexamined by data in this chapter. It is in this sense that our understanding of civil religions will be advanced even if only a plausible *reason* for their existence can be given. With these two qualifications, then, I present and test the narrower of the two theories.

The Theory

John Courtney Murray put the first part of this narrower theory as well as it can be put: Civil discourse or civil unity is complicated and laborious enough, but under conditions of religious pluralism it is more so because discussion of concrete affairs goes on in abstract terms—in "realms of some theoretical generality"—and pluralism creates different sets of these realms. Discourse becomes "incommensurable" and confused.[1] Such confusion is easy to imagine since some taken-for-granteds get called into question. Would-be partners cease to be sure of each other's commitments and thus trustworthiness. The relative strength of loyalties to kin, neighborhood, status group, and such are possibly challenged by one's loyalty to one or another (or no) religious group. To the simple categories of believer and heretic get added the various ways to be a nonbeliever. Religious pluralism, to put it simply, complicates matters by ripping the once intact sacred canopy. Interaction, we might suppose, thereby is inhibited.

For this reason, and perhaps contrary to one's initial guess, we can expect *greater* pluralism at the religious level to be associated with *lesser* amounts of social development (or "societal complexity"). At least we can expect no positive relationship between religious pluralism and societal complexity. This is the first proposition.

It is important to realize the meaning attached to "societal complexity" in this proposition, however. Since religious pluralism itself represents one kind of complexity, it should be clear that kind of complexity is excluded from this variable. The reference in the present complexity variable is rather to those "secular" activities that, if religious considerations can be ignored or overcome, may proceed unimpeded but into which religious considerations are likely to intrude *unless special efforts are made.* The type case is the market transaction wherein two parties can strike a bargain suitable to both if particularistic factors such as religion do not interfere. But the whole range of contacts generally regarded as "socioeconomic" also apply here. I recognize that the usual formulation is somewhat different, that is, as secular activities develop, such particularistic factors as religion diminish. In either view particularistic factors are held in abeyance to some degree; I am arguing that the condition of religious pluralism makes it more important for people to hold religious consideration in abeyance. What little difference exists between these two views revolves around whether religion's diminution (secularization) occurs *automatically* with pluralization or instead will occur only if the "holding in abeyance" is *helped along* (as by a changing legal order).

In any event, though religious heterogeneity may very well appear alongside or as part of general social complexity, I expect a plurality of meaning systems or "sacred canopies" will inhibit development of those social interactions that typically *cross* religious lines, that is, secular or socioeconomic activities.

The second part of the theory deals with situations wherein secular activities *have been or are in a position to be* inhibited by religious pluralism. It states that the (threat of) impasse may be lessened by the existence of legal institutions that foster universalistic norms. In effect, this requires of the law some procedures to enable diverse parties to interact in spite of otherwise inhibiting characteristics. For example, two persons who are prohibited by religious scruples from transactions with each other may find it possible, through law, to use third parties (for example, the impersonal, universalistic procedures of a bank). Or, as another example, two groups who define themselves as "believers" and "heretics" or as "faithful" and "infidel" may nevertheless be convinced they will receive fair treatment in the courts and thus allow themselves to buy and sell, enter into contract, and so forth.

Max Weber's distinction between substantive and formal rationality sets the terms for this part of the theory:

> In general terms . . . the rationality of ecclesiastical hierarchies as well as of patrimonial sovereigns is substantive in character, so that their aim is not that of achieving the highest degree of formal juridical precision which would maximize the chances for the correct prediction of legal consequences. . . . The aim is rather to find a type of law which is most appropriate to the expediential and ethical goals of the authorities in question. . . . Yet in the course . . . of rationalization of legal thinking on the one hand and of the forms of social relationships on the other, the most diverse consequences could emerge from the

non-juridical components of a legal doctrine of priestly make. One of these possible consequences was the separation of *fas*, the religious command, from *jus*, the established law for the settlement of such human conflicts which had no religious relevance. In this situation, it was possible for *jus* to pass through an independent course of development into a rational and formal legal system. . . . Juridical formalism enables the legal system to operate like a technically rational machine. Thus it guarantees to individuals and groups within the system a relative maximum of freedom, and greatly increases for them the possibility of predicting the legal consequences of their actions. Procedure becomes a specific type of pacified contest, bound to fixed and inviolable "rules of the game."[2]

Weber, as usual, is speaking here of ideal-typical forms of legal systems. Nevertheless, he sees the strategic importance played by the shift from particularistic to universalistic standards—from what he calls substantive to formal rationality. Related to this shift is the obvious fact that *religious* particularism is not the *only* particularism. Thus Weber refers to "patrimonial" as well as "ecclesiastical" sovereigns.[3] The proper interpretation is to recognize that whatever loyalties and commitments people may have —to kin, guild, caste, and so on—are likely, when institutionalized, to be expressed religiously. It is in this sense that the opening paragraphs of this chapter refer to meaning systems or sacred canopies *as* religion. In a totemistic, endogamous, clan society, for example, the "kin" loyalty and "religious" loyalty would be identical. But in any society kin loyalty is likely to find expression in religious language, rituals, and so forth.

The proposition in this second half of the theory can be stated as follows, therefore: The higher the level of religious pluralism in a society, the more will societal complexity depend upon, and thus be associated with, the presence of a universalistic legal system.

This second proposition appears almost to represent common knowledge. A rationalized, generalized, predictable legal system will foster social interaction and thus societal complexity.[4] The claim here is more than this, however; it is that, while a rationalized legal system may facilitate societal complexity in *any* situation, it may be *even more helpful* for people who are otherwise religiously different. Here is the argument locating this chapter in the context outlined in the opening paragraphs: *The legal order in some significant measure becomes a substitute for the religious order*— the order that supplies meaning—and thus sets the stage for the emergence of civil religion.[5]

Granted, the outcome may not be a sharply defined "civil religion"—one that could be universally recognized as such—but at the least it can be anticipated that some kind of "political religion" will be more likely to emerge in societies where legal structures take on meaning-bestowal qualities.[6] Obviously such political religion can emerge in "totalitarian" as well as "democratic" societies, but in either setting it will be the law and not mere coercion that facilitates social development. This is Kozolchyk's point regarding "fairness" in the law. *If* law is to facilitate societal complexity, it must instill trust, which means it cannot deviate far from the will of those governed. Nation-states of considerable as well as meager development are variously located along the pluralism axis. I shall show that regardless of political style, the societal complexity of religiously plural societies is helped along *more* by universalistic legal systems than is the complexity in religiously homogeneous societies.

Testing the Theory

In an ambitious project to assess the correctness of Talcott Parsons's theory of evolutionary universals, Gary Buck accumulated masses of data for 115 contemporary nation-states from every part of the world.[7] He developed elaborate indices (as of 1960 wherever possible) of the ten variables Parsons discussed: (1) communication, (2) kinship organization, (3) religion, (4) technology, (5) stratification, (6) cultural legitimation, (7) bureaucratic organization, (8) money and market complex, (9) generalized universalistic norms, and (10) democratic association.[8] Information was taken from such sources as the *United Nations Statistical Yearbook,* the *Yearbook of Labor Statistics,* and UNESCO's *World Survey of Education.* One index (kinship organization) was measured by only three indicators, but the others were more extensively measured, some by over a dozen separate pieces of information. I have borrowed five of Buck's ten indices in order to measure two of the three variables.

Societal Complexity

Societal complexity refers to the degree of complexity in "secular" activities, of which the market transaction is the prime example. Perhaps socioeconomic development is a suitable alternative phrase. Four of Buck's indices—communication, technology, bureaucratic organization, and money and market complex— seem to measure this variable very well. Altogether they entail fifty indicators (making their listing here too space consuming), but one indicator from each of the four indices will give an idea of their nature (see Table 2).

Table 2. Four Indices of Societal Complexity and Sample Indicators of Each

For the index of:	An illustrative indicator is:
Communication	Motor vehicles in use
Technology	Percentage of gross domestic product originating outside of agriculture
Bureaucratic organization	Ratio of salaried employees to wage earners.
Money and market complex	Imports and exports per capita

While Buck found it necessary to keep these four indices separate—if he was to test the sequential nature Parsons claimed for them—I have no such requirement. Therefore since each measures a different but important aspect of "complexity," I merge all four indices. Each had a range of scale scores from one to seven, which means the composite index used here ranges from four to twenty-eight. For simplicity I have subtracted three from every unit, making the range from one to twenty-five. Countries were found at every score level. It is important to remember that all fifty indicators, despite their differences, refer to "secular" activities, that is to say, activities that can be engaged in by persons whether or not they "like" or "know" or "frequently see" each other. They measure how easily "strangers" are brought into interaction.

Legal Development

Buck also has an index he called, following Parsons's terminology, "generalized universalistic norms." A legal system is generalized, Parsons says, to the degree it is "an integrated system of universalistic norms, applicable to the society as a whole rather than to a few functional or segmental sectors, highly generalized in terms of principles and standards, and relatively independent of both the religious agencies that legitimize the normative order of the society and vested interest groups in the operative sector, particularly in government."[9] That is, a generalized legal system facilitates social relations. Such a process can be regarded as legal development (in the sense I have been using that concept here), and I therefore use the Buck index of generalized universalistic norms as its measure. He, in turn, built his index on eight pieces of information about each society contained in one of two sources.[10]

Seven of these pieces of information deal with the degree to which the law is used to "eliminate" opposition rather that to facilitate concerted action by disparate groups. Thus from Banks and Textor, Buck recorded the degree of freedom opposition groups enjoy, and from Feierabend and Feierabend he recorded (for the period 1948–1962) the amount of "repressive action against specific groups," "arrests of significant persons for political reasons," "arrests of insignificant persons," "significant changes of general laws," "politically motivated killing by the government," and the frequency with which the constitution is suspended and martial law is declared. The eighth indicator, from Banks and Textor, reflects a characterization (with the help of a legal scholar) of each nation's legal system as ranging from "indigenous" (indicating low development) to "common law" (reflecting high development). While this final indicator can be criticized as being subjective (at least on the part of the legal scholar, if not on the part of those who appended the labels on each country's legal system), it is worth pointing out that as only one of eight indicators, this one influences the index very little. Were it to be eliminated altogether, the *relative* scores on legal development in 115 nations would change hardly at all.

It may well be asked whether an index mainly of *negative* instances fairly measures the degree of something positively stated. Political reprisals and closing off opposition may reflect the *absence* of a widespread legal order, it might be argued, but is the nonappearance of such phenomena to be taken as indicating its *presence?* Two responses might be made. (1) The expedient one is that the Buck measure *is* available, and no preferable measure based on recorded data is known. (For example, information on the number of lawyers, law schools, and so forth in a society could be a substitute measure of legal development, but in that case the relationship with societal complexity would be well-nigh tautological.) (2) Moreover, I am not so much interested in the *existence* of law and lawyers as I am their effectiveness in subjecting persons' behavior—without coercion—to legal rules. The record of legal repression seems, then, a reasonable measure of legal development, much repression indicating little legal development, and little repression more legal development.

Religious Pluralism

The third index measures the degree of religious pluralism with information from various sources.[11] Because a certain amount of arbitrariness was involved in this procedure, I want to be certain it is explicit. First, it became apparent that the highest levels of pluralism as measured by any available method are *not* found in those societies regarded today as very pluralistic (the Western industrialized democracies). To be sure, in the scoring scheme the United States would be quite plural—with Catholics, Jews, and Protestants all in considerable number. But it is surpassed by a number of nations in Asia, Africa, and the Near East, where there exist not only Protestant and Roman Catholic or Christian and Jew but maybe Islam, Hindu, Animist, Shintō, and Buddhist as well. I decided therefore that though one could enumerate many sectarian expressions of Protestantism, the same information did not exist for Buddhism, Islam, Animism, and so forth; so I counted only the major groupings just listed (plus Eastern Orthodox and Confucianism), giving one point for the presence in any society of each of these ten religious categories.

Second, since even the most religiously uniform society is going to have a smattering of "deviants," it was decided that a religion must be represented by at least 2 percent of the population if it was to get counted. Without any firm evidence for selecting that cutoff point, I reasoned that clashing definitions of ultimate reality are likely to clash only when supported by at least a handful of opposing "believers." Moreover, it can be assumed the data are more imprecise on religious minorities; with a minimum of 2 percent the chances are good they are at least noticed.

The upshot, however, as already indicated, was that those societies generally regarded as most plural—even to a point of the widespread exercise of religious freedom—were categorized along with newly developing societies where tribal religions compete with the legacies of numerous missionaries. It was as if one were comparing a present-day African or Asian nation with the United States of 1825 (with Protestants and some Jews entrenched on the East Coast, Catholics entrenched in the Southwest, and "Animists" spread out in between). But in fact the measures of legal development and societal complexity are contemporary, thus making that comparison impossible or at least illegitimate.

The only solution seemed to be to eliminate those nations that had already "developed." Granted, this move has an arbitrariness about it, *but the effect is to subject the theory to an immensely more stringent test.* If societies like the United Kingdom, Canada, Sweden, Luxemburg, France, United States, and New Zealand are known in advance to be (1) highly complex, (2) highly developed legally, and (3) religiously plural, it is not much of a test to determine if legal development and societal complexity are strongly related in religiously plural societies. But what of Burma, Sudan, North Vietnam, Bulgaria, Camaroun, Trinidad, and Ceylon? It seemed reasonable to treat all these latter nations as develop*ing* rather than develop*ed* and to inquire about their legal and religious circumstances.

Consequently, eliminated are the 23 nations (of the original 115) that scored twenty or higher on the societal complexity index (these are all so-called developed nations). The remaining 92 nations ranged in scores on religious pluralism from one (low) to four (high).

Another obvious weakness characterizes the religious pluralism index; it counts only orthodox, traditional, universally
recognized religions. These may, but probably do not, exhaust
the variety of "meaning systems" in a society. Thus to take an
example, Belgium is nominally all Roman Catholic; yet the Wal-
loon-Flemish distinction is known to pervade all social behavior. India, to take a different kind of example, contains sizable
adherents of several "religions," but the adherents of any one
religion are themselves divided by language, ethnic, and regional loyalties of great depth. The pluralism index measures
none of these religious (but not orthodox religious) differences,
though it can be hoped that errors are distributed randomly.
To the extent they are, they mute the corelationships that do
show up.

It is also worth noting that, while these variables were measured with data from around 1960, the relationships between
variables are not necessarily time-bound. Particular scores for
particular nation-states change through time, but the tendency
for one characteristic of a nation to associate with another characteristic changes only very slowly if at all. A pattern of relationships found at one time, therefore, is likely to be the pattern
found at other times as well.

Results

The first part of the theory states that religious pluralism and
societal complexity are inversely related, the reasoning being
that while religious pluralism is itself a kind of complexity, it has
an inhibiting influence on those "secular" interactions necessary
for the kind of development I have called societal complexity.
Table 3 shows the findings on this first question.

A statistical fundamentalist would insist no guaranteed negative relationship exists in Table 3 because the number of cases
is small and the differences are slight indeed. So be it. The argument is only that, contrary to idle speculation perhaps, religious
pluralism is not just another aspect of social differentiation but
is, if anything, inimical to societal complexity. The data seem to
support this part of the theory.

Table 3. Religious Pluralism and Societal Complexity

	Religious Pluralism			
	Low			High
	1	2	3	4
Average Societal Complexity Scores	10.8	10.0	9.8	8.9
(Number of Nation-States)	(25)	(24)	(24)	(19)

The second part of the theory is more difficult to test. It is not enough to show that legal development facilitates societal complexity, though Table 4 suggests it does.

Table 4. Legal Development and Societal Complexity

	Legal Development						
	Low						High
	1	2	3	4	5	6	7
Average Societal Complexity Scores	6.5	7.6	11.6	11.5	9.1	13.3	16.5
(Number of Nation-States)	(11)	(17)	(19)	(17)	(21)	(3)	(4)

The less than perfect relationship reminds us societal complexity is an enormously involved phenomenon and therefore subject to a multitude of forces in addition to legal development. Had the relationship in Table 4 been reversed, I would have had to revise my thinking. But in a major way the finding of Table 4 is just what is expected: Nations with the least legal development are least complex; high legal development is associated with high complexity. Bear in mind, too, that putting back in the twenty-three nations already eliminated would, because they are both legally developed and societally complex, greatly sharpen the relationship in Table 4.

The evidence so far, then, supports the proposition that a universalistic legal system facilitates societal complexity. The theory states more than this, however. It states a universalistic legal system will be *more* facilitating of societal complexity the *higher* the level of religious pluralism. Operationally, this amounts to the prediction that with each increase in religious pluralism the association between societal complexity and legal development will also increase. Table 5 contains the evidence.

Table 5. Religious Pluralism, Legal Development, and Societal Complexity*

	Religious Pluralism			
	Low 1	2	3	High 4
Degree of Association Between Legal Development and Societal Complexity (Gamma)	.16	.26	.53	.74
(Number of Nation-States)	(25)	(24)	(24)	(19)

*The nations contained in this table are found in Table 6.

It would appear that the theory finds considerable support (recognizing, of course, that mere association does not necessarily signify the causal path the theory claims). One possible criticism comes immediately to mind, however: Might the increasing association between legal development and societal complexity be artifactual? Might earlier colonial regimes, for example, have left both the makings of an industrial (complex) society *and* a legal system somewhat more developed than what they found? Table 6 suggests not. The four societies at once most plural, most complex, and most developed legally (Bulgaria, Malaysia, the Philippines, and Trinidad) are drawn from widely divergent areas of the world. They represent different ways to be religiously plural, but so also are their legal development scores arrived at in different ways. Common law traditions are found in the background of one or two, and modern-day colonialism existed in two or three, but neither attribute characterizes all four. In other words these four nations are not closely aligned historically, geographically, politically, legally, or religiously. Similar statements can be made of the other eleven groups of societies listed in Table 6. As with all research using static data, of course, such arguments do not "prove" the theory being advanced, but they do make it plausible. To reiterate, legal development does appear to make more of a difference in the complexity of religiously plural societies.

Implications for Civil Religion

The question then arises as to what civil religious implications there may be in the role played by legal institutions in religiously

Table 6.

	Low Societal Complexity: (scores of 1–7)	Legal Development Score	Medium Societal Complexity: (scores of 8–12)	Legal Development Score	High Societal Complexity: (scores of 13–19)	Legal Development Score
Very High Religious Pluralism						
	Burma	4	Camaroun	2	Bulgaria	5
	Central African Republic	1	Ceylon	5	Malaysia	5
	Chad	3	Ghana	3	Philippines	7
	Dahomey	1	Malagaysay	4	Trinidad	7
	Nigeria	2	North Korea	1		
	North Vietnam	1	South Korea	3		
	South Vietnam	1				
	Sudan	3				
	Uganda	5				
Medium High Religious Pluralism						
	Burundi	2	Albania	3	Hungary	3
	Congo (Brazza)	2	China (P.R.)	4	Jamaica	6
	Ethiopia	5	Congo (Leopold)	2	Japan	7
	Gabon	2	Guinea	1	Lebanon	3
	Laos	5	Haiti	4	South Africa	3
	Rwanda	2	India	5	Yugoslavia	4
	Togo	1	Ivory Coast	4		
	Upper Volta	1	Panama	5		
	Senegal	2				
	Tanzania	2				

Medium Low Religious Pluralism

Country		Country		Country	
Cambodia	5	Indonesia	2	Brazil	4
Guatemala	4	Libya	5	Chile	4
Jordan	3	Morocco	5	Costa Rica	5
Liberia	5	Nicaragua	4	Cuba	4
Mali	2	Paraguay	4	Cyprus	7
Nepal	1	Syria	2	Rumania	3
Niger	1	Egypt	2	Uruguay	4
Pakistan	3			Venezuela	3
Sierra Leone	5				

Very Low Religious Pluralism

Country		Country		Country	
Afghanistan	5	Bolivia	3	Algeria	2
Iran	4	Ecuador	5	Argentina	3
Somalia	3	El Salvador	3	Colombia	4
Thailand	2	Honduras	6	Dominican Repub.	5
Yemen	2	Iraq	2	Greece	6
		Mauritania	3	Mexico	5
		Mongolia	1	Peru	4
		Saudi Arabia	5	Poland	3
		Tunisia	5	Portugal	5
				Spain	4
				Turkey	3

plural society. It can be ventured that if people experience conflict, they attempt to resolve it. If the conflict itself includes a clash of "resolution systems" (meaning systems or "sacred canopies")—if, in other words, A and B cannot agree because neither accepts the other's basis for agreement—then some other resolution will be sought. It is here that the law may be turned to, especially to the degree it is "universalistic," thus overriding whatever parochial conditions have stood in the way. Insofar as the law responds satisfactorily—its procedures respected, its orders obeyed, its sanctions upheld—a legal "order" can be said to exist. But if in addition the agencies of this legal order use the language and imagery of purpose and destiny, if they not only resolve differences but also *justify* their resolutions, it is easy to see how something identifiable as civil religion could emerge. There would exist already a cadre of "clergy," a set of "rituals," places for "worship," and a number of directives for behavior. Add to these a "theology"—an ideology of purpose and destiny or theodicy—and a civil religion may be close behind. Whether Bulgaria, Malaysia, the Philippines, and Trinidad are further along in the development of civil religions than other societies in Table 6 I do not know. But it seems reasonable to suggest, on the basis of the theory here, that whatever level of civil religion they may possess at this time will, more so in their cases, be reflected by their legal systems. At least such a perspective directs us to further research into the issue of civil religion.

NOTES

1. John Courtney Murray, *We Hold These Truths* (Garden City, N.Y.: Doubleday, 1964), pp. 27–29. See also Talcott Parsons, "Religion in a Modern Pluralistic Society," *Review of Religious Research,* 7 (1966), pp. 125–146; Peter Berger, *The Sacred Canopy* (Garden City, N.Y.: Doubleday, 1967), pp. 48–49, 135–138.

2. Max Weber, *On Law in Economy and Society,* trans. Edward Shils and Max Rheinstein (New York: Simon and Schuster, 1967), pp. 225–227.

3. And Cowan speaks of "legal pluralism." "A second great complex of problems to which legal pluralism gives rise is that which has generally come to be known under the heading of inter-personal conflict of laws, internal

conflict of laws, or inter-gentile law. . . . How should one regulate disputes between members of different ethnic or religious groups living within the same political unit under different laws?" Denis V. Cowan, "African Legal Studies," in Hans W. Baade, ed., *African Law: New Law for New Nations* (Dobbs Ferry, N.Y.: Oceana Publications, 1963), p. 18.

4. Compare with Kozolchyk's statement: "The main function of a legal system in bringing about economic development is to instill trust in legal institutions." Boris Kozolchyk, "Commercial Law Recodification and Economic Development in Latin America," *Lawyer of the Americas*, 4 (1972), p. 2.

5. Thus Kozolchyk, ibid., whose research is based on Latin American societies, goes on, "And this trust results not only from the efficient operation of legal institutions, that is to say, when these institutions perform predictably and in the least costly manner, but also from their fairness." The point, of course, is that "fairness" automatically spills over into the religious sphere.

6. See David Apter, "Political Religion in New Nations," in Clifford Geertz, ed., *Old Societies and New States* (New York: Free Press, 1963).

7. Talcott Parsons, "Evolutionary Universals in Society," *American Sociological Review*, 29 (1964), pp. 339–357.

8. Gary Buck, *A Quantitative Analysis of Modernization*, Office of Research Analyses, Holloman Air Force Base, New Mexico, 1969. Buck found by scalogram analysis, incidentally, that the evolutionary sequence Parsons suggests (that is, the order in which I listed the ten variables) is strongly supported by the data on these 115 societies. I am indebted to Buck for his cooperation in this research.

9. Parsons, "Evolutionary Universals," p. 351.

10. Arthur S. Banks and R. B. Textor, *A Cross-Polity Survey* (Cambridge, Mass.: MIT Press, 1963); I. K. Feierabend and R. L. Feierabend, "Aggressive Behaviors Within Polities, 1948–1962: A Cross-National Study," *Journal of Conflict Resolution*, 10 (1966), pp. 249–271.

11. S. W. Coxill and Sir Kenneth Grabb, *The World Christian Handbook* (London: Lutterworth, 1968); Elisa Daggs, *All Africa* (New York: Hastings House Publications, 1970); *Deadline Data on World Affairs* (Greenwich, Conn.: D.M.S., Inc., 1971); *Facts on File* (New York: Facts on File, Inc., 1971); John S. Mbiti, *African Religions and Philosophy* (New York: Praeger, 1969).

6. Pluralism and Law in the Formation of American Civil Religion

PHILLIP E. HAMMOND

While Rousseau is generally credited with coining the term "civil religion," analysis of civil religion in sociology has been influenced more by Emile Durkheim. Durkheim was, of course, an intellectual heir to Rousseau, but nevertheless a gap of great proportions separates them: For Rousseau civil religion is a sensible thing for leaders to create and encourage; for Durkheim it is an emergent property of social life itself.

On this rather simple difference hangs a conceptual issue obscuring almost all contemporary analyses of modern-day civil religion. Those influenced by Rousseau often begin with a bias *against* civil religion on the grounds that it is or easily can be an idolatrous fraud perpetrated on naive believers. Those influenced by Durkheim, by contrast, often begin with a bias *in favor* of civil religion on the grounds it is inevitable in any case and may —in its finest forms at least—be the transcendental expression of the profoundest values of a people.

Each of these points of view is therefore likely to have a blind spot, an aspect of civil religion left unquestioned and thus never made problematic in theory. For those largely in the Rousseau

This chapter is a considerably revised version of "Religious Pluralism and Durkheim's Integration Thesis," in *Changing Perspectives in the Scientific Study of Religion*, ed. Alan Eister (New York: John Wiley, 1974). Used by permission of John Wiley & Sons, Inc.

camp this blind spot is their difficulty in taking seriously the claims of a civil religion. Durkheim's followers, on the other hand, give little thought to the question of *how* a civil religion comes to be. This chapter addresses the latter question by looking at the role played by religious pluralism and law in the formation of America's civil religion.

Durkheim's Conception of Religion

Generally speaking, Durkheim's civil religion theory has been understood to mean that, to the degree a collection of people *is* a society, it will exhibit a common ("civil") religion. A corrupt, though understandable, interpretation of this theory holds that religion therefore unites a people or integrates the society. Such an interpretation is plausible, of course, if one reads literally Durkheim's definition of religion (what "unites into one single moral community"). Other statements in *The Elementary Forms* are just as conducive to that interpretation (for example, *"Rites are means by which* the social group reaffirms itself periodically").[1]

But it is the fact of unity more than the fact of religion with which Durkheim begins. Religion is more the *expression* of an integrated society than it is the *source* of a society's integration. "Men who feel themselves united, partially by bonds of blood, but still more by a community of interest and tradition, assemble and become conscious of their moral unity," Durkheim goes on. "They are led to represent this unity."[2] Here is the key passage. It is in this kind of reasoning that Durkheim connects religion and integration—not that religion produces the cohesive society but rather that the phenomenon of cohesion has a religious quality.

This argument is not at all unknown. In 1937 Talcott Parsons observed that the real significance of Durkheim's work on primitive religion lay in his recognition not that "religion is a social phenomenon" but that "society is a religious phenomenon."[3] In other words, the very existence of society—the fact of stable social interaction itself—implies religion. The question is whether and how it is expressed.

Durkheim, of course, found religion expressed in the totemistic practices of the Arunta. The persuasiveness of his argument lies in the rather direct link between the *experiences* of unity al-

legedly felt by the Arunta and their ritualistic *expressions* of that
unity. But Durkheim did not mean his theory to rest on the
directness of this link. ("We cannot repeat too frequently that the
importance which we attach to totemism is absolutely independent of whether it was universal or not."[4]) Had Durkheim lived
longer, he very likely would have pursued the religious significance of societal integration in a modern context. When he asked
rhetorically, "What essential difference is there between an as-
sembly of Christians celebrating the principal dates of the life of
Christ . . . and a reunion of citizens commemorating . . . some
great event in the national life?" he was certainly hinting at this
issue.[5] But it was only a hint. Was he noting that Christianity is
no longer the language by which unity is expressed? Did he
believe he could identify the "religions" that do express for modern societies what totemism expressed for the Arunta? Would he
agree that these are "civil" religions?

Answers to these questions are not easy to come by. The analysis of modern civil religion gives evidence of one rather direct
application of Durkheim's thesis—expecting in any society a reasonably close analogue to totemism. This work in civil religion,
however, fails to deal with the "linkage" that totemism so con-
veniently provided. Why should a people, *dis*united by denomi-
nationalism, multiple ethnic traditions, class differences, and
such be led to represent their unity anyway? Around what are
they unified? Arguing they are unified by a civil religion may be
a difficult task, but it is made easier if a plausible case can be made
for why a civil religion might develop in the first place.

This chapter therefore attempts to outline two related issues:
(1) How has a single, uniting religion emerged out of the variety
of Christian (and non-Christian) groups in American society?
(2) Is this religion simply "there," to be expressed by those
Americans who choose to do so, or are there structural settings
(analogous to the "effervescent" phases in Durkheim's Arunta)
where its enunciation is, so to speak, fostered, even compelled?

The common interpretation of Durkheim's thesis—that a society is integrated to the degree it possesses a common religion—
is therefore given two twists in what follows: First, the major
terms in the thesis are reversed and taken to mean that to the
degree a society is integrated the expression of its integration will

occur in ways that can be called religious. And second, because conflict obviously endangers societal integration, wherever resolution of conflict occurs is a likely scene for the expression of this religion. In the religiously plural society, churches cannot resolve conflicts, at least between parties from different churches. But legal institutions *are* called upon to do so. Without claiming that legal institutions—and they alone—are responsible for American civil religion, I argue only that law has played a critical role in that civil religion's development.

In developing this argument I shall (1) take a close look at the notion of religious pluralism, finding it to mean much more than mere multiplicity of groups defined by ecclesiastical characteristics; (2) look at the historical form taken by pluralism in American society as a set of pressures to which responses were required; and (3) identify the "religiousness" of the response made by legal institutions. In so doing I am attempting to apply Durkheim's thesis to religiously plural societies and thereby show how a civil religion can develop.

Religious Pluralism

The term "pluralism" is widely used today by social scientists. At a minimal level it refers simply to heterogeneity. In the hands of political scientists, anthropologists, and political sociologists, for example, arguments occur over whether pluralism impedes or secures democratic government. Theorists also differ in their understanding of how pluralism works—whether it provides multiple channels to power holders or supplies group anchorage for would-be alienated individuals. And there is the intricate argument that pluralism permits multiple but contradictory group memberships, thus making political conflict erupt more often within an individual or a group than between contending political factions.

For all the specifications of "pluralism," however, the concept as used in political analysis almost always refers to heterogeneity of *groups*. And since modern societies commonly contain several religious groups, the notion of religious pluralism has been seen as analogous to or even synonymous with racial or ethnic pluralism.

There is, of course, nothing incorrect in this usage. Methodists *are* a different group from Presbyterians, just as Catholics are different from Protestants or Christians from Jews. Still, the incompleteness of this notion of religious pluralism is apparent if instead of denominational differences one looks at historicocultural differences: the Judeo-Christian tradition versus the Islamic tradition, a Western versus an Oriental religious outlook, a mystical versus an ascetic perspective. What can religious pluralism mean if reference is not to denominational or group heterogeneity but to a multiplicity of nonempirical belief systems? Understood this second way, religious pluralism builds on the classical understanding of religion in sociology and therefore requires fuller discussion.

Whether formulated by Durkheim (a system of beliefs and practices related to sacred things), by Weber (that which finally makes events meaningful), or by Tillich (whatever is of ultimate concern), religion in its "classical" sense refers not so much to labels on a church building as to the imagery (myth, theology, and so forth) by which people make sense of their lives—their "moral architecture," if you will.[6] That human beings differ in their sensitivity to and success in this matter of "establishing meaning" there can be no doubt. Moreover, people certainly differ in the degree to which they regard historic, institutionalized formulations as personally satisfactory. Thus some are churchgoers and some are not; some would change the prevailing theology or ritual and others would not. Societies might be said to differ in whether they offer only one or more than one system for bestowing ultimate meaning.

Teggart asserted social change results from "the collision of groups from widely different habitats and hence of different idea-systems."[7] And if Teggart assumed human history records few stable "pluralistic" situations (that is, single habitats with multiple idea systems), he was very likely correct. The word "religion" in its plural form does not even enter the language of the West until the mid seventeenth century and does not become common until the eighteenth. Closely related words—piety, obedience, reverence, and worship—never do develop plural forms.[8]

Religious pluralism (in the sense "religion" is used here) is not equivalent, then, to a choice between Rotary and Kiwanis, the

Cubs or the White Sox, the Methodists or the Presbyterians. Rather, as Teggart notes, the consequence for the individual of confronting competing idea systems is liberation from "traditional group constraints" and "enhanced autonomy."[9] Correlatively, Smith observes the word "religions" (plural form) comes into use only as one "contemplates from the outside, and abstracts, depersonalizes, and reifies the various systems of other people of which one does not oneself see the meaning or appreciate the point, let alone accept the validity."[10] In other words, though religious pluralism can mean the existence simply of religious differences, it can also refer to a situation qualitatively different from other pluralisms: When one meaning system confronts another meaning system, the very meaning of "meaning system" changes.

In the Western world this change is most readily seen in the separation of church from state—the explicit differentiation at the structural level of religion and polity. But as MacIntyre, referring to British society, contends, "It is not the case that men first stopped believing in God and in the authority of the Church, and then subsequently started behaving differently. It seems clear that men first of all lost any over-all social agreement as to the right ways to live together."[11] The accuracy of this time sequence determines the viability of the notion of religious pluralism being presented here: If the separation of church and state is regarded as only a political event, then churches are seen as voluntary associations, and pluralism indicates merely the presence of multiple religious groupings. Alternatively, if the separation of church and state arises from a situation of competing meaning systems (that is, is essentially a political response to a *religious* state of affairs), then the existence of multiple churches indicates something far more profound than simply a choice of religious groups. Needless to say, this latter interpretation of religious pluralism is the one used here.

My previous comments are no mere attempt to legislate the use of terms in sociological discourse. They mean to suggest that viewed in a certain way the concept of religious pluralism can have new theoretical importance.

John Courtney Murray, in discussing the "civilization of pluralist society," uses the notion of religious pluralism in both senses outlined.[12] First, religious pluralism implies different people's different histories—here Murray essentially is merely relabeling those differences. Second, because discussion of concrete affairs goes on in abstract terms—in "realms of some theoretical generality"—pluralism implies the existence of different sets of terms, different realms. Discourse, Murray says, thus becomes "incommensurable" and confused. Compare MacIntyre's analysis: "If I tell you that 'You ought to do this,' . . . I present you with a claim which by the very use of these words implies a greater authority behind it than the expression of my feelings. . . . I claim, that is, that I could point to a criterion . . . you too ought to recognize. . . . It is obvious that this activity of appealing to impersonal and independent criteria only makes sense within a community of discourse in which such criteria are established, are shared."[13] Kingsley Davis says it more succinctly yet: "As between two different groups holding an entirely different set of common-ultimate ends, there is no recourse."[14]

Religious pluralism need not imply *entirely* different sets of "common-ultimate ends," of "impersonal and independent criteria," or of "moral architectures." But it may be argued that *some* level of sharedness must exist for institutions to exist, and religious pluralism would appear to reduce that sharedness.

But does it? Once a society permits multiple meaning systems to exist side by side, does it cease to *be* a society? Doubtless that can happen, but it is more normal for a society to work toward a new, more generalized, common meaning system. It is easier to form a social contract than for all to go to war against all. Still, as is now recognized, "mere" social agreement, a rationally derived document, is insufficient. Commitment to its rightness is also required. Every contract has its noncontractual element, Durkheim said; every legal order possesses its charismatic quality, Weber noted. And that noncontractual element, that charismatic quality, that commitment is articulated finally in terms that are (by definition) "religious." In a single society, then, can more than one set of religious terms exist? And if they coexist, can they continue to function as they are thought to function in a society with a religious monopoly?

Obviously, individuals do not generally confront each other's "moral architectures" in any direct fashion. Such situations do arise, of course, but manifestations of moral commitment more often occur as *institutional* conflicts and conflict resolution. The city government decides between road improvement and welfare payments. The corporation chooses to reward longevity or quality of service. The church elects to immerse or sprinkle. The citizenry is ordered to stop plowing and go to war. In all such instances (assuming the absence of sheer coercion) persons feel —or can come to feel—an *obligation* to justify their behavior. But this is not because of any prerecognized specific norm; there is no detailed prescription for every conceivable act. Rather, the obligation is in "realms of some theoretical generality," to use Murray's phrase. It is, as Talcott Parsons notes, a "generalized obligation" that is morally binding. A person or an institution demonstrates integrity not only by choosing right from wrong in a concrete situation but by maintaining a "commitment to the pattern over a wide range of different actual and potential decisions, in differing situations, with differing consequences and levels of predictability of such consequences."[15]

Such commitment in any but the simplest, thoroughly ascribed society must be to a "generalized symbolic medium," not to specific norms.[16] Given the integrative potential of such a generalized symbolic medium—of action to action, policy to policy, person to person—the question can be raised whether in a single society more than one such medium can exist. Or if "pluralism" exists, can any one medium command the same commitment it might in a monopolistic situation?

The relation between a "generalized symbolic medium of values" and what I earlier referred to as "moral architecture" or "set of religious terms" is quite clear and has long been recognized. The "primary moral leadership in many societies," Parsons writes, "has been grounded in religious bodies, especially their professional elements such as priesthoods."[17]

Religious pluralism, as just interpreted, clearly has had enormous impact on those institutions regarded as religious before pluralization: churches, clergy, theology, and so forth. In some sense they become "less" religious if they no longer enjoy a monopoly in articulating the ideology by which ultimate meaning is bestowed. Reduction in ecclesiastical power, the transformation of ritual into a "leisure" time activity, and the "privatizing" in general of theology into pastoral counseling or religious "preference" all reflect this altered status.

If churches become less religious in some ways, some other places in the social structure may become *more* religious. If pressures are great in a society for a single generalized symbolic medium, a single reality-defining agency, and churches no longer are the targets of those pressures, the pressures will be exerted elsewhere. It is my contention that in America *legal* institutions feel those pressures greatly, that portrayal of the sacred or articulation of the charismatic tends to be expected of them. In this special sense the law has become more "religious." The pages that follow show how a "common American religion" emerged from religious pluralism and illustrate how current legal institutions express that common religion. In these efforts the Durkheimian blind spot is overcome; I will be investigating just how a civil religion—in this case America's—came to be.

Religion and Law

The impact of Puritanism on the common law is now widely acknowledged.[18] David Little has traced the close connections between Puritan theology and early seventeenth-century common law.[19] Considering the volatility of the seventeenth century, it is hardly surprising that religious and legal reformation possessed common elements. But tracing out those elements in detail is, as Little shows, an exceedingly difficult task. For example, the codifying common lawyer, Sir Edward Coke, remained a loyal Anglican all his life, paying no special attention to Puritan theological debates going on at the time. And yet in the jurisdictional struggle between church courts and common law courts Coke not only claimed the latter's superiority but justified the claim by reference to common law tradition.[20] In so doing he effectively sided with Puritanism in its struggle against Anglican traditionalism.

Pound's assertion of Puritanism's "impact" is not well documented. It does little more than show how "individualism" in the common law had analogues in Puritanism, but as Pound himself makes clear, this individualism in the common law has many other roots. Moreover, Puritanism may have contributed (or did

contribute) as much to a renewed interest in "collectivism" in the
law, considering the stress it placed on the covenant, on the
"contractualism" it posited between man and God or man and
man. David Little claims "explicit Puritan influence on the particulars of common law was nil." Nevertheless, he continues, "It
is my contention that the concurrence of important tensions and
changes in legal and religious outlook toward the end of the
sixteenth and at the beginning of the seventeenth centuries is
more than coincidence. In this I believe I am not far from
Pound's interest . . . [in his effort] to understand how a system
of law comes to embody and perpetuate a general way of looking
at social life—a special system of values."[21]

The argument by which Little so carefully weaves together
these two entities—Puritanism and common law—does not follow Pound, then, in method. He does not see a *direct* impact of
one on the other. Instead Little argues the common law was in
a fluid state at the time, seeking principles of legal interpretation
for frequent new activities and conflicts. Where might such principles be found? More accurately, perhaps, how might they be
articulated? Little's answer is twofold: First, the religious revolution of the seventeenth century—a revolution that defined new
"order" in the church, in the parish, in the "priesthood of all
believers," and in social life generally—provided an ideologically
parallel case. Second, Puritan theological conceptions found outlet in the common law's articulation of its principles. "Obviously,
the crown and the courts could not work together indefinitely so
long as each was making the kind of claims to authority it was.
A solution had to be found, but it would have to come from
sources other than the old English order [that is, the "ancient
realm or the Angelican tradition"]. . . . The deep-seated tensions
of early seventeenth-century English society had to be solved by
some rather novel rearrangements of political and legal institutions."[22] In other words, Puritanism was an "ordering" ideology
available to a common law seeking theoretical foundation.

What is underplayed in this approach, however, is the additional role Puritan theology played in *legitimizing* religious pluralism. Calvinism, Anabaptism, and subsequent "Protestantisms"
contributed a new interpretation of order; but *they also provided a
theological rationale for ending church monopolies on articulating that*

order, thus pressuring legal institutions into the attempt themselves. As one historian of nationalism puts it: "The Protestant
Revolution, by disrupting the Catholic Church and subjecting the
Christian community to national variations of form and substance, dissolved much of the intellectual and moral cement
which had long held European peoples together. At the same
time it gave religious sanction to the notion, already latent, that
each people, and each alone, possessed a pure faith and a divine
mission."[23]

Puritanism, then, did more than offer an alternative articulation of social values for seventeenth-century England even as it
did more than provide parallel support to common lawyers in
their fight against traditionalism. In addition, though not all at
once, of course, Puritanism forced onto society's agenda the item
of pluralism, the question of "religious liberty," the separation
of church and state, the matter of "intellectual and moral cement." In so doing it left legal systems, especially the common
law tradition, the task of formulating a new religion, so to speak.
This process is most clearly evidenced in the activity surrounding
the U.S. Supreme Court, to which I turn presently. First, however, I must take two intermediate steps.

The first concerns the doctrine of religious liberty. I have just
argued that Protestantism provided a theological rationale for
ending church monopoly. Any doctrine of religious liberty will
lead to the separation of civil authority from matters of faith,
hence possibly to pluralism. But inasmuch as Zwingli's Zurich,
Calvin's Geneva, or Puritan New England are ordinarily seen as
having been religiously *in*tolerant, the task of tracing the establishment of religious liberty is a critical one.

The first *idea* of religious freedom is, of course, lost to history,
but it may be accurate to suggest 1523 as a significant date in the
social structuring of the idea in the West. In October of that year
Conrad Grebel and others (who "became" the Anabaptist movement) challenged Zwingli's use of civil power to enforce religious
conformity. Bender highlights it thus: "Here is where the first
break in the Reformation occurred that led inevitably to the
founding of Anabaptism. In 1523–25, at Zurich, are the cross-
roads from which two roads lead down through history: the road
of the free church of committed Christians separated from the

state with full religious liberty, and the road of the state church, territorially fixed, depending on state support, and forcibly suppressing all divergence, the road of intolerance and persecution."[24]

The "logic" of religious toleration was established, then, even though occasions of reneging were obviously frequent. Thus Geneva must be considered a theocracy by all accounts, but Calvinism's English counterparts, the Presbyterians, really had no rebuttal for their "leftist Puritan" challenger, Henry Robinson. A real commitment to the doctrine of predestination, he said, precluded religious persecution. Those not elected by God could not possibly be saved; "uniformity of profession" cannot be confused with "certainty of grace."[25] A doctrine of religious liberty and therefore of pluralism was clearly implied here, even if its widespread institutionalization was a long time in coming.

Soon after Henry Robinson came another Robinson—this one the Reverend John—who also symbolizes the Protestant theology of pluralism. As spiritual leader of what became the Mayflower Pilgrims (though he remained in Leyden, never coming to Massachusetts), John Robinson is remembered today as the author of the phrase, "The Lord hath more truth and light yet to break forth." One does not have to believe the Massachusetts colonists *wanted* to be religiously tolerant; it is enough merely to acknowledge that a theology allowing religious liberty (or legitimating pluralism) was being clearly enunciated, however long before it became practical reality.

The second step concerns law and authority in colonial America. Not surprisingly, without many of the traditional encumbrances the emerging American society was freer than old societies to manifest religious pluralism and its consequences. This is especially apparent in the Supreme Court's articulation of the newly emerging "common" religion. As will presently be shown, the history of the Court can be interpreted as a halting, hesitant, but "inevitable" effort to perform for American society the religious task of providing a common moral understanding. Before I deal with that dependent variable, however, I must take a second intermediate step, this time into colonial history.

American colonial life has been highly romanticized. With respect to the subject at hand, should one remember witch hunts or Roger Williams? Was Massachusetts Bay a theocracy or the fount of town meeting democracy? Historians' judgments on these questions vary, but it seems important to my thesis to maintain that the pressures of pluralism and their impact on legal institutions did not wait for the revolution and constitutionmaking. Is there evidence in colonial America, then, that these pressures were felt from the beginning?

C. K. Shipton points out "there never was an established church in Massachusetts, there was no agreed-upon body of dogma, and serious moral deviation was punished by the state, not the church. . . . Many of the normal functions of the established churches in Europe were here transferred to the state." Towns maintained a minister at public expense, it is true, but all inhabitants, including vocal Quakers, Baptists, and Presbyterians, participated in his selection, "with the result that the minister's theological difficulties were usually with the civil body rather than with the church."[26] Meanwhile the civil body—township or colony —was able to escape the "chaotic confusion of laws" in England by administering them "in one tribunal," according to Howe. "Ecclesiastical, maritime, statutory, and equitable" laws were subsumed under the common law, which Bay colonists recognized "as a set of unchanging principles of public law, principles which our usage would describe as 'constitutional.' "[27] G. L. Haskins goes further; the common law was the "cornerstone," the Bible merely the "touchstone," of early Massachusetts.[28]

It may have been an intensely moralistic atmosphere, therefore, but churches had no monopoly in defining what was moral. Anticipating the distinction between "professed doctrines of religious belief" and "actions" as it arose in *Reynolds* v. *United States* (98 US 145 [1879])—a case resulting in the prohibition of plural marriage—a number of persons came to see that religious "liberty" could become behavioral license unless the obligations between people were subject to the jurisdiction of a secular tribunal. By mid eighteenth century in New Haven, William Livingston rephrased a "Puritan principle" to read "The civil Power hath no jurisdiction over the Sentiments or Opinions of the subject, till such Opinions break out into Actions prejudicial to the Community, and then it is not the Opinion but the Action that is the Object of our Punishment."[29]

Shipton suggests this principle of freedom of thought, often believed to be state policy first in Virginia, whence it entered the U.S. Constitution as a "natural right," may have been borrowed from Puritan New England. If the revivalistic Great Awakening (1730–1745) was a last ditch effort to reinstate the "old order" against the onslaught of the coming denominational pluralism, it would be accurate to say the cause was hopeless. The Puritan "old order" itself quite clearly contained the ideas that had already destroyed its ordering capability.

But "ordering" could not be avoided. "Natural rights mean simply interests which we think ought to be secured," but it is clear that legal institutions increasingly had the task not only of securing those rights but of defining them as well.[30] Laws, that is to say, not only would inform citizens what to do and what not to do but would have to serve as well to assess the *morality* of what they did. The common law as influenced by Puritanism in England, then, was transferred to America, but in the transfer its moral-architectural ("religious") features stand out because the pressures of pluralism also stand out. To a degree hitherto unknown in the West, people were free to adopt any religion. The consequence, however, was that the simultaneously emerging common law was forced to take up the slack, giving it, as Pekelis insists, a "religious and moralistic character."[31] That is to say, the pressures for a single moral architecture (single "reality-defining" agency, single "generalized symbolic medium") were felt in common law institutions. American society well illustrates the effect of those pressures.

The Religious Character of Legal Institutions

The institutions of the common law seem to have had their "religious" flavor for a long time. The law for Edward Coke, writes David Little, "is more than the measure of reason. It is . . . the measure and source of virtue as well."[32] Just as Puritanism had the effect of making every issue a moral question, so also, as Pound noted, did every moral question become a legal question.[33] The notion of "contempt of court," as found in English and American law, illustrates the point well:

The Anglo-American idea . . . means that the party who does not abide
by certain specific decrees emanating from a judicial body is a con-
tumacious person and may, as a rule, be held in contempt of court,
. . . fined and jailed. . . . Now, this very concept of contempt simply
does not belong to the world of ideas of a Latin lawyer. It just does
not occur to him that the refusal of the defendant . . . may, as soon
as a judicial order is issued, become a matter to a certain extent
personal to the court, and that the court may feel hurt, insulted,
"contemned."[34]

Where the law is highly codified, where, so to speak, the law
is asked to specify duties—the situation more nearly found in
"civil law" or Latin cultures—the courts can act more administra-
tively, less "judgmentally." But where the task of justifying, articulating, or "interpreting" the law is asked of the courts—where
"aspirations" as well as "duties" are at issue—courts must take
on a "religious" character.[35] Only in a sense, Pekelis reminds us,
does the United States have a written constitution. "The great
clauses of the Constitution, just as the more important provisions
of our fundamental statutes, contain no more than an appeal to
the decency and wisdom of those with whom the responsibility
for their enforcement rests."[36] Whether courts are thought to
"interpret" or to "make" the law, the fact remains that common
law courts find and give *reasons* for their decisions. And in the act
of reasoning they do more than cite statutes; they also develop
the single symbolic moral universe—the moral architecture. The
common law, then, has a "collective" character as pronounced as
the individualism more often viewed as its distinctive feature.
Any *concerted* effort, even to promote individual interests, will
yield a collective enterprise. But if religious liberty is among the
promoted interests, the concerted effort takes on an interpreta-
tive task *on behalf of* the collective.

We must say that the aspects of legal life in England and America
. . . do not substantiate the contention of the individualistic character
of the common-law technique. On the contrary, the strength of the
enforcement devices, the clerical and moralistic character of the legal
approach at large, the duty of disclosure, the close control exercised
by the community upon the individual and upon the law, if compared
with the analogous legal institutions of the Latin countries, seem to
disclose rather a more collectivistic than a more individualistic charac-

ter of the common-law system. . . . It seems to us that what is generally considered as and taken for the individualistic aspect of American life is simply the existence and coexistence of a plurality of communities and—let's not be afraid of this quantitative element—of an extremely great number of communities of various types.[37]

Though this chapter's central notion, religious pluralism, is rendered by Pekelis simply as "communities of various types," the elements of the argument are all there by implication: (1) Plurality of the religious systems requires redefinition of order but does not escape the need for order. (2) Legal institutions therefore are called upon not only to secure order but to give it a uniformly acceptable meaning as well. (3) The result is a set of legal institutions with a decided religiomoral character. The historical context of these forces in the West has led the common law to become their medium, the legal philosophy of the Enlightenment their symbols, and the U.S. judicial system most concretely their vehicle of expression.

No clearer illustration can be found than Nelson's analysis of the legal situation in Massachusetts during the years just before and after the revolution. In prerevolutionary times, he notes, juries reached verdicts and applied the law consistently "largely because men selected to juries shared a . . . set of ethical values and assumptions."[38] By the 1760s, however, this ethical unity no longer obtained because Puritan theology itself contained the seeds of pluralism; the Great Awakening was but the early eighteenth-century flowering of those seeds, leading to religious diversity in New England. The result was that as soon as "jurors could no longer agree whether a community gained or lost when, for instance, a millpond flooded a meadow, jury verdicts indeed became 'fluctuating estimates' that were 'utterly indefinite and uncertain,' and *it became essential to transfer to the judiciary the power of finding law"* (italics added). Moreover:

> By the beginning of the nineteenth century . . . judges were abandoning the notion that they should adhere rigidly to precedent. . . . [The difference] was less in what the courts did than in their understanding of what they properly could do. . . . As long as juries had found the law . . . adherence to precedent had imposed little burden on the legal system. . . . But once the law-finding power passed to judges, who began to exercise it by rendering written opinions that remained

available for all to read, precedent threatened to impose a straight-jacket on future legal development and to bar all future legal change.[40]

One can inquire whether other institutions also served to express those moral standards. Thus, "Congress quickly assumed a theological function and began interpreting events in religious terms and exhorting other patriots on doctrine and morality. . . . But as the early years faded and the years of war began to pass, Congress made progressively fewer pronouncements which required any reference to the foundation of things in God and busied itself more and more with mundane affairs such as the disposition and pay of the Continental Army."[41]

More importantly, however—and more in keeping with the Durkheimian spirit of this chapter—one can ask if any agency in American society has been *required* to express those moral standards. I assert here that such a "theological function" was unavoidably thrust upon the judicial system. Ethical diversity then, or what I have called religious pluralism, had the effect of putting onto the judicial agenda the task of declaring, indeed promulgating, the moral standards for the community at large. The culture may yet have been Puritan at its roots, but the courts replaced the churches as the vehicle for expressing the moral standards of that culture.

Religion in the Legal System: A Disappearing Rhetoric

Little documentation is needed for the claim of an expanding judiciary in American history. "Actually, between 1820 and 1890 the judges were already taking the initiative in lawmaking. Far anticipating the leadership of the executive or administrative arms, the courts built up the common law in the United States—a body of judge-made doctrine to govern people's public and private affairs."[42]

The present thesis, however, contains a critical corollary less widely acknowledged: With this expansion the judiciary adopted the task of articulating the collective's moral architecture. Federal judges, as Albanese puts it, "rode circuit with the gospel of the civil religion and preached sermons in which the Constitution, its virtue and its promise, figured prominently."[43] Of course, many have spoken of "the nine high priests in their black robes" and of the sacredness imputed to the Constitution and other artifacts of the legal order. But in keeping with Eugene V. Rostow's characterization of the contemporary Supreme Court as a "vital national seminar," it is worth noting that the original charge to the Court was only that it render an aye or a nay.[44] It quickly began handing down written opinions also, however, and under Marshall began the practice of trying for a single majority opinion, which gave "judicial pronouncements a forceful unity they had formerly lacked."[45]

With the expansion of judicial explanation came the difficult problem of knowing what religious rhetoric, if any, was allowed in the explanation. I have already referred to the *Reynolds* v. *United States* case (1879) wherein Mormon polygamy was outlawed. "Can a man excuse his practices . . . because of his religious belief?" asked Mr. Chief Justice Waite. "To permit this would be to make the professed doctrines of religious belief superior to the law of the land. . . ." Were "religious" exceptions to be made, the opinion held, "then those who do *not* make polygamy a part of their religious belief *may be found guilty* and punished" (98 US 145 [1879], italics added).

Here in a single decision is exemplified the paradox confronting American courts because they are in a religiously plural society—a paradox that hands to them the erstwhile religious task of articulating a moral architecture. On the one hand citizens cannot use religious beliefs to justify any and all actions. On the other hand truly religious belief, it is thought, *ought* to be manifest in action; else why assume in finding Reynolds innocent society might find nonpolygamists guilty? Protestantism enhanced the development of the concept of religious liberty and thus religious pluralism. But this in turn led, as Pound and others saw, to making everything a moral question yet also a legal question. Courts, then, could not resolve legal questions without resorting to moral answers. But the rhetoric and imagery available for expressing these moral answers could not be drawn from the language of orthodox religion as the implications of religious pluralism became clearer. Instead the rhetoric—if it was to have *general* meaning—had to be drawn from another sphere, but from a sphere no less religious in its functioning.

Thus says Bickel:

> The function of the Justices . . . is to immerse themselves in the tradition of our society and of kindred societies that have gone before, in history and in the sediment of history which is law, and . . . in the thought and the vision of the philosophers and the poets. The Justices will then be fit to extract 'fundamental presuppositions' from their deepest selves, but in fact from the evolving morality of our tradition. . . . The search for the deepest controlling sources, for the precise 'how' and the final 'whence' of the judgment . . . may, after all, end in the attempt to express the inexpressible. This is not to say that the duty to judge the judgment might as well be abandoned. The inexpressible can be recognized, even though one is unable to parse it.[46]

It would be difficult to find a better description of "religion" as it is outlined in classical sociology.

This change in rhetoric that the courts have felt obliged to use is readily illustrated in so-called church-state cases.

1. *Church of the Holy Trinity* v. *United States,* 143 US 226 (1892). Events in our national life, wrote Mr. Justice Brewer, "affirm and reaffirm that this is a religious nation." Moreover, in holding that a statute prohibiting aliens from being imported for labor was not intended to prevent a church from hiring a foreign Christian minister, the Court quoted approvingly from two previous judicial opinions showing "we are a Christian people, and the morality of the country is deeply ingrafted upon Christianity" and "the Christian religion is a part of the common law of Pennsylvania."

2. *United States* v. *Macintosh,* 283 US 605 (1931). Forty years later the Court was faced with a question of whether citizenship could be denied a person because he held reservations about taking arms in defense of his country. It is evident, said Mr. Justice Sutherland, "that he means to make his own interpretation of the will of God the decisive test which shall include the government. . . . We are a Christian people, according to one another the equal right of religious freedom, and acknowledging with reverence

the duty of obedience to the will of God. But, also, we are a nation with the duty to survive." Citizenship was denied.

3. *Zorach* v. *Clauson,* 343 US 306 (1952). Two decades later in its decision that released-time religious instruction is permitted provided it occurs off public school grounds the Court asserted—in Mr. Justice Douglas's words—that "We are a religious people whose institutions presuppose a Supreme Being." This statement, as well as the result, drew the dissent of Mr. Justice Black, who claimed, "Before today, our judicial opinions have refrained from drawing invidious distinctions between those who believe in no religion and those who do believe."

4. *United States* v. *Seeger,* 380 US 163 (1965). Here, in another conscientious objection case, the Court decided "belief in relation to a Supreme Being," thus exemption, is to be determined by "whether a given belief that is sincere and meaningful occupies a place in the life of its possessor parallel to that filled by the orthodox belief in God of one who clearly qualifies for the exemption." More than monotheistic beliefs qualify—Mr. Justice Clark noting the "vast panoply of beliefs" prevalent. Seeger's beliefs qualified, therefore, and he was exempted. In a concurring opinion, Douglas went further in acknowledging how pluralism forces rhetorical change. Hawaii, he noted, at the time the Selective Service law was passed (1940), probably had more Buddhists than members of any other "faith," and how could a concept like Supreme Being be helpful in determining a Buddhist's eligibility for exemption? This from the Justice who thirteen years earlier had written that American institutions "presuppose" a Supreme Being.

5. *Welsh* v. *United States,* 398 US 333 (1970). The result in *Welsh* was identical with that in *Seeger,* the Court finding the facts to be the same so that the legal application was the same. The opinion, by Mr. Justice Black, contained an even more expanded notion of religion, however. Exemption from Selective Service is to be allowed on "registrant's moral, ethical, or religious beliefs about what is right and wrong," provided "those beliefs be held with the strength of traditional religious convictions." Moreover, inasmuch

as the government had argued that Welsh's beliefs were less religious than Seeger's, the Court responded this "places undue emphasis on the registrant's interpretation of his own beliefs. The Court's statement in *Seeger* that a registrant's characterization of his own belief as 'religious' should carry great weight . . . does not imply that his declaration that his views are nonreligious should be treated similarly . . . very few registrants are fully aware of the broad scope of the word 'religious' [as interpreted by law since *Seeger*]."

It is instructive to see what developed in the course of a century. In *Reynolds* the Court recognized that "religion" is not defined in the Constitution but agreed that even if the state had no power over opinion, it was free to regulate actions. And polygamy, it said, has always been "odious" to Western nations, leading as it does to "stationary despotism." Therefore though there is no implication that Mormon *opinion* is punishable by law, Mormon *action* clearly is. A few years later the Court can speak of the "Christianity" of the nation, of its people, and of its morality, which therefore permits a church (though not a secular employer) to import alien labor. Though a *church* is entitled to special exemption from a law for religious reasons, an *individual* is not. Even if "We are a Christian people," and even if Macintosh is a professor in a Christian seminary, the government's interest in self-preservation is greater than a person's right to religious free exercise.

In *Zorach* v. *Clausen* the remark that "We are a religious people" might be seen as gratuitous—this is the only case here involving the establishment rather than the free exercise clause—except that what is allowed by the Court is a *religious* program. Black, in dissent, wonders about the rights of *irreligious* people; are they protected by the First Amendment mention of "religion?" They might be, it would appear from the *Seeger* and *Welsh* cases, since what is "religion" gets an even broader interpretation, to the point in *Welsh* where Black says the law may have to regard as religious something persons themselves claim is nonreligious.

At this point it would seem the definition of religion is so broad as to be meaningless in deciding cases, at least free exercise cases. From a time when the rhetoric used to justify a decision could be presumptively Christian, there comes the time when it cannot even be presumptively religious. *Seeger* and *Welsh* set out a distinction—any sincere and meaningful belief occupies a place parallel to that of orthodox belief. As Harlan argued in his concurring opinion in *Welsh,* however:

> My own conclusion . . . is that the Free Exercise Clause does not require a State to conform a neutral secular program to the dictates of religious conscience of any group. . . . [A] state could constitutionally create exceptions to its program to accommodate religious scruples. That suggestion must, however, be qualified by the observation that any such exception in order to satisfy the Establishment Clause of the First Amendment, would have to be sufficiently broad to be religiously neutral. . . . This would require creating an exception for anyone who, as a matter of conscience, could not comply with the statute.

"Religion" for legal purposes becomes simply "conscience," and Congress, if it is to grant conscientious exemptions, "cannot draw the line between theistic or nontheistic beliefs on the one hand and secular beliefs on the other." For all intents, assuming the eventual "triumph" of Harlan's position or something like it, the law simply dispenses with the notion of religion as commonly understood. Having tried for a century to regard it on its own terms—as sacred, special, and compelling—courts realize the attempt is futile. All efforts to allow "free exercise" of religion *because it is religion* conflict with the requirement of "no establishment" or special treatment. Religious pluralism requires articulation of "highest obligation" not in orthodox religious language but otherwise. What form does this take?

Religion in the Legal System: An Emerging Civil Religious Rhetoric

If the analysis here is correct, a new rhetoric is still in developing stages. Were this new civil religion—this new moral architecture —fully mature, it would be part of the common culture, but instead considerable doubt is expressed over the shape, authenticity, even the existence of an American civil religion. I do not postulate a fully mature civil religion here, however. Instead I argued commitment to religious liberty (pluralism) makes impossible the use of the rhetoric of any *one* religious tradition; so pressures are great to create a new rhetoric, that is, find a new religion. In the American case this new rhetoric is found in the common law and develops in legal institutions. Procedure takes precedence over substantive precepts and standards, not because *procedures* are uniquely required in plural societies—*all* societies require procedures—but because the *rhetoric* of procedure is required to justify outcomes between parties whose erstwhile religions are different.[47] The rhetoric of procedure thus becomes the new common or civil religion.

It is in this context that the jurisprudence of Lon Fuller can best be understood. When he remarks on the impossibility of distinguishing the law that *is* from the law that *ought* to be or when he discusses the imperceptible line between the "morality of duty" and the "morality of aspiration," he is insisting the law itself has concretely the task of portraying the ideal, whether it wants to or not.[48] And though Fuller has not included this point in his argument, I argued here that the "law" takes on this task to the degree that "religion" is denied it as a result of pluralism. Thus the "internal morality" of the law informs and guides a judge even though the "external morality" (interests) of contending parties must remain of no concern to him.[49] Fuller finds a "natural law" rubric congenial for analyzing this process, a fact that bespeaks even more the degree of transcendency that the law takes on.

Conclusion

Legal institutions do not take on this transcendent or civil religious task single-handedly, of course. Public schools certainly play a critical role in socializing youngsters into the "transcendence" of the law. As Kohlberg has framed the issue:

> It has been argued . . . that the Supreme Court's Schempp decision [prohibiting school sponsorship of prayer and Biblereading] calls for the restraint of public school efforts at moral education since such education is equivalent to the state propagation of religion conceived

as any articulated value system. The problems as to the legitimacy of moral education in the public schools disappear, however, if the proper content of moral education is recognized to be the values of justice which themselves prohibit the imposition of beliefs of one group upon another. . . . [This] does not mean that the schools are not to be "value-oriented." . . . The public school is as much committed to the maintenance of justice as is the court.[50]

One can, however, usefully distinguish agencies for socialization into the civil religion from agencies for articulating or elaborating it. Public schools are the new "Sunday schools," it might be said, whereas courts are the new pulpits.

NOTES

1. Emile Durkheim, *Elementary Forms of Religious Life*, trans. Joseph Swain (New York: Collier, 1961 [originally published in French in 1912]), pp. 62 and 432.
2. Ibid., p. 432.
3. Talcott Parsons, *Structure of Social Action* (New York: McGraw-Hill, 1937), p. 427.
4. Durkheim, *Elementary Forms*, p. 114.
5. Ibid., p. 475.
6. P. L. Berger and Thomas Luckmann, "Secularization and Pluralism," *Yearbook for the Sociology of Religion*, 2 (1966), pp. 73–85, refer to "sacred comprehensive meanings for everyday life."
7. Fredrick J. Teggart, *The Processes of History* (New Haven, Conn.: Yale University Press, 1918), p. 118.
8. Wilfred Cantwell Smith, *The Meaning and End of Religion* (New York: Macmillan, 1963), p. 43.
9. Teggart, *The Processes*, p. 118.
10. Smith, *The Meaning*, p. 43.
11. Alasdair MacIntyre, *Secularization and Moral Change* (London: Oxford University Press, 1967), p. 54.
12. John Courtney Murray, *We Hold These Truths* (Garden City, N.Y.: Doubleday, 1964), p. 27.
13. MacIntyre, *Secularization*, p. 52.
14. Kingsley Davis, *Human Society* (New York: Macmillan, 1950), p. 143.
15. Talcott Parsons, *Politics and Social Structure* (New York: Free Press, 1969), p. 445.
16. Ibid., p. 455.
17. Ibid., p. 452.

18. Roscoe Pound, "Law in Books and Law in Action," *American Law Review,* 44 (1910), pp. 12–34, and *The Spirit of the Common Law* (Francetown, N.H.: Marshall Jones, 1921).

19. David Little, *Religion, Order and Law* (New York: Harper & Row, 1969).

20. Ibid., p. 185.

21. Little, *Religion,* pp. 239 and 240.

22. Ibid., p. 225.

23. C. J. H. Hayes, *Nationalism: A Religion* (New York: Macmillan, 1960), p. 36.

24. Harold S. Bender, *The Anabaptists and Religious Liberty in the Sixteenth Century* (Philadelphia: Fortress Press, 1953), p. 8.

25. Little, *Religion,* pp. 255–256.

26. C. K. Shipton, "The Locus of Authority in Colonial Massachusetts," in G. A. Billias, ed., *Law and Authority in Colonial America* (Barre, Mass.: Barre Publishers, 1965), pp. 137 and 138.

27. Mark De W. Howe, "The Sources and Nature of Law in Colonial Massachusetts," in Billias, *Law and Authority,* pp. 14–15.

28. G. L. Haskins, *Law and Authority in Early Massachusetts* (Hamden, Conn.: Archon Books, 1968), esp. chap 10.

29. Shipton, "The Locus," p. 143.

30. Pound, *The Spirit,* p. 92.

31. Alexander Pekelis, *Law and Social Action* (Ithaca, N.Y.: Cornell University Press, 1950), p. 56.

32. Little, *Religion,* p. 177.

33. Pound, *The Spirit,* p. 43.

34. Pekelis, *Law,* pp. 45–46.

35. Lon Fuller, *The Morality of Law* (New Haven, Conn.: Yale University Press, 1964).

36. Pekelis, *Law,* p. 4.

37. Ibid., pp. 66–67.

38. William E. Nelson, *Americanization of the Common Law: The Impact of Legal Change on Massachusetts Society, 1760–1830* (Cambridge, Mass.: Harvard University Press, 1975), pp. 165–166.

39. Ibid., p. 166.

40. Ibid., p. 171.

41. Catherine Albanese, *Sons of the Fathers* (Philadelphia: Temple, 1976), p. 194.

42. J. Willard Hurst, *The Growth of American Law* (Boston: Little Brown, 1950), p. 85.

43. Albanese, *Sons,* p. 218.

44. Eugene V. Rostow, "The Democratic Character of Judicial Review," *Harvard Law Review,* 66 (1952), p. 208.

45. Robert McClosky, *The American Supreme Court* (Chicago: University of Chicago Press, 1960), p. 40.

46. Alexander Bickel, *The Least Dangerous Branch* (Indianapolis: Bobbs-Merrill, 1962), pp. 236–238.

47. Talcott Parsons, *Societies: Evolutionary and Comparative Perspectives* (Englewood Cliffs, N.J.: Prentice-Hall, 1966), p. 27.

48. Lon Fuller, *The Law in Quest of Itself* (Boston: Beacon Press, 1966), and *The Morality*.
49. Fuller, *The Morality*, pp. 131–132.
50. Lawrence Kohlberg, "Education for Justice: A Modern Statement of the Platonic View," in J. M. Gustafson et al., eds., *Moral Education* (Cambridge, Mass.: Harvard University Press, 1970), pp. 67–68.

IV. Civil Religion and New Religious Movements

7. New Religious Consciousness
and the Crisis in Modernity

ROBERT N. BELLAH

Signs of Crisis

The disturbances and outbursts in America in the 1960s are
hardly unique in modern history. Indeed, in reviewing a century
where irrationality and horror of all sorts—mass executions,
mass imprisonments, wars of annihilation, revolutions, rebel-
lions, and depressions—have been common, the events of that
decade might even be overlooked. But it is precisely the significance of that decade that the irrationality and horror of modern

This chapter was originally published as Chapter 15 in *The New Religious Consciousness* (University of California Press, 1976), edited by Charles Y. Glock and myself.
It has been somewhat revised for inclusion here. *The New Religious Consciousness*
is a report of research that Glock and I directed from 1971 to 1974 on new
religious groups in the San Francisco Bay Area. In this chapter I attempt to sum
up the meaning of our study. Our research project was an effort to understand
the cultural and political upheaval of the 1960s. We chose to study what we
believed to be the deepest dimension of that upheaval, that is to say its religious
dimension, and to interpret that meaning in the context of modern American
history. As it turned out, our study got under way just when the upheaval in its
most dramatic forms had subsided. We studied the successor movements to the
counterculture rather than the counterculture in its effervescent stage. But to
interpret our findings I must begin with the developments of the 1960s that lie
immediately behind our study and with the nature of the society in which those
developments occurred. If, as I argue, the 1960s represent a break in the line of
continuity in American culture generally, they certainly also represent a break in
the line of continuity of American civil religion. Toward the end of this chapter,
I speculate on the meaning of that break.

history were seriously borne in upon Americans—so seriously
that for the first time mass disaffection from the common understandings of American culture and society began to occur. Far
more serious than any of the startling events of the decade was
the massive erosion of the legitimacy of American institutions—
business, government, education, the churches, the family—that
set in particularly among young people and that continued, if
public opinion polls are to be believed, in the 1970s even when
overt protest had become less frequent.

The erosion of the legitimacy of established institutions among
certain sectors of the populations of many European countries—
particularly the working class and the intellectuals—began at
least a hundred years ago. In many of the newer third-world
countries the nation-state and modern institutions have not yet
gained enough legitimacy to begin the process of erosion. But in
America, in spite of a civil war, major social and religious movements, and minor disturbances of occasionally violent intensity,
the fundamental legitimacy of the established order had never
before been questioned on such a scale. This is in part because
that order was itself a revolutionary order, the result of one of the
few successful revolutions in the modern world. The messianic
hope generated by the successful revolution and nurtured by the
defeat of slavery in the Civil War for long made it possible to
overlook or minimize the extent to which the society failed to
achieve its own ideals. The promise of early fulfillment, which
seemed so tangible in America, operated to mute our native
critics and prevent mass disaffection, at least for a long time. But
in the decade of the sixties for many, not only of the deprived but
of the most privileged, that promise had begun to run out.

Biblical Religion and Utilitarian Individualism

By way of background we may consider those interpretations of
reality in America that had been most successful in providing
meaning and generating loyalty up until the sixties: biblical religion and utilitarian individualism. The self-understanding of the
original colonists was that they were "God's new Israel," a nation
under God. (From this point of view the addition of the phrase
"under God" to the pledge of allegiance in the 1950s was an

indication of the erosion of the tradition, not because it was an innovation but because it arose from the need to make explicit what had for generations been taken for granted.) In New England this understanding was expressed in the biblical symbol of a covenant signifying a special relationship between God and the people. American society was to be one of exemplary obedience to God's laws and subject to the grace and judgment of the Lord. The notion of Americans as an elect people with exemplary significance for the world was not abandoned but enhanced during the revolution and the period of constructing the new nation. It was dramatically reaffirmed by Lincoln in the Civil War and continued to be expressed in the twentieth century in the thought of men like William Jennings Bryan and Woodrow Wilson. This biblical aspect of the national self-understanding was strongly social and collective, even though it contained an element of voluntarism from its Protestant roots. Its highest conception of reality was an objective absolute God as revealed in scriptures, and its conception of morality was also based on objective revelation.[1]

A second underlying interpretation of reality that has been enormously influential in American history, utilitarian individualism, was never wholly compatible with the biblical tradition, complex as the relations of attraction and repulsion between the two were. This tradition was rooted ultimately in the sophistic, skeptical, and hedonistic strands of ancient Greek philosophy but took its modern form initially in the theoretical writings of Thomas Hobbes. It became popular in America mainly through the somewhat softer and less consistent version of John Locke and his followers, a version deliberately designed to obscure the contrast with biblical religion. In its consistent original Hobbesian form, utilitarianism grew out of an effort to apply the methods of science to the understanding of man and was both atheistic and deterministic. While the commonsense Lockian version that has been the most pervasive current of American thought has not been fully conscious of these implications, the relation between utilitarianism and Anglo-American social science has been close and continuous from Hobbes and Locke to the classical economists of the eighteenth and early nineteenth centuries to the social Darwinists of the late nineteenth century and finally to such influential present-day sociologists as George Homans. Whereas the central term for understanding individual motivation in the biblical tradition was "conscience," the central term in the utilitarian tradition was "interest." The biblical understanding of national life was based on the notion of community with charity for all the members, a community supported by public and private virtue. The utilitarian tradition believed in a neutral state in which individuals would be allowed to pursue the maximization of their self-interest and the product would be public and private prosperity. The harshness of these contrasts was obscured, though never obliterated, by several considerations. The biblical tradition promised earthly rewards as well as heavenly for virtuous actions. The utilitarian tradition required self-restraint and "morality," if not as ends then as means. But the most pervasive mechanism for the harmonization of the two traditions was the corruption of the biblical tradition by utilitarian individualism so that religion itself finally became for many a means for the maximization of self-interest with no effective link to virtue, charity, or community. A purely private pietism, emphasizing only individual rewards, that grew up in the nineteenth century and took many forms in the twentieth, from Norman Vincent Peale to Reverend Ike, was the expression of that corruption.[2]

The increasing dominance of utilitarian individualism was expressed not only in the corruption of religion but also in the rising prestige of science, technology, and bureaucratic organization. The scientific instrumentalism that was already prominent in Hobbes became the central tenet of the most typical late American philosophy, pragmatism. The tradition of utilitarian individualism expressed no interest in shared values or ends, since it considered the only significant end to be individual interest maximization, and individual ends are essentially random. Utilitarianism tended therefore to concentrate solely on the rationalization of means, on technical reason. As a result the rationalization of means became an end in itself. This is illustrated in the story about an American farmer who was asked why he worked so hard. To raise more corn, was his reply. But why do you want to do that? To make more money. What for? To buy more land. Why? To raise more corn. And so on ad infinitum.

While utilitarian individualism had no interest in society as an end in itself, it was certainly not unaware of the importance of society. Society like everything else was to be used instrumentally. The key term was organization, the instrumental use of social relationships. "Effective organization" was as much a hallmark of the American ethos as technological inventiveness.

The central value for utilitarian individualism was freedom, a term that could also be used to obscure the gap between the utilitarian and the biblical traditions since it is a central biblical term as well. But for biblical religion, freedom meant liberation from the consequences of sin, freedom to do the right, and was almost equivalent to virtue. For utilitarianism it meant the freedom to pursue one's own ends. Everything was to be subordinate to that: nature, social relations, even personal feelings. The exclusive concentration on means rendered that final end of freedom so devoid of content that it became illusory and the rationalization of means a kind of treadmill that was in fact the opposite of freedom.

That part of the biblical tradition that remained uncorrupted or only minimally corrupted found itself deeply uneasy with the dominant utilitarian ethos. Fundamentalism in America is not simply an expression of backward yokels. Even Bryan's opposition to evolution was in part an opposition to the social Darwinism he saw as undermining all humane values in America. But that opposition remained largely inchoate, in part because it could not penetrate the facade of biblical symbols the society never abandoned even when it betrayed them.

The Challenge of the 1960s

It was this dual set of fundamental understandings that the eruption of the 1960s fundamentally challenged. It is important to remember that the events of the sixties were preceded and prepared for by a new articulation of Christian symbolism in the later fifties in the life and work of Martin Luther King. King stood not only for the actualization of that central and ambiguous value of freedom for those who had never fully experienced even its most formal benefits. Even more significantly he stood for the actualization of the Christian imperative of love. For him society was not to be used manipulatively for individual ends. Even in a bitter struggle one's actions were to express that fundamental love, that oneness of all men in the sight of God, that is deeper than any self-interest. It was that conception, so close to America's expressed biblical values and so far from its utilitarian practice that, together with militant activism, was so profoundly unsettling.

We are accustomed to think of the "costs" of modernization in the developing nations: the disrupted traditions, the breakup of families and villages, the impact of vast economic and social forces that can neither be understood nor adapted to in terms of inherited wisdom and ways of living. Because it is our tradition that invented modernization, we have thought we were somehow immune to the costs or because the process was, with us, so slow and so gradual, we had successfully absorbed the strains of modernization. The sixties showed that in America, too, the costs have been high and the strains by no means wholly absorbed. In that decade, at least among a significant proportion of the educated young of a whole generation, occurred the repudiation of the tradition of utilitarian individualism (even though it often persisted unconsciously even among those doing the repudiating) and the biblical tradition, too, especially as it was seen, in part realistically, as linked to utilitarianism. Let us examine the critique.

The criticisms of American society that developed in the sixties were diverse and not always coherent one with another. What follows is more an interpretation than a description. In many different forms there was a new consciousness of the question of ends. The continuous expansion of wealth and power, which is what the rationalization of means meant in practice, did not seem so self-evidently good. There were of course some sharp questions about the unequal distribution of wealth and power, but beyond that was the question whether the quality of life was a simple function of wealth and power or whether the endless accumulation of wealth and power was not destroying the quality and meaning of life, ecologically and sociologically. If the rationalization of means, the concern for pure instrumentalism, was no longer self-evidently meaningful, then those things that had been subordinated, dominated, and exploited for the sake of rationalizing means took on a new significance. Nature, social relations, and personal feelings could now be treated as ends rather than means, could be liberated from the repressive control of technical reason.

Among those who shared this general analysis there was a division between those who emphasized overthrowing the present system as a necessary precondition for the realization of a more human society and those who emphasized the present embodiment of a new style of life "in the pores," so to speak, of the old society. The contrast was not absolute, as the effort to create politically "liberated zones" in certain communities such as Berkeley and Ann Arbor indicates. And for a time in the late sixties opposition to the Vietnam War, seen as an example of technical reason gone mad, took precedence over everything else. Yet there was a contrast between those mainly oriented to political action (still, in a way, oriented to means rather than ends, though it was the means to overthrow the existing system) and those mainly concerned with the actual creation of alternative patterns of living. The difference between demonstrations and sit-ins on the one hand and love-ins, be-ins, and rock festivals on the other illustrates the contrast. Political activists shared some of the personal characteristics of those they fought—they were "uptight," repressed, and dominated by time and work. The cultural experimenters, represented most vividly perhaps by the "love, peace, groovy" flower children of the middle sixties, believed in harmony with man and nature and the enjoyment of the present moment through drugs, music, or meditation. In either case there was a sharp opposition to the dominant American ethos of utilitarian instrumentalism oriented to personal success. There was also a deep ambivalence to the biblical tradition, to which I will return.

The question of why the old order began to lose its legitimacy just when it did is not one I have felt equipped to answer. Clearly in the sixties there was a conjuncture of dissatisfactions that did not all have the same meaning. The protests of racial minorities, middle-class youth, and women had different causes and different goals. In spite of all the unsolved problems, the crisis was brought on by the success of the society as much as by its failures. That education and affluence did not bring happiness or fulfillment was perhaps as important as the fact that the society did not seem to be able to solve the problem of racism and poverty. The outbreak of a particularly vicious and meaningless little war in Asia that stymied America's leadership both militarily and politically for years on end acted as a catalyst but did not cause the crisis. The deepest cause, no matter what particular factors contributed to the actual timing, was, in my opinion, the inability of utilitarian individualism to provide a meaningful pattern of personal and social existence, especially when its alliance with biblical religion began to sag because biblical religion itself had been gutted in the process. I would thus interpret the crisis of the sixties above all as a crisis of meaning, a religious crisis, with major political, social, and cultural consequences to be sure.

The New Revival

Religious upheaval is not new in American history. Time and time again after a period of spiritual dryness there has been an outbreak of the spirit. But the religious crisis was in more ways a contrast to the great awakenings of the eighteenth and nineteenth centuries than a continuation of them. By all the measures of conventional religiosity the early 1950s had been a period of religious revival, but the revival of the fifties proved to be as artificial as the cold-war atmosphere that may have fostered it. The sixties saw a continuous drop in church attendance and a declining belief in the importance of religion, as measured by national polls. It is true that conservative and fundamentalist churches continued to grow and that the major losses were in the mainline Protestant denominations and in the Catholic church after the full consequences of Vatican II began to sink in. But in terms of American culture the latter had long been more important than the conservative wing. Although clergy and laity of many denominations played an important part in the events of the sixties, the churches as such were not the locale of the major changes, even the religious ones.

Indeed, it was easier for many in the biblical tradition to relate to the political than to the religious aspect of the developing counterculture. The demand for social justice fitted closely with the prophetic teachings of Judaism and Christianity. The struggle for racial equality and later the struggle against the Vietnam War drew many leaders from the churches and synagogues, even though the membership as a whole remained passive. But in spite of the leadership of Martin Luther King and the martyrdom of divinity students in the civil rights movement and in spite of the leadership of the Berrigans and William Sloane Coffin in the peace movement, those movements as a whole remained indifferent if not hostile to religion. By the end of the sixties those churchmen who had given everything to the political struggle found themselves without influence and without a following. For most of the political activists the churches remained too closely identified with the established powers to gain much sympathy or interest. As dogmatic Marxism gained greater influence among the activists during the decade, ideological antireligion increased as well.

But the churches were even less well prepared to cope with the new spirituality of the sixties. The demand for immediate, powerful, and deep religious experience, which was part of the turn away from future-oriented instrumentalism toward present meaning and fulfillment, could on the whole not be met by the religious bodies. The major Protestant churches in the course of generations of defensive struggle against secular rationalism had taken on some of the color of the enemy. Moralism and verbalism and the almost complete absence of ecstatic experience characterized the middle-class Protestant churches. The more intense religiosity of black and lower-class churches remained largely unavailable to the white middle-class members of the counterculture. The Catholic church with its great sacramental tradition might be imagined to have been a more hospitable home for the new movement, but such was not the case. Older Catholicism had its own defensiveness, which took the form of scholastic intellectualism and legalistic moralism. Nor did Vatican II really improve things. The Catholic church finally decided to recognize the value of the modern world just when American young people were beginning to find it valueless. As if all this were not enough, the biblical arrogance toward nature and the Christian hostility toward the impulse life were both alien to the new spiritual mood. Thus the religion of the counterculture was by and large not biblical. It drew from many sources, including the native American. But its deepest influences came from Asia.

In many ways Asian spirituality provided a more thorough contrast to the rejected utilitarian individualism than did biblical religion. To external achievement it posed inner experience; to the exploitation of nature, harmony with nature; to impersonal organization, an intense relation to a guru. Mahayana Buddhism, particularly in the form of Zen, provided the most pervasive religious influence on the counterculture; but elements from Taoism, Hinduism, and Sufism were also influential. What drug experiences, interpreted in oriental religious terms, as Timothy Leary and Richard Alpert did quite early, and meditation experiences, often taken up when drug use was found to have too many negative consequences, showed was the illusoriness of worldly striving. Careerism and status seeking, the sacrifice of present fulfillment for some ever-receding future goal, no longer seemed worthwhile. There was a turn away not only from utilitarian individualism but from the whole apparatus of industrial society. The new ethos preferred handicrafts and farming to business and industry and small face-to-face communities to impersonal bureaucracy and the isolated nuclear family. Simplicity and naturalness in food and clothing were the ideal, even though conspicuous consumption and oneupmanship ("Oh, you don't use sea salt, I see") made their inevitable appearance.

Thus the limits were pushed far beyond what any previous great awakening had seen: toward socialism in one direction, toward mysticism in the other. But perhaps the major meaning of the sixties was not anything positive at all. Neither the political movement nor the counterculture survived the decade. Important successor movements did survive and they have been the focus of our study, but the major meaning of the sixties was purely negative: the erosion of the legitimacy of the American way of life. On the surface what seems to have been most drastically undermined was utilitarian individualism, for the erosion of the biblical tradition seemed only to continue what had been a long-term trend. The actual situation was more complicated. Utilitarian individualism had perhaps never before been so divested of its ideological and religious facade, never before recognized in all its naked destructiveness. And yet that very exposure could become an ironic victory. If all moral restraints are illegitimate, then why should I believe in religion and morality? If those who win in American society are the big crooks and those who lose do so only because they are little crooks, why should I not try to be a big crook rather than a little one? In this way the unmasking of utilitarian individualism led to the very condition from which Hobbes sought to save us—the war of all against all. Always before, the biblical side of the American tradition has been able to bring antinomian and anarchic tendencies under some kind of control, and perhaps that is still possible today. Certainly the fragile structures of the counterculture were not able to do so. But out of the shattered hopes of the sixties there emerged a cynical privatism, a narrowing of sympathy and concern to the smallest possible circle, that is truly frightening. What happened to Richard Nixon should not obscure for us the meaning of his overwhelming victory in 1972. It was the victory of cynical privatism.

The Successor Movements

In this rather gloomy period of American history—and the mood of the youth culture in the period of our study has been predominantly gloomy; not the hope for massive change that characterized the sixties but the anxious concern for survival, physical and moral—the successor movements of the early seventies take on a special interest. We may ask whether any of them has been able to take up and preserve the positive seeds of the sixties so that under more favorable circumstances they may grow and fructify once again. Some of the successor movements clearly do not have that potential. The Weathermen and the Symbionese Liberation Army on the one hand, the Krishna Consciousness Society and the Divine Light Mission on the other, are parodies of the broader political and religious movements they represent, too narrow and in some cases too self-destructive to contribute to the future solution of our problems. About others there may be more hope.

   To some extent the successor movements, especially the explicitly religious ones, have been survival units in a quite literal sense. They have provided a stable social setting and a coherent set of symbols for young people disoriented by the drug culture or disillusioned with radical politics. What Synanon claims to have done for hard-core drug users, religious groups—from Zen Buddhists to Jesus people—have done for ex-hippies. The rescue-mission aspect of the successor movements has had tangible results. In many instances reconciliation with parents has been facilitated by the more stable life-style and the religious ideology of acceptance rather than confrontation. A new, more positive orientation toward occupational roles has often developed. In some cases, such as followers of Meher Baba, this has meant a return to school and the resumption of a normal middle-class career pattern.[3] For others, such as resident devotees of the San Francisco Zen Center or ashram residents of the 3HO movement, jobs are seen largely as means to subsistence, having little value in themselves.[4] While the attitude toward work in terms of punctuality, thoroughness, and politeness is, from the employer's point of view, positive, the religious devotee has no inner commitment to the job nor does he look forward to any advancement. In terms of intelligence and education the job holder is frequently "overqualified" for the position he holds, but this causes no personal distress because of the meaning the job has for him. For many of these groups the ideal solution would be economic self-sufficiency so members would not have to leave the community at all; but few are able to attain this. As in monastic orders some full-time devotees can be supported frugally by the gifts of sympathizers, but they are exceptions. Many of the groups also insist on a stable sexual life, in some instances celibate but more usually monogamous, with sexual relations being confined to marriage. Such norms are found not only among Jesus people but in the oriental groups as well.

These features of stability should not be interpreted as simple adaptation to the established society, though in some cases that may occur. The human-potential movement may serve such an adaptive function, and perhaps Synanon also does to a certain extent. But for the more explicitly religious groups, stable patterns of personal living and occupation do not mean acceptance of the established order. Our survey found that sympathizers of the oriental religions tend to be as critical of American society as political radicals, far more critical than the norm. While the survey shows that people sympathetic to the Jesus movement are less critical of American society, the Christian World Liberation

Front, a Berkeley group, is atypical in being quite critical. All these movements share a very negative image of established society as sunk in materialism and heading for disaster. Many of them have intense millennial expectations, viewing the present society as in the last stage of degradation before the dawning of a new era. 3HO people speak of the Aquarian age, which is about to replace the dying Piscean age. Krishna Consciousness people speak of the present as the last stage of the materialistic Kali Yuga and on the verge of a new age of peace and happiness. More traditionally biblical expectations of the millennium are common among Jesus people. All these groups, well behaved as they are, have withdrawn fundamentally from contemporary American society, see it as corrupt and illegitimate, and place their hope in a radically different vision. We should remember that early Christians too were well behaved—Paul advised them to remain in their jobs and their marriages—yet by withholding any deep commitment to the Roman Empire they helped to bring it down and to form a society of a very different type.

Both our survey and our qualitative observations indicate sympathizers of the human-potential movement are less alienated from American society than followers of oriental religions or political radicals. They are, nonetheless, more critical than the norm, and many of their beliefs contrast sharply with established American ideology. A tension exists within the movement over the issue of latent utilitarianism. If the techniques of the human-potential movement are to be used for personal and business success (the training-group movement out of which the human-potential movement in part derives had tendencies in that direction), then it is no different from the mind cures and positive thinking of the most debased kinds of utilitarian religion in America. But for some in the movement the whole idea of success is viewed negatively, and the training is seen in part as a way of gaining liberation from that goal. The high evaluation of bodily awareness and intrapsychic experience as well as nonmanipulative interpersonal relations place much of the movement in tension with the more usual orientations of American utilitarian individualism. Here as elsewhere in our field of research we have found utilitarian individualism is a hydra-headed monster that tends to survive just where it is most attacked.

Common Themes

I have already considered some of the common themes of the counterculture of the sixties. I shall now consider how they have survived and been elaborated in the successor movements. Immediate experience rather than doctrinal belief continues to be central among all the religious movements, including the Jesus movements, and in the human-potential movement as well. Knowledge in the sense of direct firsthand encounter has so much higher standing than abstract argument based on logic that one could almost speak of antiintellectualism in many groups. Yet it would be a mistake to interpret this tendency as rampant irrationalism. Even though science is viewed ambivalently and the dangers of scientific progress are consciously feared by many in our groups, science as such is not rejected. There is a belief that much of what is experienced could be scientifically validated. Indeed, the human-potential groups (and Transcendental Meditation) believe their teachings are in accord with science broadly understood. The study of the physiology of the brain during meditation is seen not as a threat but as a support for religious practice. Since reality inheres in the actual experience, explanatory schemes, theological or scientific, are secondary, though scientific explanations tend to be preferred to theological ones because of the general prestige of science. At a deeper level the lack of interest in critical reflective reason may be a form of antiintellectualism, but the conscious irrationalism of groups such as the romantic German youth movement is missing. Similarly, there is a complete absence of primordial loyalties and hatreds based on race, ethnic group, or even, usually, religion.

In spite of the primacy of experience, belief is not entirely missing. In some groups the stress on doctrine may be increasing. The early phase of the New Left was heavily experiential: Unless you had placed your body on the line you could not understand the reality of American society. Consciousness raising in racial and women's groups continues to emphasize the experiential aspect of oppression and the struggle against it. But New Left groups became increasingly doctrinal toward the end of the 1960s and remain today more oriented to doctrine than experience in comparison with religious and human-potential groups.

A central belief shared by the oriental religions and diffused widely outside them is important because of its sharp contrast with established American views. This is the belief in the unity of all being. Our separate selves, according to Buddhism, Hinduism, and their offshoots, are not ultimately real. Philosophical Hinduism and Mahayana Buddhism reject dualism. For them ultimately there is no difference between myself and yourself, and this river and that mountain. We are all one and the conflict between us is therefore illusory.

While such beliefs are diametrically opposed to utilitarian individualism, for which the individual is the ultimate ontological reality, there are elements in the Christian tradition to which they are not entirely opposed. Christian theology also felt the unity of being and the necessity to love all beings. The New Testament speaks of the church as one body of which we are all members. But Christianity has tended to maintain the ultimate dualism of creator and creation that the oriental religions would obliterate. Christian mystics have at times made statements (viewed as heretical) expressing the ultimate unity of God and man, and in a mediated form the unity of God and man through Christ is an orthodox belief. Still, American Christianity has seldom emphasized the aspect of the Christian tradition that stressed the unity rather than the distinction between the divine and the human; so the oriental teachings stand out as sharply divergent.

Much of the countercultural criticism of American society is related to the belief in nondualism. If man and nature, men and women, white and black, rich and poor are really one, then there is no basis for the exploitation of the latter by the former. The ordination of women by Zen Buddhists and 3HO, even though not warranted in the earlier traditions, shows how their American followers interpret the fundamental beliefs. It is significant that from the basis of nondualism conclusions similar to those of Marxism can be reached. But because the theoretical basis is fundamental unity rather than fundamental opposition, the criticism of existing society is nonhostile, nonconfrontational, and often nonpolitical. Nonetheless the effort to construct a witness community based on unity and identity rather than opposition and oppression can itself have critical consequences in a society based on opposite principles.

Another feature of oriental religions that has been widely influ-

ential is their view of dogma and symbol. Believing, as many of
them do, that the fundamental truth, the truth of nondualism, is
one, they also accept many beliefs and symbols as appropriate for
different groups or different levels of spiritual insight. Dogma-
tism has by no means been missing in the oriental religions and
has been traditionally more important than many of their American followers probably realize. But in relation to Christianity and
biblical religions generally, the contrast holds. Belief in certain
doctrinal or historical statements (Jesus is the son of God, Christ
rose from the tomb on the third day) has been so central in
Western religion that it has been hard for Westerners to imagine
religions for whom literal belief in such statements is unimportant. But the impact of oriental religion coincides with a long
history of the criticism of religion in the West in which particular
beliefs have been rendered questionable but the significance of
religion and myth in human action has been reaffirmed. Postcritical Western religion was therefore ready for a positive response
to Asian religions in a way different from any earlier period. Paul
Tillich's response to Zen Buddhism late in his life is an example
of this. Thomas Merton's final immersion in Buddhism is an even
better one. Such tendencies, however, are not to be found in the
Christian World Liberation Front or other Jesus movements.

But in many of the oriental groups and certainly in the human-
potential movement there has been a willingness to find meaning
in a wide variety of symbols and practices without regarding them
literally or exclusively. The danger here as elsewhere is that
postcritical religion can become purely utilitarian. This can happen if one fails to see that any religious symbol or practice,
however relative and partial, is an effort to express or attain the
truth about ultimate reality. If such symbols and practices become mere techniques for "self-realization," then once again we
see utilitarian individualism reborn from its own ashes.

The New Religious Consciousness and the Future

Our study began with the thought that the new religious consciousness that seemed to be developing among young people in
the San Francisco Bay Area might be some harbinger, some straw
in the wind, that would tell us of changes to come in American

culture and society. We were aware that studies of American religion based on national samples could tell us mainly about what was widely believed in the present and perhaps also in the past, since religious views change relatively slowly. Such samples, however, could not easily pick up what was incipient, especially what was radically new and as yet confined to small groups. Even our Bay Area sample, weighted as it was to youth, picked up only a tiny handful of those deeply committed to new forms of religion, although it did lead us to believe the new groups had gotten a hearing and some sympathy from a significant minority. Our qualitative studies of particular groups, based on participant-observation field studies, have told us a great deal about them.

But to assess what we have discovered with respect to possible future trends remains terribly hazardous. The future will certainly not be determined mainly by the groups we studied. What role they can play will depend largely on other developments in the society as a whole. Thus in trying to assess the possible meaning and role of our groups in the future I would like to outline three possible scenarios for American society as a whole: liberal, traditional authoritarian, and revolutionary.

The future most people seem to expect and the futurologists describe with their projections is very much like the present society only more so. This is what I call the liberal scenario. American society would continue as in the past to devote itself to the accumulation of wealth and power. The mindless rationalization of means and the lack of concern with ends would only increase as biblical religion and morality continue to erode. Utilitarian individualism, with less biblical restraint or facade than ever before, would continue as the dominant ideology. Its economic form, capitalism, its political form, bureaucracy, and its ideological form, scientism, would each increasingly dominate its respective sphere. Among the elite, scientism—the idolization of technical reason alone—would provide some coherent meaning after traditional religion and morality had gone. But technical reason would hardly be a sufficient surrogate religion for the masses. No longer accepting the society as legitimate in any ideal terms, the masses would have to be brought to acquiesce grudgingly by a combination of coercion and material reward. In such a society one could see a certain role for oriental religious groups and the human-potential movement—perhaps even for a small radical political fringe. All these could be allowed within limits to operate and provide the possibility of expressing the frustration and rage the system generates but in a way such that the individuals concerned are pacified and the system itself is not threatened. The utilitarian individualism latent in all the countercultural successor movements, political and religious, makes this a real possibility. This scenario depicts the society as heading, mildly and gradually, into something like Aldous Huxley's *Brave New World.*

Lately, however, questions have been raised as to the viability of this direction of development. Perhaps there are inner contradictions that will lead to a drastic breakdown in the foreseeable future. Robert Heilbroner has predicted such a collapse, largely as a result of ecological catastrophe.[5] But Heilbroner also envisages the possibility that tensions between the rich and the poor nations could bring disaster sooner than would ecological attrition. Even since Heilbroner wrote, the proliferation of atomic weapon capacity in India and the Middle East has strengthened this possibility. Another distinct possibility is worldwide economic collapse bringing social convulsions in train. No matter how the breakdown of the "modernization" syndrome might occur, Heilbroner envisages a relapse into traditional authoritarianism as the most likely result—providing, that is, the worst outcome, total destruction of life on the planet, is avoided. Simpler, poorer, and less free societies might be all humans would be capable of in the wake of a global catastrophe. The social and personal coherence modernizing societies never attained might be supplied by the rigid myths and rituals of a new hierarchical authoritarian society. To put it in terms of the present discussion, the collapse of subjective reason, which is what technical reason ultimately is, would bring in its wake a revival of objective reason in a particularly closed and reified form.[6] Technical reason, because it is concerned not with truth or reality but only with results, not with what is but only what works, is ultimately completely subjective. That its domineering manipulative attitude to reality in the service of the subject leads ultimately to the destruction of any true subjectivity is only one of its many ironies. But a new traditional authoritarianism would set up some single orthodox version of what truth and reality are and enforce agreement. Some historically relative creed, belief, and ritual would be asserted as identical with objective reality itself. In this way social and personal coherence would be achieved, but ultimately at the expense of any real objectivity.

If a relapse into traditional authoritarianism is a distinct possibility in America, and I believe it is, we might ask what are the likely candidates for the job of supplying the new orthodoxy. Perhaps the most likely system would be right-wing Protestant fundamentalism. We already have a good example of such a regime in Afrikaner-dominated South Africa.[7] Conservative Protestant fundamentalism has a large and by some measures growing following in America. It has the religious and moral absolutism a traditional authoritarianism would require, and it is hard to see any close rival on the American scene today. The Catholic church, which might at an earlier period have been a candidate for such a role, is certainly not, in its post–Vatican II disarray. Some of the more authoritarian Asian religions might provide a sufficiently doctrinaire model, but their small following in comparison with Protestant fundamentalism virtually rules them out. The future for most of the groups we have studied, all but the Jesus movements, would be bleak indeed under such a neotraditional authoritarianism. It is doubtful if even a group as open as the Christian World Liberation Front could survive. Neoauthoritarian regimes are hard on nonconformity in every sphere. The Chilean government, for example, not only sets standards of dress and hair style but also persecutes oriental religions.

There remains a third alternative, however improbable. It is this I am calling revolutionary, not in the sense that it would be inaugurated by a bloody uprising, which I do not think likely, but because it would bring fundamental structural change, socially and culturally. It is to this rather unlikely outcome that most of the groups we have studied, at least the most flexible and open of them, would have most to contribute. Such a new order would involve, as in the case of traditional authoritarianism, an abrupt shift away from the exclusive dominance of technical reason; but it would not involve the adoption of a reified objective reason either. In accord with its concern for ends rather than means alone, such a revolutionary culture would have a firm commitment to the quest for ultimate reality. Priorities would shift away from endless accumulation of wealth and power to a greater concern for harmony with nature and between human beings. Perhaps a much simpler material life, simpler, that is, compared to present middle-class American standards, would result; but it would not be accompanied by an abandonment of free inquiry or free speech. Science, which would ultimately have to be shackled in a traditional authoritarian regime, would continue to be pursued in the revolutionary culture, but it would not be idolized as in the liberal model. In all these respects the values, attitudes, and beliefs of the oriental religious groups, the human-potential movement, and even a group like the Christian World Liberation Front, as well as the more flexible of the radical political groups, would be consonant with the new regime and its needs. Indeed, many of the present activities of such groups could be seen as experiments leading to the possibility of such a new alternative. Neither safety valve nor persecuted minority, the new groups would be, under such an option, the vanguard of a new age.

Such an outcome would accord most closely with the millennial expectations rife among the new groups. Even if an enormous amount of thought and planning were devoted to such an alternative, thought and planning the small struggling groups we have been studying are quite incapable at the moment of supplying, the revolutionary alternative seems utopian. Perhaps only a major shift in the established biblical religions, a shift away from their uneasy alliance with utilitarian individualism and toward a profound reappropriation of their own religious roots and an openness to the needs of the contemporary world, would provide the mass base for a successful effort to establish the revolutionary alternative. To be politically effective, such a shift would have to lead to a revitalization of the revolutionary spirit of the young republic so that America would once again attract the hope and love of its citizens. This outcome too at present seems utopian. It may be, however, that only the implementation of a utopian vision, a holistic reason that unites subjectivity and objectivity, will make human life in the twenty-first century worth living.

NOTES

1. See Robert N. Bellah, *The Broken Covenant: American Civil Religion in Time of Trial* (New York: Seabury Press, 1975), for an analysis of the role of biblical religion in the formation of American society and also for the relations between biblical religion and utilitarian individualism. Two related essays are "Reflections on Reality in America," *Radical Religion*, 1, no. 3 (1974); and "Religion and Polity in America," *Andover Newton Quarterly*, 15, no. 2 (1974), pp. 107—123.

2. An excellent treatment of the deep inner cleavage in American culture is Wilson Carey McWilliams, *The Idea of Fraternity in America* (Berkeley: University of California Press, 1973).

3. See the interesting study of Thomas Robbins and Dick Anthony, "Getting Straight with Meher Baba," *Journal for the Scientific Study of Religion*, 11, no. 2 (1972), pp. 122–140.

4. My information on the San Francisco Zen Center comes mainly from David Wise, "Zen Buddhist Subculture in San Francisco," Ph.D. dissertation, Department of Sociology, University of California, Berkeley, 1971.

5. Robert Heilbroner, *An Inquiry into the Human Prospect* (New York: W. W. Norton, 1974).

6. The contrast between subjective and objective reason has been developed by members of the Frankfurt School. See, for example, Max Horkheimer, *The Eclipse of Reason* (London: Oxford University Press, 1947; Seabury Paperback, 1974).

7. See Dunbar Moodie, *The Rise of Afrikanerdom* (Berkeley: University of California Press, 1974), for an excellent analysis of Afrikaner civil religion and its Dutch Calvinist dimension.

8. Civility and Civil Religion: The Emergence of Cults

PHILLIP E. HAMMOND

On recent occasions one or another university student has asked if I am a Christian, a question I find bothersome. Anyone who words the question that way in my campus office is, I assume, possessed of a world view different from mine, so I have resisted answering with a single word. But, it has not seemed appropriate to square off and establish ground rules for moving from theology to metaphysics and back to theology again. Instead I mutter something about heritage and background, culture and socialization, and current denominational affiliation. Questioners walk away with *an* answer but not *the* answer; they must still try to decipher whether I am *with them* or not, for that is what such a question is really asking. It is not my parish affiliation but my tribal loyalty they inquire about by asking if I am "a Christian." In questionnaires that ask if one is Christian, Jew, Hindu, or whatever, I employ no circumlocution. But the answer marked there is not a satisfactory response to the question these occasional students ask. They can already infer, of course, that I grew up a "Judeo-Christian," and the church of my choice is not really of interest to them. What they seek, in asking the question, are my convictions. Are they Christian convictions?

Any reluctance I feel in answering a question about my Christian identity is not because it pries into my convictions, however. It stems rather from two things: first, from my impatience with the forced-choice nature of the question—either yes, my convictions are adequately conveyed by this single word, or no, Christianity has nothing to do with my convictions—second, from my impatience (perhaps irritation is a better word now) with the assumption that convictions are real if declared but are not otherwise knowable through behavior, everyday speech, general intellectual stance, and so forth.

No student has ever asked if I "believe in" the American civil religion. If that were to happen, I think I would be forthright in my declaration of assent. Oddly enough, I would not stumble about for a way around that question.

Why this difference? The answer lies in an irony: The commitment I feel to the civil religion (and thus the commitment I am willing to express in a single word) is the very sentiment that makes awkward any forced-choice inquiry into my Christian commitment. The public civil religion, in other words, presumes a private church religion. Indeed, as I have argued in other chapters in this volume, the tolerance many church religions developed toward each other is itself one of the central tenets of a robust American civil religion. But this tolerance developed at the cost of making church religion a private affair and thus in some measure made church religion off limits for casual inquiry. One's religion did not necessarily become politically irrelevant, but only the quaintest of civic claims could be made in its name. (As I write this, for example, I am in Honolulu, and the local newspaper carried a story of some construction workers who walked off the job. Their task was to erect a chain link fence around an ancient *heiau* [Polynesian temple] site, but enough strange events occurred that the workers walked away, fearful they were disturbing the gods. The president of the contracting firm thus called in a Pentecostal clergyman to "pray a little to purify the place and chase the evil spirits away," and the workers resumed working, "very relieved."[1] Had the job been bigger, it is not too cynical to suggest, such consideration probably would not have been shown; conscientious objection is allowed only if it isn't too inconveniencing.)

The religious freedom resulting from this tolerance is real enough; what is unreal is the assumption that religious convictions that cannot be acted on in public will nonetheless continue to function in private as if they could be. Instead there develops a commitment to what John Murray Cuddihy calls the Protestant etiquette—a ritualized belief that no religion should offend another—and this commitment constitutes a major plank in the American civil religion. It is a point, moreover, where civil religion and civility become much the same thing.[2] I do not feel comfortable with the student's question of whether I am a Christian because the claims I make in the name of Christianity, while real, are nevertheless importantly limited. By knowing that label, the student may legitimately infer little else about me and thus should not inquire into the label in so casual a manner. This rule of etiquette, when elevated to a matter of principle and thus of religion, becomes a commitment to which I readily pledge allegiance.

It can be misleading to call this civility/civil religion the Protestant etiquette, however, for that allows the impression that the phenomenon might just as well have been the Catholic etiquette or Jewish etiquette but happens in America, because of who got established first, to be Protestant in flavor. In fact the relationship between Protestantism and the civility/civil religion of which I speak is far more than coincidental. Edward Shils explains the relationship this way: "The notion that every man has a spark of divinity in him, that all men participate in a common substance —sacred in the last analysis but civil in its concrete and mediated forms—has grown out of the conjunction of the modern national state and Christian Protestantism. From this conjunction grew the idea of citizen, and from it our modern idea of the civil order as a stratum of being in which all the members of a state participate."[3]

Of course Protestants have no monopoly on this civility, nor is there reason to suppose they necessarily possess it in greater proportion than non-Protestants. What is reasonable to suppose is that the separate loyalties citizens feel—to religion certainly but also to class, ethnic group, profession, party, or whatever— will be regulated on behalf of the common good. Insofar as this regulation is self-imposed, it can be called civility, and insofar as this civility is believed to inhere in the nature of social life itself, civility merges into civil religion.

Thus civility means far more than good manners. Granted,

democratic society requires manners if it is to contain diverse religious, ethnic, or party groups. But it also requires an orientation that locates these manners in the moral order. The democratic citizen must be partisan if politics is to function at all, but partisanship must be pursued under rules so important, so sacred, they apply to oneself as well as to one's opponents.

Whether called Protestant, middle class, or bourgeois, therefore, the civility that becomes the civil religion is a set of ground rules permitting civil harmony in the midst of political diversity, religious peace in the midst of ecclesiastical pluralism. In its particulars it can no doubt be tinkered with, but in its fundamentals there exists an immutability so inherent in the process itself that it warrants the label of natural law. And it is this fundamental, immutable, "natural" quality that so readily encourages a religious orientation toward what otherwise appear to be mere rules of order. One does not believe in this kind of civility because it is convenient, middle class, or Protestant but because it is true. (One view has it that sociology is the discovery of the natural laws underlying this civility, that is, the principles governing persons' behavior in social settings that inhibit conflict and promote harmony. It is perhaps odd that those sociologists most ready to accept the mantle of "science" for their work are least comfortable with this view of sociology.) Civility is true, as Lon Fuller reminds us, in the same sense that the rules of carpentry are true ("natural"); if the house is to stand, the rules must be followed.[4]

Does this mean for full citizenship in a democracy a person must be civil? Does this mean for full ecclesiastical rights a person must relinquish all unique social claims for his religion? The answer is deceptively simple: Yes. Moreover the answer is yes in at least two senses. One of these senses is almost mechanical in that without *behaving* in a civil manner toward others' claims a person is restrained from exercising his own claims. At the extreme this means that even the defendant in a murder case, if he is to have a fair trial at the bar of society, must behave as if he believes in observing proper procedure. (Thus the U.S. Supreme Court in its 1970 *Allen* decision [164 US 492] ruled that until a defendant agreed to refrain from further disruptive courtroom tactics, his constitutional right to confront his accusers could be waived, and the trial could proceed without him.)

The other sense in which one must relinquish superior claims for one's own stance in favor of the civil procedure whereby all stances are at parity is often called secularization. That is to say, the certainty with which we hold *our* convictions is eroded when we find ourselves according others equal right to *their* convictions. "All of us," writes Cuddihy, "are witness to the profanation of our sacred particularities; all of us suffer the pathos of the secularization process."[5] It is not that sacred particularities disappear altogether but rather that they become private or noncivil, matters of preference only and thus no longer socially compelling. The Protestant doctrine that only Jesus saves, the Catholic doctrine that salvation is only through the Church, and the Jewish doctrine of the Chosen People do not disappear. Instead, as Cuddihy shows, those doctrines in American society get transformed; their hard edges get softened; their claims and implications get muted. In short they cease to be central identifying ideologies for their respective devotees and become instead part of the history of people who "happen to be" Protestant, Catholic, or Jew. What was once sacred is now secular.

What is not so clear is why people, having secularized their various sacred particularities, would sacralize the very procedures that brought about the secularizing. Why, in other words, would civility become civil religion? I have tried elsewhere in this volume to answer this question and won't repeat all the reasoning here. Briefly put, the argument follows Emile Durkheim's observation that even the contract has a noncontractual element. If a people who are so diverse that pursuit of their commonwealth would be precluded learn ways to engage in that pursuit, it is not surprising to find them honoring—even worshipping—those "ways." The collective, Durkheim insisted, *will* be represented. (Mystery surrounds not so much *this* process, then, but rather the process by which a collective determines what its boundaries are.)

For whatever reasons, Americans became religiously diverse and tolerant, and religious pluralism became a fact of life. It is therefore no more surprising to find Protestants uncomfortable with the particularistic claims of a Billy Graham, Catholics with those of a Father Feeney, or Jews with those of a Rabbi Kahane than it is to find lawyers embarrassed by the courtroom antics of their clients, politicians chagrined by the failure of election losers to acknowledge defeat, or members of the winning ball club joining those they defeated in complaining about the officiating. Who, after all, wants to win through broken rules?

There are pressures, then, both to relinquish particularisms and to exalt the procedures whereby diverse particularisms exist together harmoniously. There are reasons, in other words, why civility becomes civil religion. This might even occur smoothly were it not for two problems. One problem arises because civility, while real enough, is easily ignored. Persons or groups *can* strive to achieve private goals at the expense of the collective welfare, bypassing procedural rules as they do so. Oftentimes those very rules delay or inhibit altogether challenges from those who otherwise would surely challenge. Civility is fragile, as is often noted, and one reason is because individuals who would dismantle it may protect themselves by the rules they would dismantle.

Another problem with the civil religious standing of civility is the constant tendency to trivialize civility, thus making it absurd as civil *religion*. This in turn happens in two ways. The first is by treating as sacred the trappings of civil religion rather than its principles, as in the case of superpatriots, for example. Persons can trivialize the civil religion through idolworshipping. Second, not civility as the natural laws of procedure but civility as merely etiquette can be elevated to sacred status, thus trivializing the civil religion by legalisms. In either case appearance predominates over principle, and civility, now corrupted, loses its transcendent quality.

It is my contention that the trivialization or corruption of the American civil religion has been an important factor in the explosion of cults in this society during the last fifteen years. There are several links in this relationship.

It is easy to forget that during the decade immediately before the mid 1960s the single most common observation about Americans dealt with their conformity or other-direction. The importance of sensitivity to others was stressed (and sometimes regretted) as necessary for advancement in the bureaucratic, corporate, button-down world. Suburbia was the great homogenizer. The middle class was on the march, drawing into itself members from both above and below, and if that meant everybody gave up some of his or her ethnic, class, and religious particularities, so be it. Middle-class morality called for politeness, gentility, and etiquette. In short it was trying to sacralize civility. Before the gray flannel suit became a monk's robe, however, the superficiality of this kind of civility was made obvious, and generations of unbelievers, not just nonbelievers, began to appear.

All this was set in the context of a cold war, however, in which a rhetoric of national honor, national security, and national purpose was everywhere. It was a period during which, in the name of democracy, our nation upheld dictators. Therefore when in the name of peace it waged war in Vietnam, that war became a symbol of the absurd to everyone. For supporter and opponent alike, the absurdity could be stated: If we're going to fight a war, then let's fight to win in the name of national honor, even if we don't know what it is we're fighting about.

Thus throughout a lengthy period the line was drawn between the "patriots" who defended such U.S. actions in the name of national purpose and those who, believing the national purpose was being violated, were forced by their protests to be "unpatriots." Once again generations of unbelievers in the American civil religion had reason to appear.

The status quo always benefits some more than others. If the civil religion—its symbols, rituals, and tenets—are captured by those in power and invoked on behalf of present arrangements, it becomes all the more difficult to advocate change in the name of civil religion. If waving the American flag becomes a gesture only of those happy with the current situation, for example, then burning the flag remains a countergesture by those unhappy with the situation. But burning the flag gains neither converts nor an increased commitment to the civil religion for which the flag stands. Still again generations of unbelievers had cause to appear.

My contention is also exemplified, negatively, by the case of Martin Luther King, Jr., a person seemingly destined to go down in history as a true interpreter and prophet of the American civil religion. The nonviolent character of King's protests, his readiness to accept penalties imposed by the very system he was challenging, reflect precisely civility elevated to civil religion. There were moments therefore when optimism was justifiably high, when the bestowal of benefits was to be rearranged and the status quo altered in the name of America's noblest ideals. But it was not to be. A president, in the name of national honor, shoved civil rights off track by superpatriotic moves in Southeast Asia; an FBI director, in the name of national security, assisted in the derailment by sowing seeds of distrust in the civil rights movement; and others then "merely" committed the murder. Optimism easily gave way to despair, and the times were ripe for yet more unbelievers in the Americal civil religion.

Finally, among these links between an eroded civil religion and the rise of cults, can be mentioned the publicity of Watergate. The scandal itself was hardly significant; what it stood for was the depth of cynicism to which the American people had sunk. President Nixon happened to get caught but in getting caught forced on us all the recognition that "dirty tricks" had become our way of life. Fidelity to the rules of the game could not even be a pretense anymore.

Cynics argue that such events, while real, do not play the dramatic role I give them. The gray flannel suit, they point out, was a phenomenon in only a few urban areas and in only a few occupations. Most people, even if they know about it, don't regret U.S. support to dictators but applaud it in the name of anticommunism. Despair at King's murder was the response of many blacks and some white liberals, but others were not distressed, and most did not care. Watergate, these cynics admit, led to a decline in the prestige of the presidency, but then they point to how fast it was restored by Nixon's successor. Such matters, it is contended, are only superficial, easily swayed by headlines, but therefore not the stuff of which civil religion is made.

Although a little cynicism is always healthy, too much perverts the view. Civil religion, like any religion when it flows, flows in and through the interstices of life. It is not likely that any concrete event will by itself therefore significantly alter the status of America's civil religion. Rather, the civil religion is always in the process of accretion or erosion. Commitment to it and faith in it are always expanding or contracting, deepening or shallowing, being celebrated or being ignored. The events just reviewed, then, are more properly seen as symptoms, not causes of a trivialized and corrupted civil religion. If one thinks of synonyms for "civil religion"—for example, belief in the good intentions of one's nation, optimism about the future of that nation, faith in the legitimacy of its historic institutions, conviction that its errors can and will be corrected—then it is obvious that many events could and did trivialize the American civil religion. Some persons perhaps, crushed by the burden of medical expenses, had no objection to a cold-war garrison state as such, yet they could wonder about a nation that spent far more on weapons than on health coverage. Others, perhaps unmoved by any civil rights rhetoric, were nevertheless bewildered by their government's inability to guarantee jobs, create housing, or control crime in the streets.

It is my argument that in a period of a quarter of a century the American civil religion was eroded by many such events; it lost far more than it gained. But further, this loss occurred even as civil religious symbols and rhetoric were being self-consciously invoked. Thus in the 1950s we added "under God" to the pledge and "in God we trust" to our coins, perfectly innocent gestures in some contexts but trivializing in this instance because of their political, not religious, origins. Similarly with our national anthem, a sacred symbol trivialized. The national hymn of Mexico is considered so sacred that only on extraordinary occasions is it played (and never recorded), whereas the U.S. national anthem is commonly performed. Sports enthusiasts are expected to perform the ritual on a daily basis almost, and as a result even a star singer blowing out her lungs in Yankee Stadium stirs up not patriotic fervor but impatience with the game's delay.

During the twenty-five years following World War II, therefore, there was no letup in the use of civil religious symbols, but there was a series of events that trivialized those symbols, which made outright rejection of them attractive to some and idolatrous embrace of them attractive to others. The impact on successive generations of young Americans was a decline in their commitment to all kinds of practices reflecting mainline American values: from demure dress and gentile language to orderly career and civic responsibility. Included in these rejected practices—regarded as hollow exercises in being "middle-class American"—was, of course, churchgoing. Part of the attack on suburban conformity had included precisely the criticism that churchgoing was but a social ritual, not a sign of deep commitment. As Andrew

Greeley and others make clear, the radical change in churchgoing since the 1950s has not occurred across the board. It is a change created almost exclusively by the young, who in great numbers just never started churchgoing.

Here, then, is where cults stepped in, offering an opportunity to commit oneself and to do so in ways that were neither middle class nor even particularly American. No doubt the cults of Eastern import illustrate the assertion best, but so do "cults" devoted to political radicalism, communalism, mind-altering drugs, or Protestant fundamentalism. Indeed, of all the cultish opportunities for the uncommitted to commit themselves, only the environmentally concerned groups, the women's movement, and the human-potential movement are designed to envelope people into mainline America, not alienate them further. Other cults are distinctive for being centrifugal, not enveloping forces; they are in significant ways therefore subversive of core American (that is, civil religious) values. In other words they are uncivil. They make outrageous claims. They demand their members be obsessed, when Americans are not to be religiously (or politically) obsessed. Civil religion (like civil politics) permits all beliefs to exist provided none makes excessive claims, but here are cults making excessive claims. They challenge the civil religion, therefore, but in order for that to have happened, the civil religion had to have been eroded through trivialization and corruption.

Cults' outrageous claims are often enough benign. Being pressed with a flower petal in an airport is only irritating, not demoralizing or destructive. Chanting, sloganeering, even dominating certain airways or TV channels can be ignored as but the bizarre behavior of those on the fringe. Cultists can be dismissed, in other words, as eccentrics, the way their Hindu-flavored predecessors in America were dismissed before the 1960s.[6]

The extraordinarily negative response by many Americans to these cults in the present day suggests they are not merely being dismissed. Cult members are not simply eccentrics. Instead many are believed to be "brainwashed," forcibly enjoined from "returning" to society, "fooled" or "hypnotized" into their beliefs. They are, in short, threats to "our" values. The mass suicide in Jonestown is but the extreme case in point, with a general reluctance by the public to believe that hundreds of people would knowingly reject life altogether in favor of an ideal. But "moon-

ies" who must be "deprogrammed," Children of God who must
be parentally "kidnapped," or devotees who are "forced" into
mass marriages are additional instances of our inability to think
of cult members as just ordinary church members. They are
instead subversives.

This changing role of cults—from the haven of a few eccentrics
to a real threat to core American values—is possible because the
American civil religion has itself been made precarious by trivialization and corruption. Younger generations, finding it precarious, are thus attracted by cults offering certitude of a particularistic sort; older generations, finding it precarious, respond with
fear and hostility rather than with the certitude provided by a
robust civil religion. What better example than a society prepared to violate the constitutional rights of its members (in some
instances the rights of one's own sons and daughters) in the name
of "religious freedom"? Seeming success at being nervy leads to
a nervy response—and both because of a failure of nerve.

Of course that is an exaggeration. Many factors are involved in
the rise of new religious movements and the reactions to them.
Moreover, I have merged as cults a number of groups, many of
which others would call something else and each of which would
resist being classified with the others. It was not these differences
I wanted to highlight here, however, but the characteristic these
groups share. After all, the popularity, if not the origins, of all
these groups dates to a relatively brief time span. All have been
attractive primarily to young, not old, people. And all evoke in
their followers if not total dedication, at least a fervor and commitment (I previously called it "obsession") uncharacteristic of
major American religious bodies. Thus I offered as the common
characteristic of these cults their *un-*Americanism, finding in that
un-Americanism both some of the attraction to those attracted
and the source of the hostility of those repelled.

Cultists are pushy, and Americans are not supposed to push—
at least not push ideologies. To do so is uncivil. But the ideology
that says it is uncivil and thus makes possible the coexistence of
many ideologies—when conceived as in the nature of things and
not just as a matter of etiquette—is itself then a civil religion.
Only if this civil religion is in reasonable working condition will
civil order be maintained. We see around us that civil order is
precarious indeed.

In 1960, when Daniel Bell published *The End of Ideology: On the Exhaustion of Political Ideas in the Fifties,* he had in mind that Americans were more or less agreed on this ideology that makes civility possible. Thus no other, particularistic, ideology was likely to be pushed at the expense of the overarching ideology. We have seen since 1960 that is not quite accurate. In the decade following Bell's book all manner of ideologies burst forth. It is true that Americans did not long remain in open ideological warfare; there are too many cross-cutting and therefore self-restraining loyalties in America for that. So there is little reason to suppose any of these cultish ideologies now competing will ever win out. But in recent years these ideologies have ceased being the havens of mere kooks, which is the position they were assigned in the 1950s when those ideologies were believed exhausted. Instead that over-arching ideology, the civil religion, has become exhausted. As a result some Americans are taking a new religious plunge while others regret how uncivil the plungers are. It is this lack of civility in the question of whether I am a Christian—and all that such lack of civility might mean for the civil religion of the present day— that bothers me.

NOTES

1. *Honolulu Star-Bulletin,* 1 August 1979.
2. John Murray Cuddihy, *No Offense: Civil Religion and Protestant Taste* (New York: Seabury, 1978).
3. Edward Shils, "Ideology and Civility," *Sewanee Review,* 66 (Summer 1958), p. 480.
4. Lon Fuller, *The Morality of Law* (New Haven, Conn.: Yale University Press, 1964).
5. John Murray Cuddihy, *The Ordeal of Civility* (New York: Basic Books, 1974), p. 235.
6. For a vivid example see John Lofland, *Doomsday Cult* (Englewood Cliffs, N.J.: Prentice-Hall, 1966), an engaging analysis of a group of society's outcasts attracted by an oriental offbeat claiming to be the new savior but who a decade later turns out to be Sun Myung Moon. The revised version of this book (1977) has something to say about the transformation of Moon's public image from that of a harmless eccentric known only to a few to what some regard as a cunning, even dangerously conspiratorial, messiah.

Epilogue:
The Civil Religion Proposal

PHILLIP E. HAMMOND

The civil religion debate, to which Robert Bellah refers in the Introduction to this volume, has in some measure mellowed into dispassionate analysis. An issue that at first evoked more heat than light has become a serious item on research agendas. Civil religion has survived quarrels over its utility as a concept—even its existence as a phenomenon—and gone on to become a major topic of textbooks, monographs, and learned journals. Sociologists have picked up the theme, of course, but so have theologians, political scientists, and historians. The *Journal of Church and State* devoted all of its Winter 1980 issue to the matter, to name just one recent example.

Yet even with this mellowing, civil religion discussions retain something of an advocacy quality. They often have an urgent air, a whiff of the pulpit. Why is this the case? What is it about civil religion, especially American civil religion, that not only attracts scholarly interest but lends a sense of advocacy?

John F. Wilson addresses this question after noting the proliferation of what he calls "public religion proposals." He suggests that such proposals are "potential revitalization movements occasioned by widespread loss of internal confidence in American society and changed external cultural relationships."[1] They are efforts, he says, "to distill the old political culture of the United States which was supported by a broadly Protestant establishment. The purpose is to conserve that culture even as it, and the associated establishment, is threatened from within and without."[2]

His is a worthy insight. Interest in American civil religion probably does reflect not just a scholarly interest but also a nostalgic yearning for something that happened to be importantly Protestant. Even more certainly, that interest has arisen at a time of considerable confusion in the nation's values. More certainly still, civil religion analysts often sound like Old Testament prophets.[3] There is undoubted merit, then, to Wilson's explanation.

If the preceding chapters are correct, however, the public religion proposal we are making is not *sufficiently* described as a revitalization movement. It may be that all right, but it is far more as well, and requires an understanding that does not simply equate it with the Ghost Dance or a Cargo Cult.

Revitalization movements, we might agree, *are* efforts to recover something sacred out of the past, spurred by the sense of a deteriorated present. Any people experiencing the erosion of their cultural core are extremely vulnerable, and they might well look backward and find a spiritual legacy that hardly seemed to exist when the culture was healthy. Many examples of just this process are readily found in the social scientific literature on religion.

A central conception behind such analyses of revitalization movements, however, is their futility. Whatever optimism they inspire is assumed to be misplaced, their believers misguided. Thus, Wilson points out, black and Spanish-speaking Americans, having a different interpretation of *their* American past, do not want to recover the religious legacy of the Protestant Establishment. Any appeal in the name of the American civil religion is therefore—on this score at least—futile; the inclusiveness it seeks is the very feature it cannot have.[4] Moreover, for Wilson, the American civil religion proposal is an ineffective way to bind people and nations together. Other methods, most notably economic exchange, are better. Wilson writes, "A broadly economic framework which seeks to relate perceived self-interests to awareness of interdependence probably has promise of being more effective than explicitly universal religious or political world views."[5]

Here is the rub. The civil religion of which Bellah and I speak does not play down, let alone rule out, the integrating potential of any framework—racial, economic, or otherwise—relating "self-interests to awareness of interdependence." But—and this is the sizable difference—we regard "awareness of interdependence" as far more problematic than a purely secular framework alone can resolve. What *allows* self-interest to be perceived as inextricably bound up with the collective welfare? Whatever the answer, it will not be found by rummaging around among self-interests alone. Even multinational corporations have reason to unleash their constituent units against each other if it appears in their economic interest to do so. Awareness of interdependence is hard to come by.

To be sure, the link between self-interest and the collective good is not necessarily religious.[6] But that link, if it achieves legitimacy and is not merely coercive, must be seen as in the nature of things, as transcending human choice, and thus as more than secular. In human history, this link has more often than not been embedded in the same metaphysical apparatus by which persons interpreted their fate, made sense of their sacred rituals, understood good and evil in their lives, and so forth. In other words, the link *has* commonly been religious (even though it was not necessarily so).

But if the link between self-interest and collective good does not have to be religious—if, to put it differently, there need not be a public theology—this link is nonetheless inescapably sacred. Underlying any contract, Durkheim observed, is a "non-contractual element," meaning in this context that the contract between citizen and state—if it is binding—necessarily involves more than mutual self-interest. Thus, in discussing "the public philosophy," Walter Lippmann was identifying the noncontractual element in American society—the code of civility, he called it—making democratic social organization possible.[7] This code, he pointed out, exists in the natural law, however imperfectly discerned. It transcends human choice. It goes beyond individual self-interest. It bears the same relationship to civic behavior that the laws of carpentry bear to the stability of the house.[8] One *may* view such a code in religious terms, though again one *need* not. One *cannot*, however, see it as a mere social contract in which everyone's self-interest coincides and which therefore exists by agreement alone.

The American civil religion proposal rests in a major way, then, on the conviction that the American founding figures gained important insights into this public philosophy and conveyed those insights in certain documents, sermons, speeches, and so forth. These documents are not simply records of a few people's self-interests. No doubt they are that in part, but they are also expressions of a theory of how "self-interest is related to awareness of interdependence," to use Wilson's phrase. They are windows onto the sacred code making democratic society possible.

As happened in the American case, the expression of this public philosophy is grounded primarily in Protestant theological language. One reason for this Protestant flavor is the simple fact that the founders were almost entirely Protestant: when they expressed noncontractual ideas, they employed familiar (Protestant) terms. Another reason is to be found in the nature of the Protestant—especially Puritan—view of individual, church, and society interrelationships. Centered on a notion of convenant, while at the same time denying ecclesiastical claims to exclusiveness, this view seeped into and informed the American code.

It has therefore been easy to perceive as the American civil *religion* a public philosophy that, despite its undeniably theological tenor, can be expressed as readily in nontheological terms.[9] Failure to see this problem as but a labeling squabble has led some to doubt the merit of the civil religion proposal. How, they ask, if we are not all Protestant, not all Christian, not even all believers in God, can one speak of a civil religion employing Protestant, Christian, theistic ideas?

Underlying such a question is the conception that the American civil religion, like the Ghost Dance or Cargo Cult, exists only to the degree people believe in it. How strange! No one would think that about the laws of carpentry, let alone the laws of physics. Yet so perversely secular have we become that sacredness appears to many to reside in the word, not in a reality of which the word is but an imperfect expression. The American civil religion *is,* whether or not we recognize it as such, and irrespective of the language in which it is expressed. The code of civility making democratic society possible *exists,* however remote may be our understanding of it in the present day.

That remoteness of understanding is, of course, precisely what leads some analyses of civil religion to become "proposals" as well. A cultural crisis, perhaps not unlike that of the Plains Indians or the Melanesians, is upon us, and one can sense the weakening of those values by which individuals with self-interests become responsible citizens. And not just citizens of a nation but of the world. But unlike the Ghost Dance proposal or the Cargo Cult proposal, the civil religion proposal is not, I would argue, futile optimism. It is no mere invention of fanciful minds awaiting deliverance.

To return to the opening question, then, we ask: Why the scholarly interest in the civil religion proposal? It is not a naive belief that America can return to a colonial past, let alone a belief that such a past is preferable because it was "Protestant." Rather, the civil religion proposal is a reluctance to succumb to cynicism. It is an assertion of hope grounded in an unusual kind of reality. "Of course the ideal 'Republic' dreamed by the founders never existed in actuality," Sydney Mead reminds us. "It was a vision, an artist-people's creative idea that imbued them with the Energy to strive—and with considerable success—to incarnate it in actuality."[10] The civil religion proposal is to strive once again to incarnate that artist-people's creative idea.

As discussed in Chapters 7 and 8, the current wave of religiousness in America seems to represent an alternative response to present-day civil malaise. Yet whether in evangelical or cultic form, this new surge of piety may not be an antidote to political atomization so much as another symptom of it. In their theological particularism and ethic of individualism, many popular religious movements today appear to intensify, not neutralize, the mood of self-interest over all. This kind of religious response, then—this way of being hopeful in the face of national lethargy —seems to be no solution at all.

Onto the agenda thus comes a revitalized—and, one hopes, revitalizing—concern for civil religion. Prompted by despair in the present, it holds out hope for the future by renewing an understanding of the past. Kenneth Underwood expresses it well:

Once historical events become the source of judgment, and their uniqueness an occasion for review of assumptions which do not quite fit reality, time loses its monotony, its quality of uniform succession. History takes on excitement and hope; and events, mystery and depth. This is the context of a creative society. People no longer just endure time; they have problems to solve, issues to win, causes to espouse.[11]

Interest in civil religion is both parent and heir to this point of view.

NOTES

1. John F. Wilson, *Public Religion in American Culture* (Philadelphia: Temple University Press, 1979), p. 171.
2. Ibid., pp. 174–175.
3. Exemplified best by Robert N. Bellah, *The Broken Covenant* (New York: Seabury, 1975), which Edwin S. Gaustad called a "jeremiad with footnotes," *Church History,* 45 (September 1976), p. 399.
4. Wilson, *Public Religion,* p. 171.
5. Ibid., p. 173.
6. Unless one makes it so by definition, as some have tried to do. The consequence is a misreading of Durkheim, as Chapter 6 tries to show.
7. Walter Lippmann, *The Public Philosophy* (Boston: Little, Brown, 1955).
8. This felicitous analogy is borrowed from Lon Fuller, *The Morality of Law* (New Haven: Yale University Press, 1964).
9. For one excellent illustration, see Richard John Neuhaus, "Law and the Rightness (and Wrongness) of Things," *Worldview* (September 1979), pp. 40–45.
10. Sidney E. Mead, "American History as a Tragic Drama," *Journal of Religion,* 52 (October 1972), p. 60.
11. Kenneth W. Underwood, *The Church, The University, and Social Policy,* Vol. I (Middletown, Conn.: Wesleyan University Press, 1969), p. 497.

Index